THE BOROUGH PARK PAPERS

SYMPOSIUM II

The Deity of Messiah and the Mystery of God

THE BOROUGH PARK PAPERS

SYMPOSIUM II
The Deity of Messiah and the Mystery of God

April 12 – 14, 2010

Borough Park Symposium
An imprint of
Messianic Jewish Publishers
Clarksville, MD 21029

15 14   6 5 4 3

Library of Congress Control Number: 2012951378

ISBN 978-1-936716-60-9

The Borough Park Papers, Symposium II

The Deity of Messiah and the Mystery of God

Printed in the United States of America

Copyright © 2012

Published by
Borough Park Symposium
An imprint of
Messianic Jewish Publishers
6120 Day Long Lane
Clarksville, Maryland 21029

Distributed by
Messianic Jewish Resources Int'l.
www.messianicjewish.net
Individual and Trade Order line: 800-410-7367
Email: lederer@messianicjewish.net

******

COVER DESCRIPTION:
"Brooklyn Bridge with Manhattan buildings in background by night" (purchased from istockphotos.com)
The Brooklyn Bridge connects Brooklyn, New York, with downtown Manhattan. Brooklyn is home to many Orthodox Jews who have not recognized Yeshua as their promised Messiah . . . yet.
******

TABLE OF CONTENTS

HOW THE BOROUGH PARK SYMPOSIUM CAME TO BE AND
WHAT IT IS
The Borough Park Steering Committee... i

THE DEITY OF MESSIAH AND THE MYSTERY OF GOD:
INTRODUCTION OF THE THEME
Darrell L. Bock, Ph.D... 1

REMINDER ON RESPECTFUL THEOLOGICAL DISCUSSION
David Rudolph, Ph.D. 5

COMMUNICATING THE DIVINITY OF YESHUA TO OUR JEWISH
PEOPLE "BETWEEN A ROCK AND A HARD PLACE"
Rabbi David Rosenberg, M.Div. 13

THE SIGNIFICANCE OF THE DEITY OF YESHUA
Mark S. Kinzer, Ph.D. 23

THE SIGNIFICANCE OF THE DEITY OF YESHUA
Mitch Glaser, Ph.D.. 31

JEWISH HISTORY AND THE DEITY OF YESHUA
Elliot Klayman, M.A., LL.M... 41

THE CANON OF SCRIPTURE AND THE DEITY OF CHRIST:
IS IT KOSHER TO SUBSTITUTE JESUS INTO GOD'S PLACE?
Darrell L. Bock, Ph.D.. 77

JEWISH TRADITION AND THE DEITY OF YESHUA
Joseph Shulam, M.A. 93

COMMUNICATING THE DEITY OF YESHUA TO THE JEWISH
PEOPLE
Daniel F.J. Nessim, B.Th., MCS 103

WORSHIP AND WITNESS TO THE DEITY OF YESHUA
Richard Harvey, Ph.D. 123

HOW TO EFFECTIVELY COMMUNICATE THE DEITY OF
MESSIAH TO A JEWISH POST-MODERN COMMUNITY
Jhan Moskowitz, D. Min. 158

COMMUNICATING THE DEITY OF YESHUA TO
POSTMODERN JEWS
Akiva Cohen, Ph.D.. 169

HOW THE BOROUGH PARK SYMPOSIUM CAME TO BE AND WHAT IT IS

The Borough Park Steering Committee

The time had come for leaders across the organizational spectrum of the Messianic Jewish/Jewish Missions world to unite as members of the Jewish community, leaders of a Remnant, with a responsibility to the God who called us his chosen people. On October 19-20, 2006, ten Messianic Jewish colleagues met in Brooklyn, New York. We agreed on a direction, a Steering Committee, and shared convictions that would determine who should actively participate:

> *We are Jews who believe in Yeshua and in God's covenant with Israel, and as members of the Jewish community, are committed to the welfare of our people.*

> *We feel compelled by the spirit of God to advance the good news of Yeshua among our people.*

> *We desire to preserve the unity and secure the future of the Messianic Jewish movement and our common mission through respectful dialogue, without acrimony, even in the face of critical disagreements.*

> *We believe in the authority of Scripture and the deity of Yeshua, and that eternal life is the gift of God in Messiah Yeshua our Lord.*

Since we held our planning meeting in an Orthodox Jewish hotel in the Borough Park neighborhood of Brooklyn, our setting provided a great name for this consultation—"the Borough Park Symposium." We scheduled it for a year later, October, 2007 and chose a topic that we knew would be controversial, but which seemed like a logical starting point for our dialogue: *The Gospel and the Jewish People.*

When the symposium arrived, we discussed the nature of the gospel itself, how it applies specifically to Jewish people, and what outreach should look like in light of all this. Participants were impassioned and not afraid of ideological clash or of expressing agreement when it was there. Leaders who had staked out opposite ends of the Messianic Jewish spectrum years earlier now sat down together and talked. Indeed, several leaders reconnected with colleagues with whom they hadn't spoken, for one reason or another, for twenty or thirty years.

When the Steering Committee evaluated the Symposium, we determined that it was a big success, not only in discussing the issues, but also in helping to "preserve the unity and secure the future of the Messianic Jewish movement and our common mission through respectful dialogue." Although we didn't want the Symposium to become institutionalized into an annual event, we started to think about a second one. The Steering Committee met in May 2008 and chose a topic that we imagined to be less controversial among us, *The Deity of Messiah and the Mystery of God.*

Paradoxically, this is the issue most controversial in the wider Jewish community, the boundary-marker that the Jewish community has set for centuries to define itself. No matter how Jewish in all other ways a person might be, a Jewish gatekeeper might say, belief in the deity of Yeshua, by itself, drives him or her out of Judaism into Christianity. And Messianic Jews are problematic (and even to be feared) because they refuse to accept that they've crossed this line.

From this perspective, all of us who gathered for BPS II, as diverse as we might have been, were on the same side of the divide, despite our differences, and even despite our lack of precise definition of the deity of Messiah. Our goal in meeting was not to produce a precise theological definition, but to discuss how we can embrace and share the truth of the deity of Messiah specifically as Jews. How do we respond to questions we often hear from non-Messianic Jewish friends? "Are you telling us to worship a man as God?" "Can it possibly be right for a Jew to acknowledge a Messiah who claims (or whose followers claim for him) to somehow be God?" "Why are you trying to bring such a non-Jewish idea into Judaism?" Much was accomplished by hearing the thoughts of others in our Community.

A clear benefit of the Symposium was the heightened sense of unity that came out of this event. Some of the panels included speakers who had been in robust debates with each other in recent years, who had widely different perspectives, and yet, at the Symposium, communicated with the greatest respect and deference. There were disagreements on many specific points, but an underlying sense prevailed that we are all in this together—marking out new territory as Jews who recognize the unique nature of the Messiah of Israel. It is our hope that this renewed awareness of our underlying unity will help the entire Messianic Jewish community to move forward. As one of the Steering Committee members remarked afterwards, "I guess this BPS Symposium was about more than our theology!"

No one expected that we'd ever have total agreement, but in the larger scope of things, we have more in common with each other than many other people in the world. We are Jews who all agree that Yeshua is the Messiah. We all believe that our people are the chosen people. We all hold that the Land of Israel was uniquely given and still belongs to the Jewish people. We all accept the Torah, and its obligations upon us as Jews, to one degree or another. Compared to the entire 6.6 billion people in the world, we have more in common with each other than many other groups in the world.

That's why these symposiums are so important. Our numbers are small, but great things can happen as we learn how to listen and work together. There's strength in unity. That's why we agreed that:

> The purpose of the Symposiums is to provide a forum for members of the broader Messianic Jewish community to articulate their beliefs with an expectation that they will receive a respectful hearing, but without the expectation that agreement concerning these beliefs will be achieved. The Symposium is designed to provide an internal platform for leaders to better understand each another and the various positions held within the Messianic movement.

So, as you read one or more of the papers in the Borough Park Symposiums, you may be challenged. You may read papers that present both sides of an argument, with few, if any, conclusions drawn. This is the way of the Jewish people.

In the Second Temple era, the time of Yeshua, there were quite a few sects of Judaism—Pharisees, Sadducees, Essenes, Zealots,

Herodians, and more—but they were all considered, and considered themselves, to be Jews. Judaism then was like Judaism today—pluralistic. Orthodox, Conservative, Reform, Reconstructionist, Hasidic, Zionistic branches may disagree today on many matters but all see themselves as part of the same people—the nation of Israel, the Jewish people.

That's the way we in the Borough Park Symposia see ourselves—Jews, albeit Messianic Jews. We are getting more comfortable talking about serious issues, in the hope of understanding God and his revelation better. You are invited to "read over our shoulders" as we have these discussions, much like when you read the New Testament, which also records discussions Jews had about critical issues. Please just remember that you are "listening in" and our discussions may not fit into your previously held pre-suppositions. You may need some paradigm shifting in your thinking.

There were response papers given to most of the papers in this volume. They can be read, as can the papers, on line at:

http://www.boroughparksymposium.com
or
http://www.boroparksymposium.com

We're pleased you are interested in the discussions we in the Messianic Jewish community are having. We believe that you will be challenged to think about these issues alongside us.

For more information, email: info@boroughparksymposium.com.

The Borough Park Symposium Steering Committee

THE DEITY OF MESSIAH AND THE MYSTERY OF GOD: INTRODUCTION OF THE THEME

Darrell L. Bock, Ph.D.

Senior Research Professor on New Testament;
Executive Director of Cultural Engagement, Center for Christian
Leadership, and Cultural Engagement; Dallas Theological Seminary

The issue of the deity of Christ is an important concern both in Christianity and in Messianic Judaism. But how exactly does this work? This has been a question in Christianity and in Messianic Judaism for a long time. Another major question is whether or not the Old Testament supports this kind of an understanding of the Son of God. Thus the relationship between the deity of Christ and mystery of God is an important question both for Christian faith and in particular for the expression of Messianic Judaism.

This same claim has been rejected by many wings of Judaism as a violation of the core confession of the one God. What is fascinating to recall is that the first believers in Jesus were Jews who held to this confession of the one God and yet somehow saw that what they believed about an exalted Jesus did not violate their ancestral faith. This belief extended to the point that Saul-Paul preached in the synagogues that what he believed was nothing more than what Moses and the prophets taught. It also allowed him to take texts from the Tanakh that described the God of Israel and place Jesus in that very same slot as he alluded to such texts. How could this possibly be?

The tension today is seen in two core ideas. First, there is the Christian doctrine of the Trinity. This is the idea that God exists in three persons, although having one nature. The unity is said to preserve the oneness of God, while the diversity is said to reflect first century Jewish messianic writings about the God of Israel, Jesus, and the Holy Spirit of God. Second, there is the core idea of God being only one, a fundamental confession of Judaism as seen in the Shema.

How does one put these two ideas together side-by-side? How can a messianic believer declare their unity with Jewish hope on the one hand, and on the other affirm the exalted position of Jesus? The nature and history of these discussions was a major concern of the second meeting of the Borough Park Symposium.

Such discussion is rooted in the writings of the New Testament, which actually are also mostly Jewish writings from the first century by messianic believers in Jesus as the Christ (of those writers, only Luke is likely to have been a Gentile and he may even have been a proselyte). The debate over Jesus and his position before God also has been the subject of discussions since that time between Jews and Christians. Messianics have argued for the exalted position of Jesus but also have insisted that this fits within the teaching of Judaism. The papers at the second meeting of the Borough Park Symposium were designed to deal with these questions and to discuss ways in which these connections work.

Key questions included: Can the deity of Christ be seen in the Tanakh? If so, exactly how do these connections work? How is one to make the case for these connections? Do they fit discussions that were taking place in Second Temple Judaism? Are there bridges in these historical points and in such background for conversations that can and should take place today? What relationship should the creeds of the Christian church have for the ideas and expressions of faith within messianic faith?

This array of questions are not only topics that have been discussed through the centuries, but also are important to sort out today in a context in which much new information exists about Judaism from the time of Jesus. In addition, there is not agreement within the messianic movement about how to answer these various questions. Even within pockets of Judaism outside of the messianic movement there is discussion of such questions and among some a recognition that such conversations were going on in very Jewish terms at the time. The recent book, *The Jewish Gospels: The Story of the Jewish Christ* (2012) by Daniel Boyarin, hardly a messianic believer, makes such observations. So the essays in this collection pursue these questions from a variety of angles and points of view about how to seek the answers. Such an anthology of views is very Jewish!

On the matter of how a confession of deity works, some argue that there is no clear evidence within the Tanakh alone for the deity of Jesus. Others, on the other side of the spectrum, argue there are many texts that point to this conclusion. Some, in a place in between those options, see development in how this argument is made as we move through the Tanakh. Still others see the background of second Temple Judaism opening up possibilities for how to make this argument to Jewish people.

On the matter of creeds, some value the creeds and see them as an important expression of faith. Others question whether the creeds really help in addressing Jewish questions in the Jewish context.

On the matter of hermeneutics, some see much direct prophecy when it comes to the issue of affirming Jesus's role as divine. Others see a bigger role for either the development of ideas across the canon and/or for the use of typology or pattern fulfillment in declaring who Jesus is.

On the matter of backgrounds, what is one to do with ideas like the Son of Man in texts like 1 Enoch? What should one do with the so-called "Two Powers in Heaven" doctrine in Judaism? Do they have anything to contribute to this discussion? Is the deity of Christ a revelatory teaching of the New Testament alone that separates one form of Judaism? Is such teaching a reflection of later development in the creeds that pushes beyond what the New Testament actually argues? Why or why not?

These kinds of questions became the focus of the second meeting of the Borough Park symposium. We think these essays have particular value both for the messianic Jewish community and the Jewish community at large. We also think that this discussion is of value to the church at large as they listen to how Jewish believers discuss how to communicate their faith to others within Judaism. After all, the Christian claim is that the two testaments belong together and have one message. A discussion about exactly how that works is important for theological reflection among Christians and among Messianics. It also may be enlightening to Jewish people open to seeing how so many Jews in the first century and today have come to believe that Jesus was and is the promised Messiah in line with hope originally expressed in the Tanakh.

So we invite you to take a look at the deity of Christ and the mystery of God. It is our hope that these essays will lead you to reflect and understand better the connection between the two.

REMINDER ON RESPECTFUL THEOLOGICAL DISCUSSION

David Rudolph, Ph.D.

Assistant Professor of Bible and Theology at
Messianic Jewish Theological Institute,
Chair of the Theology Committee of the
Union of Messianic Jewish Congregations.

Yeshua said to his disciples, "The words I have spoken to you are spirit and they are life" (John 6:63).

Words are powerful. They can heal and they can destroy. They can infuse life and they can take it away. At the 2010 Borough Park Symposium, we want to exemplify a culture of respectful theological discussion, a culture we can pass on to the next generation of leaders, a way of treating one another that honors Yeshua Adoneinu—Yeshua our Lord. How do we do this? We begin by admitting that we can all grow in this area.

With your permission, I would like to preface this reminder on respectful theological discussion by sharing with you one of the saddest stories in rabbinic literature. Then I would like to suggest some principles that I think we can learn from.

The Story of Resh Lakish and Rabbi Yochanan

As you know, Jews are involved in just about every profession. There have been Jewish boxers (in fact, there's one here in New York City who has a Star of David on his trunks and is studying to be an Orthodox rabbi). There have been Jewish basketball players, Jewish gangsters, and even Jewish pirates. But have you ever heard of a Jewish gladiator?

Well, the Babylonian Talmud relates the story of a Jewish gladiator named Shimon ben Lakish who was born around the year 200 CE. We can learn a lot from this Jewish gladiator about respectful theological discussion.

Shimon knew how to use swords and knives to kill a man or a wild animal in the arena, before a crowd of cheering spectators. That is what he did. That is what gladiators do. Then one day, according to tradition, Shimon came across Rabbi Yochanan bar Nafcha, one of the leading Torah scholars of that generation. The story of their meeting is recorded in tractate Bava Mezia 84a.

Both of these men were Jews but they were from two different worlds. Despite their differences, Rabbi Yochanan took an interest in the Jewish gladiator and said, "Strength like yours should be devoted to Torah." Rabbi Yochanan took the young man under his wing and trained him in the ways of Hashem. Shimon married Rabbi Yochanan's sister and so these two men, from two different worlds, became part of the same family.

In time, Shimon became a famous Torah scholar in the land of Israel. People called him Resh Lakish, a nickname that perhaps pointed to his being a teacher who mastered the art of asking a good question (in Aramaic, a *kushia*) in order to challenge people to think.

In Rabbinic literature, it is said that when Resh Lakish "discussed halakhic questions it was as if he were uprooting mountains and rubbing them together" (*b. Sanh.* 24a). It appears that Resh Lakish loved truth and pursued it. He was not ashamed to step back from a position when the other person's case was more convincing (*y. Git.* 3.44d). Resh Lakish was known for asking challenging questions. On numerous occasions, Rabbi Yochanan abandoned his own halakhic position after Resh Lakish showed him compelling reasons to do so (*y. Yoma* 38a; *y. 'Erub.* 18c). Rabbi Yochanan and Resh Lakish were dialogue partners (*y. Sanh.* 2.19d, 20a). A wonderful dynamic of interdependence existed between these two rabbis.

Then one day, everything changed. In the Beit Midrash, Rabbi Yochanan raised a simple halakhic question—when did metal objects like swords, knives, and daggers become susceptible to ritual impurity? Rabbi Yochanan argued that they became susceptible when hardened in the furnace. Resh Lakish retorted that they became susceptible to ritual impurity when the smith dipped them in cold water. There is no evidence in the Bavli that Resh Lakish spoke in a disrespectful way. He simply had a different point of view and explained why.

But Rabbi Yochanan took the disagreement personally. His pride got the best of him. With stinging sarcasm, Rabbi Yochanan responded by reminding Resh Lakish of his contemptible background—that he had once been someone who wielded swords and daggers—and was thus the "expert" in this halakhic matter.

Rabbi Yochanan's sharp words devastated Resh Lakish. And Resh Lakish, this gladiator turned rabbi, this powerful man, became weak and deathly sick.

Resh Lakish's wife pleaded with her brother, Rabbi Yochanan, to help her husband. She asked him at least to pray for his healing, but Rabbi Yochanan refused. Soon after, Resh Lakish died and Rabbi Yochanan fell into a deep depression.

The Rabbis sent Elazar ben Pedat, the most impressive young scholar they could find, to study Torah with Rabbi Yochanan. They hoped that this brilliant young man would cause Rabbi Yochanan to forget his grief.

Day after day, Rabbi Elazar sat with Rabbi Yochanan. And each time the older rabbi gave his opinion, Rabbi Elazar would say, "I know another source that supports what you are saying."

Rabbi Yochanan finally said to him, "Do you think you are like Resh Lakish? Whenever I stated an opinion, Resh Lakish would present twenty-four objections to what I said. He forced me to justify every ruling I gave, so that in the end, the subject was fully clarified. But all you do is tell me that you know another source that supports what I am saying. Don't I know myself that what I have said is right?"

Rabbi Yochanan tore his garments, and walked about weeping and crying out, "Where are you, son of Lakish?"

In the end, Rabbi Yochanan lost his mind. The rabbis pleaded with God to have mercy on him, and soon after Rabbi Yochanan died.

Principles

What can we learn from this story about respectful theological discussion?

1. Words can kill. This is the story of a prominent rabbi who killed another prominent rabbi with his words.

   Sadly, this is not the only instance of a death like this in Jewish history. Indeed, the counting of the omer—the season we are presently in—is an annual time on the Jewish calendar to remember other rabbis who perished because of how they treated one another. The Babylonian Talmud explains: "Rabbi Akiva had *twelve thousand pairs of disciples* between

Gabbath and Antipatris. All died during his lifetime, at the same time, between Passover and Shavuot, because they did not treat one another with respect" (*b. Yebam.* 62b).[1]

What can we learn from these Talmudic stories? They teach us the importance of communicating respect for one another and choosing our words wisely. Rabbi Jacob Telushkin writes:

An old Jewish teaching compares the tongue to an arrow. "Why not another weapon, a sword, for example?" one rabbi asks. "Because," he is told, "if a man unsheathes his sword to kill his friend, and his friend pleads with him and begs for mercy, the man may be mollified and return the sword to its scabbard. But an arrow, once it is shot, cannot be returned, no matter how much one wants to."[2]

This principle applies not only to what we say in these sessions but also to what we say in private venues—at meals, in the hallway, in our hotel rooms, in emails we send during and after the symposium, as well as in our blogs and newsletters. Words are arrows. Once released, we cannot take them back.

It is perfectly okay to express disagreement with another's point of view, but we should do it in a kind way and never invalidate the argument by invalidating the person, as Rabbi Yochanan did.

2. Let us remember that Resh Lakish was a gladiator. Physically, he was a powerful man. He must have seemed imposing. But in reality he was vulnerable. He quickly became ill because of Rabbi Yochanan's words. Some of us here—especially the New Yorkers and Israelis— may outwardly appear thick skinned and tough. But the reality is very different. Like lobbing a grenade, the words we speak can quickly blow a hole in this veneer and do great damage to the soul. Resh Lakish was killed by the words of someone very close to him, by a brother. We are *klal Yisrael*. We are brothers and sisters in the body of Messiah. Let us not murder one another with our words.

If we blow it and make the mistake of wounding someone with our words wrongfully, we should not let our pride get the best of us, as was the case with Rabbi Yochanan. We should repent immediately.

3. Rabbi Yochanan loved truth but on this particular occasion he closed the door to the possibility of learning from Resh Lakish. We need to ask the question, "Are there people in this symposium we do not want to learn from? Do we close our minds to the possibility that they can teach us?" As Russ Resnik points out, "In our passion for biblical truth in one dimension, we sometimes trample truth in another."

4. It is said that Resh Lakish was one who uprooted mountains and rubbed or grinded them together. This is a likely reference to the extent to which he grappled with different halakhic perspectives and evaluated them in relation to one another. As Artscroll puts it, "he penetratingly analyzed the laws and showed the inconsistencies between them." Let us be like Resh Lakish and grapple with the different perspectives shared in this symposium. Let us uproot these mountains and grind them together.

5. Resh Lakish and Rabbi Yochanan both exhibited an ability to step back from their positions when the other person's case was more convincing. Similarly, the disciples of Hillel and Shammai conceded at times that the other school was correct and changed their opinions. Are we able to do this? Are we willing to cross party lines at this symposium if the other person's case is more convincing?

6. Rabbi Yochanan began to think that Resh Lakish, his dialogue partner, was more of a nuisance than a blessing. And, in a sense, Rabbi Yochanan got rid of his dialogue partner by allowing him to die. But after Resh Lakish passed away, Rabbi Yochanan realized the treasure that he had lost. Rabbi Yochanan fell into a deep depression and walked about weeping and crying out, "Where are you, son of Lakish?" I want us all to look around this room. One of the wonderful things about the Borough Park Symposium is that we are leaders who do *not* see eye-to-eye on every theological issue. Truth be told, we may even at times wish in our hearts that another leader would disappear so the nuisance of their problematic teachings would go away. But our feelings do not always match our needs. When we lose our dialogue partners, and are surrounded only by the people who agree with us, we do not grow. Let us treasure each other as dialogue partners and not make the tragic mistake that Rabbi Yochanan did.

7. Finally, how can we realistically do all of this? At the root of all the principles we have been discussing is humility, the ability to condescend, to lower ourselves and think of others as better than ourselves. We can do all of this if we imitate our divine Messiah. Paul wrote in Philippians 2:

> Do nothing out of selfish ambition or vain conceit, but in humility consider others better than yourselves. Each of you should look not only to your own interests, but also to the interests of others.

> Your attitude should be the same as that of Messiah Yeshua: Who, being in very nature God, did not consider equality with God something to be grasped, but made himself nothing, taking the very nature of a servant, being made in human likeness. And being found in appearance as a man, he humbled himself and became obedient to death—even death on a cross! Therefore God exalted him to the highest place and gave him the name that is above every name, that at the name of Yeshua every knee should bow, in heaven and on earth and under the earth, and every tongue confess that Yeshua the Messiah is *ADONAI*, to the glory of God the Father. (Phil. 2:3-11)

ENDNOTES

1. Cf. *Gen. Rab.* 61.3; *Eccles. Rab.* 11.6. See Tzvi Y. Rotberg, *Sfiras Haomer* (New York: Moznaim, 1983), 84-90.
2. Joseph Telushkin, *Words That Hurt, Words That Heal: How to Choose Words Wisely and Well* (New York: Harper, 1996), xx.
3. E.g., "The School of Hillel changed their opinion and began to teach according to the School of Shammai's ruling" (m. 'Ed 1.14). Cf. Sifre Deut. 31.

COMMUNICATING THE DIVINITY OF YESHUA TO OUR JEWISH PEOPLE "BETWEEN A ROCK AND A HARD PLACE"

Rabbi David Rosenberg, M.Div.
Rabbi of Shuvah Yisrael

A great diversity of our Jewish people want to know and understand the mystery of God and the divinity of Yeshua. But . . . Messianic Judaism is often stuck in the middle of a dilemma, living in the unique Jewish space that I call: *"between a rock and a hard place."*

The Rock is the historical Christian world in all the diversity of their theological views in opposition to the Hard Place, which is our Jewish world with a very different set of theological views. Both communities claim the exclusive position as the people of God. Our Messianic Jewish community lives precariously between the Rock and the Hard Place. In response to Jhan Moskowitz's paper on Post modernism, you can also refer to this as the "soft" hard Rock and the "somewhat" hard place. Nevertheless, since we are intimately related to both worlds, we find ourselves in many ways struggling between, a little bit uncomfortable, and completely crushed. The issue of Yeshua's Divinity is one of the more uncomfortable compartments in this environment between *"a rock and a hard place."* Resolving our difficulties with one side of this equation only causes greater difficulty with the other side. This leaves us with the daunting task of solving both sides of the equation. Anything less will simply continue the pain.

OUR GOAL

We must reframe our Messianic faith to make it clearly biblical and relevant in both Jewish space and with the rest of the Body of Messiah. Although the task may seem impossible, God answers us with the same words He spoke to Abraham our Father: *"Is anything too hard for Adonai?"* (Gen.18:14, CJB). The Borough Park Symposium has taken on this impossible task by compelling our

Messianic community to gather together in the spirit of Isaiah 1:18, *"Come now let us reason together!"*

As I look over the papers being presented, it is clear that we have all been deeply impacted by our personal interactions. For Mitch Glaser it was a Lebuvitcher Rabbi in the '70s at Brooklyn College, for Jhan Moskowitz, a conversation on a plane to Israel. Many years ago, my brother Jhan and I had a conversation with a Rabbi in, of all places, Borough Park. Our youngest brother attended an Orthodox synagogue there and challenged us to talk with his Rabbi so he could help us make T'shuvah. After some time, the Rabbi became a bit agitated with our faith in Yeshua and our desire to live an observant Jewish life. When he asked why we were wearing *kippot* and not *tzi tzis*, we both replied in unison, *"You're right, we should be wearing them!"* Jhan quickly asked the Rabbi, why he had no blue techelet in his tzi tzis? He closed his eyes and put up his hands and said, *"Wait, wait, wait,"* he paused for a moment and said, *"you really aren't required to wear them."* As he danced on his own contradiction, He said, *"You're dangerous, because you are trying to build a bridge that should never be built!"* He was afraid that if we built such a bridge, people would be able to walk across from both sides, to actually communicate with one another, and that made him very uncomfortable. *"You wanna convert, convert! But, you can't be both!"*

The documents of this symposium are passionate papers written with the singular hope of solving *"the impossible dream"* of bridging the theological gap between our Jewish and Christian worlds. Our messianic Jewish community has been given the impossible task of building a bridge that no one wanted. When John Roebling set out to build the Brooklyn Bridge they said it couldn't be done. To accomplish this he had to find a way to anchor both towers on the solid bedrock found under the layers of mud below the East River. He had to invent the cables to make it work. Unfortunately he also discovered "the benz," but these are the risks of living between a rock and a hard place.

Trude Weiss-Rosmarin (author of Judaism & Christianity: The Differences) said, "The chief fundamental difference between Judaism and Christianity is that the former is committed to pure and uncompromising monotheism and the latter subscribes to the belief in the Trinitarian nature of the Divine being."

So, a gulf exists between Jewish and Christian ideas about the mystery of God, Messiah and His Divinity. But, why is the gap so large and how did it get that way? Below are examples of (observant) Jewish art that are intrinsically tied to the Hebrew language and the Hebrew alphabet creatively used to avoid the transgressing of making a "graven image."

 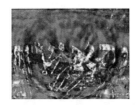 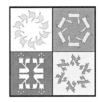

How Christian images in art shaped
Jewish perceptions: "Not a true monotheism."

The discussion and dispute over the Divinity of Yeshua has a long history! Below, a depiction of the Trinity by Domenico Beccafumi (left), and an earlier effort at the Borough Park Symposium, called *the Disputation over the Trinity* by del Sarto (Church fathers working out their differences).

Holy Trinity,
St. Jerome, and two Saints,
The ANDREA del Castagno
Nearly 18 centuries of wrong images made Yeshua *appear* to be one of *three Gods* -a radical departure from the ancient Jewish perceptions of the Invisible G-d of Israel. Somehow, the history of Christian art and the doctrine of the trinity put us in the uncomfortable position of explaining the divinity of Yeshua to our Jewish people as "an old man, a young man, (a baby), and a bird.

15

Below, a painting called the Tricephalus (three fused heads, painted by an unknown Netherlandish artist). As if a three headed G-d isn't a problem, we then have to explain why "the old man," "the young man," and "the bird" are crowning the virgin Mary as if she is some how joining the Godhead?

Coronation of the Virgin by the Holy Trinity, Jacob The JORDAENS

"The Coronation of the Virgin" Diego Rodríguez de Silva Velázquez 1599-1660

Is it any wonder that our Jewish people have such concerns:

- *"Does G-d have an image?*
- *"G-d is invisible and no one has seen Him!"*
- *"Jews don't believe in the Trinity, we believe in **one G-d**, **not three!"***
- *"Jews don't believe in a divine Messiah"*
- *"If you claim that Messiah is G-d, then you are guilty of making G-d into Man! You are an idol worshipper"*

We need to Dispel Jewish and Christian myth about God's Image: The Dichotomy of the invisible God verses the visible God.

Jewish and Christian perceptions about Gods image developed over the centuries widening the gap of perception between Judaism and Christianity between the visible and invisible God. These mythical views about God developed into competing positions. The Jewish world defined itself as the people who worship the invisible God while the Christian world countered with the visible God in the person of Jesus Christ. As Daniel Nessim discussed it in his paper, he said, *"2000 years of dogmatic formulation which lack a Jewish sensitivity and reading of the scriptures, and theological tradition seen as hostile and other, have made communication of the fullness of the Godhead dwelling in the Body of Yeshua nigh on impossible to communicate. Nevertheless as Jewish believers in Yeshua we have never shrugged*

16

from the impossible." Together, we can *"dream the impossible dream"* of building a bridge in the bedrock of God's revealed word, and with God's help, clearly communicate the biblical truths that have transformed all our lives.

I am in agreement with Daniel Nessim, Richard Harvey and the many fine papers presented at this symposium, that our answers to this dichotomy must be based in the Tenach and the Brit Hadashah. I will limit my discussion to presenting what I believe to be **forensic evidence that God has an image.**

I have, like many of you, argued and discussed the issue again and again to only walk away frustrated. In recent years I began to use power point presentations in my sermons and soon realized that the right picture can indeed be worth a thousand words. The issue of the **invisible God** *verses* **the visible God** *was the big, frustrating* **"either, or"** *of our apologetic process. So, I set out to explain the big* **"both, and"** *apologetic, to show how God is both visible and invisible at the same time.*

Important Biblical Terms about God & His Image
God is "One" (Echad) as evidenced in the Shema

Hear oh Israel the Lord our God the Lord is on (echad)

Important Biblical Terms about God & His Image in the Tenach & New Covenant

1) *The Image of God*

Genesis 1:27 *"So God created humankind in his own image; in the image of God he created him: male and female he created them."* (CJB)

2 Corinthians 4:4 *"They do not come to trust because the god of the 'olam hazeh has blinded their minds, in order to prevent them from seeing the light shining from the Good News about the glory of the Messiah, who is the image of God."* (CJB)

James 3:9 *"With it we bless ADONAI, the Father & with it we curse people, who were made in the image of God."* (CJB)

2) *The Image of God & The Invisible God*

Colossians 1:15 CJB, *"He is the visible image of the invisible God. He is supreme over all creation,"*

Colossians 2:9 *"For in him, bodily, lives the fullness of all that God is."*

Colossians 2:15 *"He is the visible image of the invisible God. He is supreme over all creation, 2:16 because in connection with him were created all things — in heaven and on earth, visible and invisible, whether thrones, lordships, rulers or authorities — they have all been created through him and for him. 2:17 He existed before all things, and he holds everything together.*

Being made in his image and likeness, makes us like Him: We are the Forensic evidence that God has an image!

Like God, we are one part visible and two parts invisible. My body is the visible image of the otherwise invisible David. As a Rabbi I have been present many times when someone was passing away. When my mother passed away I volunteered to "watch the body" as we waited for the funeral home to come. Although I watched for over an hour it was clear that the mom I knew had left the room the moment she died. I didn't see her leave the room, but she left. The human spirit is invisible and so is the human soul. We are two parts invisible and one part visible. God the Father is invisible and so is the Holy Spirit. So, if Colossians is correct that ***"in him dwells the fullness of the God head bodily"*** then we may gain some new understanding about this profound statement concerning the visible image of the Messiah and the invisible image of the Father; ***"Philip said to him, "Lord, show us the Father, and it will be enough for us." Yeshua replied to him, "Have I been with you so long without your knowing me, Philip? Whoever has seen me has seen the Father; so how can you say, 'Show us the Father'?*** (John 14:8)

Of course, the New Covenant scriptures are easy. But the strength of our argument is best made in Genesis 1:27. Here we are able to examine the context of *"Let us"* language as God speaks within the Godhead. Despite the Jewish commentaries that insist on this as a reference to angels, we can prove otherwise by a simple examining of a few related passages in the Torah.

1. *"Let us"* language in Genesis 1:27 *"Let us make mankind in our image and likeness."*

Who is speaking to whom?
Does God the Father have an image?
Are angels actually present in the story?

2. "Let us" *language in Genesis 11:5-9, The Tower of Babel*

Who came down?
Are angels in the story?
Who is speaking to whom?

Who Came Down?
וַיֵּרֶד יְהוָה לִרְאֹת
To see   ADONAI   came down

Again, Are Angels present in the text?

Within The Godhead?

Who is God Speaking to? Himself!

3. Is "Let us" *Language in the text? Genesis 18: Three visitors to Abrams tent*

Who Appeared To Abraham?
וַיֵּרָא אֵלָיו
Adonai = יְהוָה
Appeared = וַיֵּרָא
to see/ was seen

וְהִנֵּה שְׁלֹשָׁה אֲנָשִׁים נִצָּבִים
Behold = וְהִנֵּה
Three [3] = שְׁלֹשָׁה
Men = אֲנָשִׁים
Stood = נִצָּבִים

3 Messengers:
1 called 'Lord' + 2 = identified as angels
Who else appeared to Abraham?

Genesis 18:17 ADONAI said, *"Should I hide from Avraham what I am about to do, 18:18 inasmuch as Avraham is sure to become a great and strong nation, and all the nations of the earth will be blessed by him? 18:19 For I have made myself known to him, so that he will give orders to his children and to his household after him to keep the way of ADONAI and to do what is right and just, so that ADONAI may bring about for Avraham what he has promised him."*

Is Adonai speaking in the first person? *Yes!*
Are Angels present? *Yes!*
Who is He speaking about? *Avram!*
Who is he speaking to? *The Two Angels!*

So, we find a rule:

In the presence of mankind and angels, God speaks in the first person. "I am Adonai."
When God is alone, He speaks within Himself using: "Let us" language!

4. *Is "Let us" language present in the text? Genesis 28:13 Jacobs Ladder*

Marc Chagall: "Jacobs Ladder"

Ya'akov Meets The God of His Fathers

Ya'akov went out from Be'er-sheva & traveled toward Haran. *11* He came to a certain place & stayed the night there, because the sun had set. He took a stone from the place, put it under his head & lay down there to sleep.

Ya'akov Meets The God of His Fathers

28:13 Then suddenly ADONAI was standing there next to him; and he said, "I am ADONAI, the God of Avraham your [grand]father and the God of Yitz'chak. The land on which you are lying I will give to you and to your descendants.

Man+ Angels + Adonai ='s God: Speaking in 1st Person

There are many angels ascending and descending "Jacob's Ladder."
- Man (Jacob) is present in the passage.
- Adonai is present in the text.

In the presence of mankind and angels, God speaks in the first person. "I am Adonai"

5. *God's opinion about His Image. Language about God's Image in Numbers 12:5-9*

Bamidbar/ Numbers 12:1-9 - Conflict between Moses, Aaron & Miriam

5 ADONAI came down in a column of cloud and stood at the entrance to the tent. He summoned Aharon and Miryam, and they both went forward. 6 He said, "Listen to what I say: when there is a prophet among you, I, ADONAI, make myself known to him in a vision, I speak with him in a dream. 7 But it isn't that way with my servant Moshe. He is the only one who is faithful in my entire household.

8 With him I speak face to face & clearly, not in riddles; he sees the image of ADONAI.

For some it is a bit uncomfortable to say that no one will ever see the Father. When I recently taught this material in another Messianic Synagogue, some attendees expressed a disappointment over their expectations about finally seeing the Father in eternity. Phillip had similar expectations! I believe this shows how deeply many of us have been affected by powerful images and perceptions from the Christian world, and numerous expressions of the Trinity. But our responsibility is to make the message clear for our people. Based on a thorough study of the Tenach that is far more comprehensive than this paper, I believe we can reconcile the invisible God that is embraced by so many of our Jewish people by showing them that He is both visible and invisible. In addition, there is so much more we can say about the intentional purpose of God in making mankind in His image and likeness. But how we communicate these truths can be dangerous.

This is the nature of living between a Rock and a Hard place, when we seek to communicate in Jewish space within Jewish concepts we get crushed by the Christian world and in seeking to please the Christian world by giving ascent to 'improbable" and incompatible Trinitarian imagery we then become crushed in the Hard place of Jewish space while *all of Jewish space* is watching!

I believe we as the messianic community have a mutual mandate to bring a vision for reframing Jewish space and Jewish theology while at the same time challenging the Christian World to reframe both their identity and theology within Jewish space as well.

Conclusion

Without us the Rock and the Hard Place will continue as two ships passing in the night. Occasionally they will collide, bringing much damage to both. For a season, we have to endure the uncomfortable and precarious place of living between a Rock and a Hard Place until we are fully embraced by both.

The tricephalus, the old man, the baby and the bird, along with the triplet images of God must fall by the way side as other false images and weak metaphors like water, steam and ice or the egg shell, the egg white and the yoke. They are unacceptable in Jewish space and theology, and despite whatever good biblical thinking was established at Nicaea and Chalcedon, their creedal formulas end up looking crippled in the context of the history of Christian art that claims to represent them. Long before any Jewish person seeks to investigate the

21

beliefs of these famous councils, they will have been exposed to countless formulations of the Trinity that most famous paintings in the world represent.

Our Modern Messianic movement must be willing to occupy this dangerous space for the sake of our Jewish People and the Body of the Messiah. It is a bridge that only we can build with God's help! Many will still say it can't be done. But this is our quest to find a way to communicate the good news to our Jewish world. The Messianic Jewish community is the only bedrock on which the historic towers of Jewish and Christian faith can stand together!

> *"Remaining always ready to give a reasoned answer*
> *to anyone who asks you to explain the hope you have*
> *in you - yet with humility and fear"*

THE SIGNIFICANCE OF
THE DEITY OF YESHUA

Mark S. Kinzer, Ph.D.

Rabbi of Congregation Zera Avraham
Senior Scholar and President Emeritus of
Messianic Jewish Theological Institute,
Chair of the Hashivenu Board
Chair of the Hashivenu Board Ecclesiological Significance

As Messianic Jews, we identify in various ways and degrees with both the Jewish people and with the Christian Church. This dual identification places the issue of the deity of Yeshua front and center for us as a community.

For most of those who identify themselves as Christians the results of the fourth and fifth century Church councils define the substance of their faith, even if they have never heard of Nicaea or Chalcedon and even if they consider the Bible their only doctrinal authority. Affirmation of the deity of Yeshua—and, for many, acknowledgement of the doctrine of the Trinity—constitutes both the center of their confession and the boundary that demarcates its unique character.

On the other hand, the denial of Yeshua's deity has been almost as significant for classic forms of Judaism as its affirmation has been for the Christian faith. Until the Middle Ages, acknowledgement of Yeshua's deity and worship of the Trinitarian God were considered by Jewish authorities to be *avodah zara*, i.e., idolatry. Eventually this assessment changed in regards to Gentile Christians, but not in regards to Jews who believe in Yeshua.

Jews and Christians thus have agreed on the central importance of the doctrine of Yeshua's deity. The doctrine functioned for many centuries of Jews and Christians as a mutually accepted litmus test for distinguishing authentic Judaism from authentic Christianity. It provided a doctrinal correlate to the practical issue of Torah observance, drawing an unambiguous theological line between the two feuding religious communities just as the Jewish imperative and observance (or Christian prohibition and non-observance) of circumcision, Shabbat, holidays, and *kashrut* established a clear boundary on the level of praxis. For the Jewish people, the chief community-defining positive commandment was "You shall observe the Torah" and the chief negative commandment was "You shall not believe that Jesus is the Son of God." For the Christian Church, the chief community-defining positive commandment was "You shall believe that Jesus is the Son of God" and the chief negative commandment was "You shall not observe the Torah."

The drawing and fortification of these two negative boundary lines make life difficult for Messianic Jews. We are pressed from the Christian side to give up or dilute the conviction that Torah observance is incumbent on every Jew, and are pressed even more vehemently from the Jewish side to give up or dilute the conviction that Yeshua is more than a man. Recognizing the parallel between these two issues— Torah observance and the deity of Yeshua—clarifies the immense ecclesiological significance of the doctrinal question we are discussing at this symposium.

Nicene Orthodoxy

However, the theological and spiritual significance of this question is even greater than its ecclesiological import. In order to discern what is at stake, let us look briefly at Nicene orthodoxy, as exemplified in the Nicene Creed.

Nicene orthodoxy arises as a response to and rejection of Arianism. The Arians believed that the Son of God was a creature. They accepted the biblical teaching that he existed before becoming incarnate and that the world was made through him, but they held that "there was [a time] when He [i.e., the Son of God] was not." If all reality may be classified as either eternal and uncreated or temporal (i.e., with a beginning in time) and created, the Arians place the pre-incarnate Son of God in the "temporal and created" category. He is the first created entity, the highest of the angels, the most exalted being in all creation. But he is not eternal, and he is not truly divine.

The Arian position reflected the Hellenistic philosophical assumptions dominant in the period. According to those assumptions, the eternal realm of divinity was absolutely transcendent, and could have no direct point of contact with the temporal and material world. Such a system of thought excluded divine incarnation in principle. But its implications went far beyond the exclusion of incarnation. In effect, it suggested that the transcendent God was ultimately unknowable, and could not be truly present within the created order. *Such a system of thought excluded in principle the living God of Scripture, the self-revealing One who enters into an intimate covenantal relationship with the people of Israel.* In rejecting Arianism, the Nicene Creed took a stand *against* the common philosophical notions of the day, and *for* the biblical portrayal of the God of Israel

What does Nicene Orthodoxy affirm in opposition to the Arian position? At the heart of the Nicene Creed is the confession, rooted in the teaching of the *Besorah* of John, that Yeshua is "the only begotten (*monogene*) Son of God, begotten (*gennethenta*) of his Father before all worlds."

The Creed draws two conclusions from this fundamental proposition. These two conclusions are conveyed in the phrases, "Light from (*ek*) Light, true God from (*ek*) true God." First of all, the Son draws his being from (*ek*) the Father. Their relationship has a *taxis*, a structure or form, in which the Father is the ultimate source of the Son's existence and nature. That structure is eternal rather than temporal: as a star never exists without emitting light, so the Father never exists without the Son. Secondly, the Son shares the Father's nature. As the Father is "Light," so the Son is "Light"; as the Father is "true God," so the Son is "true God." Though the Son is ordered after and in relationship to the Father, he is not a demigod, a secondary divinity at a lower level of being from the Father.

The Creed continues by describing the Son as "begotten, not made." This contrast between begetting and making is crucial for the teaching of the Creed. The Son is not like a painting or a sculpture that springs from the genius of an artist but remains fundamentally different in kind from the artist himself. Just as offspring in the temporal created order are the same kind of beings as the ones who generate them, so in the eternal uncreated order the Son is as much divine as is the Father from whom he derives his being.

The contrast between "begetting" and "making" helps explain the most famous phrase of the Creed, "having the same *ousia* (*homoousion*) as the Father." In this context *ousia* appears to mean the kind of thing that something is. Thus, the *homousion* does not add anything new to what has already been presented in the Creed. It does not provide an explanation or theory for how this could all be so.

Instead, it expresses through one technical Greek term what the Creed states elsewhere in more allusive biblical language.

The Nicene Creed offers a highly plausible rendering of the Apostolic teaching on the divinity of Yeshua, in light of controversies that had emerged in the early centuries of the Yeshua movement. Though it spoke in the language of its own time and place, it did not conform to the philosophical theories that were currently in fashion. Instead, the Creed upheld a commitment to an authentic encounter with the Living God who acts in a revelatory and redemptive manner within the world. It maintained the Jewish and biblical witness to the qualitative difference between the transcendent Creator and that which is created, the particular personal character of the Creator as the God of Israel, and the reality of this God's activity within the created order. It affirmed that God can be known and encountered in the person of Yeshua the Messiah.

Medieval Jewish Parallels to the Arian Controversy

Jewish history provides us with a surprising parallel to the Arian controversy and the Nicene response. The similarity supports our contention that what is at stake at Nicaea is not merely an orthodox Christology, but the authenticity of human encounter with the redemptive self-revealing God of Israel.

Rabbinic texts usually treat the biblical accounts of God's self-revealing presence in a realistic fashion. The Sages are not embarrassed by biblical anthropomorphism. They assume that the figure, who appeared to Moses, Isaiah, Ezekiel, and Daniel, and to all of Israel at the Sea and at Sinai, was none other than *Hashem*, the God of Israel. As part of their broader assault on rabbinic authority, the 9th century Karaites, influenced by Greek philosophical currents absorbed into Islamic thought, attacked the anthropomorphism of the rabbinic texts. To ward off these attacks, Saadia Gaon drew upon the same philosophy that guided the Karaites. He reinterpreted rabbinic thought in a way that eliminated all anthropomorphism, even from the biblical theophanies.

> But how is it possible to put such [non-anthropomorphic] constructions on these anthropomorphic expressions and on what is related to them, when Scripture itself explicitly mentions a form like that of human beings that was seen by the prophets and spoke to them . . . let alone the description by it of God's being seated on a

throne, and His being borne by the angels on top of a firmament (Ezek. 1:26). ... Our answer to this objection is that this form was something [specially] created.[1]

On the one hand, Saadia treats realistically the biblical theophanies. He does not doubt that Ezekiel, Isaiah, and Daniel truly saw an enthroned human figure, referred to in the text as *Hashem*. He also does not doubt that such a figure possessed objective existence beyond the imagination of the prophet. On the other hand, his philosophical commitment to absolute divine transcendence—which he understands as a necessary corollary of the divine unity—excludes the possibility that this enthroned human figure can in fact be the eternal uncreated One. Therefore, he concludes that the form seen by the prophets—the *Kavod* (Glory) or *Shekhinah*—must be a created entity, more exalted than the angels, but not divine.

As Gershom Scholem notes, Saadia's interpretation became "a basic tenet of the [Jewish] philosophical exegesis of the Bible." Scholem also points out its radical novelty.

> These respected authors could hardly have ignored the fact that this conception of the *Shekhinah* as a being completely separate from God was entirely alien to the talmudic texts, and could only be made compatible with them by means of extremely forced interpretation of these texts. Nevertheless, these philosophers preferred 'cutting the Gordian knot' in this way rather than endanger the purity of monotheistic belief by recognizing an uncreated hypostasis.[2]

The parallel here to the Arian interpretation of the *Logos* should be evident. The underlying concerns are identical: a desire to guard the purity of divine transcendence and unity understood in terms of Greek philosophical conceptions. The problems encountered as a result of this concern are likewise identical: the realistic biblical presentation of God's self-revelation to Israel. Finally, the strategies adopted to overcome the problems are the same: the thesis that the One who is called by the divine Name and who apparently manifests the divine Presence is a created entity, distinct from God and at a lower level in the hierarchy of being.

Just as the Jewish philosophical reinterpretation of the *Kavod/Shekhinah* parallels the Arian reinterpretation of the *Logos*, so the kabalistic response to the Jewish philosophers parallels the Nicene response to the Arians. Like the Nicene fathers, those who championed the tradition of the *Zohar* agreed with their opponents on the ineffable and transcendent nature of God. These Jewish mystics employed the term *Ein Sof* (i.e., the Infinite One) to refer to this aspect of the divine reality. However, also like the Nicene fathers, the kabbalists viewed the self-revelation of God (the biblical *Kavod*, whom they referred to as the *Sefirot*) as both distinct from and one with *Ein Sof*. The infinite and transcendent nature of God required the distinction, but the objective reality and truthfulness of divine revelation required the unity. If the *Kavod* revealed to Israel is not truly and fully divine, then God remains unknown to the world, and Israel's claim to a covenant with a redemptive self-revealing God is rendered fraudulent.

Even the language used by the kabbalists to express the relationship between the *Sefirot* and *Ein Sof* resembles the language employed within the stream of Nicene orthodoxy. "The kabbalists insisted that Ein Sof and the sefirot formed a unity 'like a flame joined to a coal.' 'It is they and they are It.'"[3] This language distinguishes both *Kabbalah* and Nicene orthodoxy from Neo-Platonic thought, in which each stage of emanation involves a gradation in the hierarchy of being, and in which everything below the ineffable "One" occupies a lower ontological status in that hierarchy.

> The hidden God in the aspect of *Ein-Sof* and the God manifested in the emanation of *Sefirot* are one and the same, viewed from two different angles. There is therefore a clear distinction between the stages of emanation in the neoplatonic systems, which are not conceived as processes within the Godhead, and the kabbalistic approach.[4]

For both the Christian and the Jewish traditions, Greek philosophy challenged the biblical presentation of the God of Israel and the living faith of the communities who worshipped that God. Nicene orthodoxy and Jewish mysticism responded by drawing insights and terminology from the challenging philosophical systems and employing them within a new framework provided by Scripture and the tradition of the worshipping community. The philosophical terminology of *ousia* and emanation now served faithful testimony to the infinite transcendent God who acts within the world to establish a covenant relationship with a people, a relationship in which this God is genuinely known.

Conclusion

Both Nicene orthodoxy and *Kabbalah* accept the philosophical acknowledgement of God as infinite, transcendent, invisible, and incomprehensible. But they also reject philosophical interpretations which negate the reality of God's involvement with and in the world, and which so separate God from creation as to render God utterly unknowable. They both accomplish this correction of the philosophical currents in their own religious traditions by distinguishing between God the Father and God the Son, or between *Ein Sof* and the *Sefirot*, while simultaneously asserting their inseparable unity.

Thus, what is at stake here is not an articulation of doctrinal truth that has no bearing on our lives. We are not debating the number of angels that can dance on the head of a pin. Instead, we are seeking to bear verbal witness to the reality of a redemptive encounter with the living God in a way that does justice to the authenticity of that encounter and which effectively invites others to share in it. This is what it means for us to confess the deity of Yeshua.

The parallel between Nicene orthodoxy and the kabbalistic treatment of the relationship between *Ein Sof* and the *sefirot* can also assist us in articulating our own understanding of Yeshua's deity in a manner that draws upon traditional Jewish wisdom. Our mission as Messianic Jews summons us to challenge the negative boundaries erected by both the Jewish and Christian communities in relation to one another, but that challenge can and should draw from the resources of the very communities that put those boundaries in place.

ENDNOTES

1. Saadia Gaon, *Book of Beliefs and Opinions*, II:10 (Rosenblatt, 121).
2. Gershom Scholem, *On the Mystical Shape of the Godhead* (New York: Schocken,1991), 154-55.
3. Daniel Matt, *Zohar* (Ramsey NJ: Paulist, 1983), 33.
4. Gershom Scholem, *Kabbalah* (Jerusalem: Keter, 1974), 98.

THE SIGNIFICANCE OF
THE DEITY OF YESHUA

Mitch Glaser, Ph.D.
President of Chosen People Ministries,

*How do we understand the deity of Yeshua, not just as
theological truth revealed in Scripture, but
particularly as Jews? What is the significance of this
truth in a Jewish context?*

Identifying the Challenge

It is our task in this first presentation to try and identify the
significant elements of our topic—the Deity of Yeshua and the mystery
of God. During the ensuing papers, responses and discussions, some of
our leading Messianic theologians and thinkers will help us grapple
with the significance of this cornerstone doctrine, both in relationship
to our movement and to the mainstream Jewish and Christian
communities. The issues we face are multilayered and span the gamut
from the theological to the sociological. It is also deeply personal, as
the way in which we understand and express our understanding of the
Deity of Yeshua and the mystery of God is critical to our own
relationship with Yeshua. Similarly, our belief and expression of the
doctrine is also important to our relationship with our own movement
and peers and with the Jewish and Christian religious communities we
relate to on a regular basis.

On a personal and devotional note, may I suggest that we avoid
allowing our discussions on the doctrine of the Deity of Yeshua to lead
us into some type of chilling theological deep-freeze. Perhaps, as we
occasionally stop to pray, these actions will remind us that we are
speaking about the nature of One who is present in our midst, as He
promised, "When two or three are gathered in my name, I will be in
their midst."

At the end of the day, to engage in purely "clinical" discussion
about the Messiah and Savior we love and to whom we have dedicated

our life is near impossible. There is not an individual in this room who has not laid their reputation, family, future and all they count dear in this life at the feet of the One whom we believe to be Deity incarnate. This is a costly discussion for many of us. It is costly, as our views on Yeshua, have been at the very root and center of deep divisions with the Jewish larger community and even within our own families. I mention this because we cannot embark on a pilgrimage of understanding regarding the Deity of Yeshua and the mystery of God with intellect alone, as our devotion to God and His Son always involves the heart and soul.

I do hope that we will keep this in mind as we discuss and deliberate during our time together.

Mark will address the broader theological, hermeneutical and historical issues at stake regarding the Deity of Yeshua and the mystery of God, while I speak to some of the more sociological issues raised by our topic. Mark recently prepared a paper for the Hashivenu Forum that is quite expansive and expresses his views on this subject in greater depth. I am appreciative to Mark for his willingness to summarize his effort.

Once again, looking at this issue through the lens of both community and communication, it is critical to recognize that our actual beliefs about the Deity of Yeshua, drawn from Scripture and the formulation of these beliefs so that others might also understand our position are related but different. It is understood that we are trying to describe matters that have minimal analogies in the every day experiences of life.

A Defining Conversation

I recall a conversation I had at Brooklyn College with a Lubavitcher Rabbi a few years ago. He must have been in his 70s and a little more mature and even-tempered than some of the more zealous younger Rabbis I would usually speak to about matters of faith. After a half hour of conversation – discussing the Rebbe's role, Messianic prophecy and much more, we began a brief discussion on the person of Yeshua. He asked if I believed Yeshua was God and I said yes. He then accused me of *avod zerah*—though nicely. I volunteered that I also believed that God was three yet one. He responded, "then you believe in three gods". I said no, that is a misunderstanding of the belief. He then looked down for a moment and in what I believe was a most sincere and somewhat anguished moment he said, "You are making God so complicated!" I smiled and said, "then, I may assume that your belief in the singularity of God's nature and that there is no possibility of a "triunity", that God in all His glory and power is less complicated". We smiled at one another and went our separate ways.

I have reflected many times on this discussion as clearly, whatever we believe about the nature of God is going to be very difficult to articulate and perhaps, as Mark actually develops in his Hashevenu paper, the Kabalistic idea of an *en soph*, which is unknowable, indescribable and only comprehended to some degree through the *spehirot* or emanations which are more easily identified makes sense.

We will be addressing both what we believe and how we express our beliefs in the Deity of Yeshua and the Mystery of God. These are two different matters, but intertwined, as we cannot possibly understand one another's beliefs unless they are articulated. Both our beliefs and the formulations of our beliefs impact and even define the ways in which we will be viewed by our fellow Messianic Jews and by the greater Jewish and Christian communities. In actuality and because of many more years of experience, the views of the Church and the Jewish community regarding the Deity of Yeshua and the mystery of God are more carefully defined than within the Messianic Jewish community. The Church is essentially Nicean in its understanding and the Jewish community is strongly opposed to the idea that a man can be God or that God can take on flesh and humanity, which would lead to a denial of any concept of there being three persons who are part of the unity of God.

At the present time, in the life of our young movement and because of the unique hybridization of our theological constructs within our Messianic community—acceptance, rejection and understanding one another is more uncertain. The Jewish community and the Church have little doubt as to how to handle our beliefs in the Deity of Yeshua and the mystery of God—we are either in or out! However, our modern Messianic movement is in the midst of deciding on its beliefs, the expression of the same, and our identification with the Christian and Jewish communities and whether or not we should embrace an orthodoxy that would allow for the exclusion of others who do not hold the acceptable beliefs.

In some ways, we have been traveling along this path for some years and though our trying to define a Messianic Jewish orthodoxy might seem elusive and unnecessary, still our corporate and congregational doctrinal statements and formulations have already become a basis for fellowship and those who deviate from what is understood as orthodox have been removed from our Messianic associations, pulpits, ministry staffs and opportunities for regular fellowship. Our BPS group has even excluded a few potential participants who felt we should not have had stated a position at all on this subject and by having one that we already overly narrowed the breadth of participants. To deny the importance of the way in which this doctrine is stated from a sociological perspective would be foolish. We have not yet decided what is within the realm of acceptability for Messianic Jews to believe or express about the Deity of Yeshua and the Mystery of God. The discussion held in Israel a few years ago on the topic, whereby Messianic Jews were asked to sign a statement affirming the Deity of Yeshua is just one illustration of the importance of this doctrine for fellowship, employment, support and incorporation within the movement. How broad we should draw the perimeter on this doctrine still remains a challenge.

Our theological statements have as much to do with the sociology of our movement as it does with the theology of our faith. How are creedal statements used within the church and within Judaism – though we could argue that Judaism has a minimum of such statements? Still, those Judaism supports are well used - especially on this very issue. They are still used as a basis of inclusion or exclusion. What we believe and even more importantly how we formulate what we believe will impact our sociology and determine our acceptance or rejection within our communities of faith. This is why our discussions are so important, as some of us have treated others of us as unbelievers based upon our profession and definition of our beliefs in the Deity of Yeshua and the Mystery of God. Is this wrong? I suggest not and that is why it is so critical to try and understand one another. So much is actually at stake.

We all confess that Scripture is our ultimate authority for faith and practice. There is not one person in this room that does not believe that their understanding of the Deity of Yeshua and Mystery of God is not foundationally Biblical. And yet, we do have differing understandings of what the Scriptures teach on this issue and we also express our faith in these theological beliefs a variety of ways. Some of us tend to echo the voice of historic Christian formulations on the Deity of Yeshua and

Trinity—though we might not use the word. Others among us prefer to express this doctrine in more identifiably Jewish terms and concepts.

We are aware of Messianic Jews who espouse a theological formulation of the Deity of Yeshua and the Mystery of God that is clearly not acceptable by the wider church and by Messianic Jews who identify with the historic creeds of the church. However, I wonder if the differences might be in language, and in fact there might be complete commonality in belief but the differences rest in the written and verbal formulation of the these beliefs. Over the next few days, we will hopefully be able to gain a deeper understanding of what we believe not only how we express these beliefs.

Please remember, that this is our goal at BPS 2. We are hoping to better understand one another and not to develop a more uniform statement of beliefs among us.

The stakes are high and not merely theological. Our belief in the Deity of Yeshua and the Mystery of God and the way in which we express this faith could either move us closer or further from one another's fellowship as what we believe and how we formulate these beliefs will have serious community as well as theological consequences.

A Defining Incident

Perhaps one of the best ways to illustrate the more sociological and community-based issues at stake is to recount a well-known incident in the corporate life of our Messianic Jewish movement.

Most of us are familiar with Hugh Schonfield, the author of the Passover Plot and the splendid little volume, the History of Hebrew Christianity. Most of us have some understanding of the events that took place in the mid-1930s within the International Hebrew Christian Alliance when Schonfield and his wife were asked to leave the Alliance because of their views on the Deity of Yeshua and the doctrine of the Trinity.

Allow me to rehearse the basic facts of the situation, which have already been written and discussed in a number of more detailed and thorough articles and mentioned briefly in the new book Mapping Messianic Jewish Theology by Dr. Richard Harvey.[1] I believe that this incident in our recent history illustrates the dilemma of identity we face as Messianic Jews even today.

The following is a brief description of the events surrounding the removal of Mr. and Mrs. Schonfield from the membership of the IHCA and are based upon the minutes of the IHCA meeting in1937.

It would seem from the Minutes, that the issue was actually brought to the forefront by Schonfield himself, as he fully understood that his views on the Deity of Yeshua the doctrine of the Trinity were in flux.

The recording secretary notes that Mr. Hugh Schonfield has made an appeal against a decision of the business committee, that in view of his inability to accept the statement of belief in bylaw number nine, relative to belief in the deity of Christ, he could not remain a member of that committee. The Rev. Harcourt Samuel moved and the Rev. Jacob Peltz seconded that it was resolved that the matter be remitted to a special judicial committee to consist of the presidents of affiliated alliances three others to be nominated by Mr. Schonfield connected decision should be final.[2]

The president called for the report of the judicial committee set up to consider Mr. Schonfeld appeal. This was handed in by Dr.Arnold Frank and stated that the committee were of the opinion that Mr. Schonfeld views were not really in conflict with article 9 of the bylaws.[3]

But, this did not conclude the matter for the delegates.

The conflict over Schonfield's belief regarding article number nine of the bylaws then came to a head during the report of the nominations committee at the IHCA meeting. As follows:

The president called for the report of the nominations committee. The committee recommended the election of Dr. Frank as president. This was proposed by Rev. Harcourt Samuel and carried unanimously. Seconded by Rev. Jacob Peltz, Dr. Frank was received with acclamation.

The committee then commended the election of the Rev. Nahum Levison as vice president. Mr. Nahum Levinson declined to allow his name to go forward because of his dissatisfaction with the judicial committee's report; he complained that the committee had not fully understood the position and wondered if possibly there were not others who did not believe the full deity of Jesus. The Reverends Harcourt Samuel and I. E. Davidson, Dr. Leslie Samuel and Mr. Mark Kagan, intimated that for the same reason he also could not allow their names to go forward for reelection. After some discussion the Rev. Jacob Peltz moved and the Rev. Nathan Levenson seconded a resolution in the following terms: "in view of the fact that the creedal faith of some members of the IHCA has been questioned, this conference reaffirms its loyalty to the Constitution. It requires from every delicate an affirmation of faith as a condition of membership in the Alliance, such affirmation to be made in terms including article 9 of the bylaws.

Persons eligible for membership must be Hebrew Christians who

(A.) Have made public confession of their faith

(B.) Have accepted Jesus as their personal Savior

(C.) Believe in the atonement and vicarious suffering, which he hath wrought on the cross at Calvary

(D.) Believe in his deity and resurrection

(E.) Declare their adherence to the Scriptures of the old and New Testament as the supreme rule of faith and life

The resolution was carried, Mr. Zeidman dissenting as one by one the delegates affirmed their faith all did so with the exception of Mr. and Mrs. Schonfield and they were declared to be excluded from membership.[4]

In this instance, the ranks closed and whether or not Schonfield actually believed in the Deity of Yeshua is unclear. Curiously, the IHCA statement did not make reference to the doctrine of the Trinity. So, it was determined that the Schonfields beliefs about the Deity of Yeshua were less than what was commonly understood as Orthodox and they were removed form membership and very active involvement with the IHCA—now the IMJA and at that time perhaps the most significant Messianic organization in the world. The results of this decision were dramatic and resulted in both immediate and long term damage to the Messianic movement at the time. Was it the right decision? Did the leaders of the IHCA use a proper standard of judgment? Should they have been broader in their perspective?

Schonfield was measured by an accepted, or orthodox formulation on the Deity of Yeshua, held by the majority and because he stepped over an acceptable line he and his wife were removed from fellowship. It does seem, historically, that he had changed his views regarding the Deity of Yeshua over the years.

Conclusion

Today, we have removed Messianic Jews from our fellowship groups, mission agencies and congregations because of their "less than Orthodox" position on the Deity of Yeshua. And so, from a purely theological and devotional perspective, our discussions of this doctrine are critical to our community.

This gives us all the more reason to listen very carefully to one another as we try to understand the breadth of beliefs and formulations we hold as a community of the Deity of Yeshua and the Mystery of God. We are all struggling, within our various micro Messianic communities, to determine what is within the pale of acceptability regarding this doctrine. Usually, the only way we have of making this decision is to evaluate the formulation of the belief, which hopefully is an accurate representative of the belief itself. It is on this basis that we might very well make decisions of inclusion or exclusion in relation to our communities, congregations and organizations etc. and even on a broader level—determining that someone is outside the faith because of their beliefs on this critical issue. Ultimately, it is not the creed that is our judge—it is Scripture, but as sinful human beings we can only judge what we understand.

This is one of the reasons I applaud these Symposiums, as they give us a chance to sift through the different positions we hold in our very young movement.

It is never easy being a hyphenated community—though, of course we prefer not to think of ourselves in this way. Yet, our theology is oftentimes hybridized. Mark will even give a name to a suggested Hermeneutical approach that takes into consideration who we are in relation to the church and also as part of the Jewish community and how we might approach this issue in light of what he terms a dialectic. Yet, still, it is difficult to forge our way forward with any degree of true unity as some of us will always lean towards one side or the other – to a more Jewish side or a more Church related side. Finding a true Messianic perspective might be difficult or impossible, but it is a worthy goal and an important pursuit. What we believe must be based upon Scripture, but also informed by both Jewish and Church history and faith in drawing our conclusions about what we believe and how we express this faith.

Finally, we will hopefully cover the important topic in this Symposium as to how we communicate our beliefs in the Deity of zooming past, zigging and zagging where necessary and making quick maneuvers. We cannot expect a barge to move like a motorboat. It is time to create a lot more motorboats and retire some of the barges.

Our education system needs to move beyond the "sage on the stage." We need to move beyond the inequity and esteem-damaging tracking system and move to an educational model that values where learners are on their journeys. We need to understand that all learners are unique and learn at their own pace, and honor those differences. We need to find ways to assess growth and development instead of measuring everyone with the same yardstick. As Einstein stated in a 1936 address, "I want to oppose the idea that the school has to teach directly that special knowledge and those accomplishments, which one has to use later directly in life. The demands of life are much too manifold to let such specialized training in school appear possible. The development of general ability for independent thinking and judgment should always be placed foremost." We need to incorporate students' interests and global challenges into our curriculum and work with our students to solve these problems. We need to promote independent thinking and judgment, not how they perform against peers on an exam.

The world is changing at an exponential pace. Technology is rapidly advancing. It will be the qualities that make us uniquely human that are relied upon in the future. Our social and emotional intelligence is equally, if not more, important than academic facts and knowledge. Let's educate our children to rise to the challenge with their critical thinking, problem-solving, collaboration skills, and possibly most importantly, their capacity for empathetic action.

Only in a world where all our strengths are leveraged and everyone is valued can we find the ability to rise to our potential. A rising tide lifts all boats. As educators, we strive to give our students the ultimate gift. We want to show each student their potential and help them reach it. That is how we make a difference in the world every day.

Yeshua to the Jewish community, traditional, post modern and secular. I am sure we will all learn a lot and enjoy the sessions together. May the next few days together lead to our common growth in love and devotion for the Lord we serve.

ENDNOTES

1. Richard also wrote the article, "Passing over the Plot? The Life and Work of Hugh Schonfield," Mishkan 37 (2002): 35-48, where this incident in the life of Schonfield is discussed in some detail.
2. Minutes of the IHCAconference Tuesday, the 6th of July 1937(6).
3. Minutes of the IHCAconference Wednesday, the 7th of July 1937(5).
4. Minutes of the IHCAconference Wednesday, the 7th of July 1937(6).

JEWISH HISTORY AND THE DEITY OF YESHUA

Elliot Klayman, M.A., LL.M.

Chairs the Board of the Messianic Jewish Theological Institute
Adjunct instructor at the Messianic Jewish Bible Institute
Editor of *The Messianic Outreach* and *Kesher*
Executive Director of Messianic Literature Outreach
Chairs the Judicial Board of Elders of the
Union of Messianic Jewish Congregations
Serves on the board of Jewish Voice Ministries International

I used to think that becoming incarnate was impossible to God. But recently I have come to the conclusion that it is un-Jewish to say that this is something the God of the Bible cannot do, that he cannot come that close. I have had second thoughts about the incarnation. Pinchas Lapide[1]

From my youth onwards I have found in Jesus my great brother. That Christianity has regarded and does regard him as God and Savior has always appeared to me a fact of the highest importance which, for his sake and my own, I must endeavor to understand. Martin Buber[2]

I. WHAT ARE THE QUESTIONS THAT THIS TOPIC PRESENTS?

From the viewpoint of a number of widely read and-well respected Jewish writers, the nexus between the Jewish people and the Deity of Yeshua (Jesus) can be covered in silence.[3] There are a number of Biblical arguments posited in affirmation of this denial position. The Hebrew Scriptures say, "God is not a man." [4] Thus, belief that Jesus was God is tantamount to embracing idol worship and a violation of the first commandment, "thou shall have no other gods before me."[5]

Moreover, no man hath seen God, and lived, and hence, they ask how could Yeshua be God (Exod. 33:20).[6]

These arguments and more hindered the Jewish masses from accepting Jesus as Divine, and continue to be a factor in his rejection within the Jewish communities. After all, how can a man be God? As the argument goes, this is simply beyond the pale of monotheism embedded in Jewish law, tradition and experience.

This is an historical paper and not a theological one. Proof of the Deity of Yeshua is not the goal, but rather an aside. The paper seeks to answer the following questions relevant to the history of the Jewish people and the Deity of Yeshua: (1) What was the monotheistic understanding of God among first century Jews? (2) When did belief in Yeshua as Deity first occur? (3) What is the evidence that the early Jewish believers recognized Yeshua as Deity? (4) How were Jewish disciples of Yeshua able to accept Yeshua as Deity given their approach to monotheism? (5) What was the precipitating cause of the Yeshua-believers' turn from a scattered band of scared disciples to an unshakable community of unbending faith in the Divinity of Yeshua? (6) What were the historical events that contributed to the widening schism between the Jewish Yeshua-believers and the Jewish non-Yeshua believers relevant to the Deity of Yeshua? (7) What events are happening today to improve relations between Yeshua believing Jews and non-Yeshua believing Jews in spite of the pronounced schism caused in part by the dispute over Yeshua's Deity?

II. WHAT WAS THE MONOTHEISTIC UNDERSTANDING OF GOD AMONG FIRST CENTURY JEWS?

Idolatry tempted the Jews throughout the First Temple period, and its practices in sharp rebellion to a jealous God, precipitated God's display of anger demonstrated by the captivities of Israel and Judah, the destruction of the Temple, and loss of sovereignty over the Land. Second Temple Jews were much more careful in their worship and were staunch reactionary monotheists, who were not in fellowship with pagans, their gods or their temples. Apotheosis, the elevation of a person to the rank of God, was sharply eschewed among first century Jews.[7] To depart from the worship of One God was to disengage from the Jewish community.

True, the Jewish people had their moments throughout history when they were attracted to the pagan world. For example, during the period of the reign of Antiochus IV, there was a great defection to a Hellenized life-style among a significant number, and class, of Jews. Even the priests became enamored with the *gymnasium*[8] to the extent of neglecting their priestly duties; and medically reversing their circumcisions so that they could participate in the games, on par with their Greek compatriots.

The Maccabean revolt was as much a civil war against the overly Hellenized Jews as it was an assertion of independence from Greco-Syrian rule. The pious defenders of the faith squared off against the "defecting Jews," who even resisted *b'rit milah* and *kashrut*. However, it is one thing for Jews to gravitate toward the temptations of a foreign culture and to forego selected Jewish praxis, and even ignore the law. But it is still another thing for Jews to depart from a belief in One God.

In Spain during the Golden Age, Jews were highly influenced by Islamic culture, engaging in a dual curriculum of Jewish and Greek-based studies, which they imbibed vigorously. They became poets, warriors, astronomers, philosophers and medical doctors. They lived the good life in Spain, influenced by Greek and Islamic culture, but still did not embrace the Greek gods. Polytheism was a taboo, enhanced by the historical memory of the cause of Israel and Judah's captivities, respectively, in the 8th and 6th centuries BCE.

In order to further understand the "monotheism of the day," it is necessary to grasp that we are not talking about a homogenous Judaism, but a heterogeneous one with great diversity of religious opinions across the sectarian expanse. Nonetheless, there was certainly at least a general exclusivist concept of monotheism among first century Jews—that Yahweh was not just one of many and superior, but that He was the only God, with no competition.[9] But even within this exclusive monotheistic position there were variations of thought among Jews on the "nature of God."[10] What is clear, however, is that the Jewish disciples, while accepting the Divinity of Yeshua, still believed that this acceptance was within the ambit of embracing the uniqueness of God, and his exclusive position as Creator and Redeemer. For example, Paul says:

> Although there may be so-called gods in heaven or on earth—as indeed there are many "gods" and many more "lords"—yet for us there is one God, the Father,

from whom are all things and for whom we exist, and one Lord, Messiah Jesus, through whom are all things and through whom we exist. (I Cor. 8:5-6)

Here Paul, without wavering, depicts a binitarian nature of God—Father and Son—while at the same time speaking of One God. This is not an isolated instance of early disciples affirming the unique Oneness of God:

You believe that there is one God; you do well. The demons also believe and tremble. (James 2:19)

Now a mediator is not a mediator of one, but God is one. (Gal. 3:20)

One God and father of all, who is above all, and through all, and in you all. (Eph. 4:6)

The early Yeshua followers received teaching from Yeshua consistent with the Oneness of God through the centrality of the Shema: "And Jesus answered him, 'The first of all the commandments is Hear, O Israel: The Lord our God is one Lord' " (Mark 12:29).

For mainline first century Jews there was a very strong adherence to a belief in the Oneness of God. The historical evidence found within New Covenant Scripture attests to this same commitment on the part of the early Jewish followers of Yeshua.

III. WHEN DID BELIEF IN YESHUA AS DEITY FIRST OCCUR?

Among scholars, orthodox believers, messianic and others, there remains controversy as to when the disciples first embraced Yeshua's Deity. Contrary to some thinking, the origin of the exaltation of Yeshua to Divine status was not a late happening, but rather an early occurrence among his followers. The mosaic necessary for embracing Jesus as Deity was rooted right in Jewish thinking and concepts. That is not to say that these concepts yielded their understanding so easily and readily when it came to first century Jews applying them to Jesus. It was still a leap for Yeshua's early disciples to embrace his Deity, and it did require a catalyst to unlock this mystery that was divinely revealed to the early Jewish disciples.

The burst of veneration by Jewish Yeshua-believers was contagious enough to be adopted by the Gentiles who may have had fewer problems because of their experience with multiple divinities.[11] Those who opt for a later veneration are more prone to find roots in Hellenistic/Paganistic influences and to backdate it to the first century disciples. This is an untenable position that has been soundly debunked by a number of scholars.[12] What is clear is that the evidence is overwhelming that the early Jewish believers recognized Yeshua as Deity.

IV. WHAT IS THE EVIDENCE THAT THE EARLY JEWISH BELIEVERS RECOGNIZED YESHUA AS DEITY?

Much is made of the fact that Yeshua never expressly claimed to be God. What is more important for this historical study is how his disciples viewed him. In their book, *Putting Jesus in His Place: The Case for the Deity of Christ*, Bowman & Komoszewski debunk the idea that the fourth century councils constructed the Deity of Jesus and imposed it on the Church through its creeds.[13] They overwhelm the reader with the proof that the disciples embraced Jesus as Deity as evidenced by their recognition of his honors, attributes, names, deeds and seat.[14]

Divine Honors

The early followers of Yeshua, as recorded in the New Covenant canon, afford Yeshua the honors that are reserved for God. He is honored just as the Father is honored (John 5:23). Glory is given to Yeshua through the invocation of doxologies patterned after the Hebrew Bible doxologies that clearly refer to God (1 Pet. 4:11; 2 Pet. 3:18). Aspects of worship contained in the Hebrew Bible and reserved for God are expressly applied to Yeshua (Heb. 1:6; Rev. 5:8-14). He is honored with religious songs (Eph. 5:19-20; Rev. 5:9-10). The post-resurrection disciples put their faith in Yeshua, even as the Hebrew Scriptures implore the people to be faithful to God (Rom.

10:11). He is honored by his disciples with fear (Eph. 5:21) and reverence (1 Pet. 3:14-16), service, and love (Eph. 6:24) in the same manner that God is to be feared, reverenced and loved.[15] These divine honors in and of themselves may not be the "end all;" however, when added to the rest of the evidence, they do become exceedingly convincing that Yeshua's first century disciples accounted Yeshua as God.

Divine Attributes

Jesus was recognized by his disciples as God manifest in the flesh.[16] That means that He is Man and Deity. Characteristics that support his manhood include hunger, thirst, sleep, emotions and limits of knowledge. The Divine side of his nature is characterized by certain attributes that are confined to God, and no one else. His disciples recognized, for example, that He is the exact image of God (Col. 1:15; Heb. 1:3); He is the eternal creator (Heb. 1:2, 10-12) and immutable (Heb. 13: 8). His love morphs God's (Rom. 8:35-39; Rev. 1:5). He is recognized as omnipotent (Col. 1:16-17; Heb. 1:2-3), omnipresent (Eph. 4:10), and omniscient (Acts 1:24).[17] These divine attributes recognized by his followers make it a very difficult case to prove that they did not think him to be Divine.

Divine Names

The uniqueness about the name is the emphasis that is placed on it in the Hebrew Bible. The name of the person quite often identifies the nature or characteristics of that person. Theophonic names—those that contain the name of God—are quite common in the Hebrew Bible. That does not mean that the person who possesses the theophonic name is Divine. However, the context and the circumstances of the assignment of the name are most critical. Yeshua is referred to repeatedly as God (John 1:1, 18; 20:28; Rom. 9:5; Titus 2:13; Heb. 2:8; 2 Pet. 1:1). Yeshua is also named in various places as Lord (Rom. 10:9; I Cor. 8:6; Phil. 2:11; 1 Pet. 3:15), Savior (Titus 2:13; 2 Pet. 1:11), and the Alpha and Omega (Rev. 1:7-8). These are not just theophonic, but Divine Names reserved for God in the Hebrew Bible. In this sense his name is above every other name,[18] and certainly so when coupled with all the evidence that Yeshua's disciples recognized him as Divine.[19]

Divine Deeds

Yeshua's disciples attributed certain deeds to him that are within the exclusive province of God. They recognized him as the Creator (John 1:3) and the Sustainer (Col. 1:16) of the universe. They marveled at his control over the wind and the sea, forces of nature (Matt. 8:25-27). They saw him perform healings and miracles on a consistent basis with no failed attempts (e.g., Matt. 14:13-33). They attributed to him the deed of forgiveness of sins, an action clearly confined to the work of God (Col. 3:13), the imparting of life (John 5:21, 26), and the judging of the people. (2 Cor. 5:10).[20] These deeds were undeniable signs of the Divinity of Yeshua, witnessed by his followers.

Divine Seat

The early disciples put Jesus on a heightened and permanent throne where He is seated in God's place. Yeshua's claim that he would sit at the right hand of God was one that the unbelieving Jews unmistakably understood as a blasphemous claim to Deity (Mark 14:61-64). His claim to "all power is given to me in heaven and in earth" (Matt. 28:18) contributes to Paul's understanding that when He is thus seated in heaven, all things will be subdued under him, that God may be "all in all." (I Cor. 15:27-28) He is clearly seated in heavenly places above all created beings including the angels (Eph. 1:21), in the seat reserved for God (Rev. 22:1, 3). And from that position of authority, He sent the Ruach haKodesh (Acts 2:33); received Stephen (Acts 7:59); and is the subject of universal worship (Rev. 5:8-14), including the angels (Heb. 1:6).[21] When this "seat" is combined with the several other recognitions by the early believers, the "deity mosaic" is complete, and it is "beyond a reasonable doubt" that the very early disciples believed Yeshua to be Divine. Richard Baukham in *Jesus and the God of Israel* supports this bottom line position, maintaining that the theology of Jesus' divinity was fully formed in the New Testament as understood through examining his divine identity with the God of the Hebrew Bible.[22]

V. HOW WERE JEWISH DISCIPLES OF YESHUA ABLE TO ACCEPT YESHUA AS DEITY GIVEN THEIR APPROACH TO MONOTHEISM?

There was clearly a dilemma posed by the dichotomous tension between the strident belief in One God, and the embracement of Yeshua as God.[23] Larry Hurtado, in *One God One Lord: Early Christian Devotion and Ancient Jewish Monotheism*, states the issue as:

> How did the early Jewish Christians accommodate the veneration of the exalted Jesus alongside God while continuing to see themselves as loyal to the fundamental emphasis of their ancestral tradition on one God? [24]

Today, Jewish believers bump up against classic anti-deity arguments solidified in post-New Testament thought. For example, in the second century, *Dialogue with Trypho*, Trypho, the Jew, emphasizes that the Messiah was to be "born," and thus be human.[25] It would be quite easy to resolve the conflict by saying that the Jews who accepted Jesus as Deity were secular Jews who were influenced by Jewish-pagan syncretism to which they had been heavily exposed throughout the Greco-Roman periods. Their susceptibility then, to binitarianism, would be obvious, and, in fact there would not be any great conflict. But this was just not the case.

Ancient Jewish concepts of *Hocham*, *Memra*, *Shekhinah*, and *Malachi Adonai*, all predating the first century, were based in Jewish writings and thought which were available to the early Yeshua believers who undoubtedly ruminated on Jewish concepts to identify the risen Yeshua, and the ramifications of his teachings and actions.[26] These were *preconditioning aspects* that contributed to the resolution of the apparent dilemma posed by the recognition of Yeshua as Deity and the Jewish classical monotheistic understanding of One God.

Hocham (Wisdom)

First century Jews had the benefit of the Hebrew Bible, the Apocrypha and Pseudepigraphic writings. Each of these sources contained the concept of the personification of Wisdom. Proverbs, the granddaddy of wisdom personified in the Hebrew Bible, reads in part:

> Does not wisdom cry and understanding put forth her voice? . . . I, Wisdom, dwell with prudence . . . I love those who love me, and those who seek me early shall find me. . . . The Lord possessed me in the beginning of his way, before his works of old. I was set up from everlasting, from the beginning, or ever the earth was. When there were no depths, I was brought forth— when there were no fountains abounding with water. Before the mountains were settled, before the hills, was I brought forth. . . . When he prepared the heavens, I was there; when he set a compass on the face of the depth; when he established the clouds above; when he strengthened the fountains of the deep. . . . Then I was by him, as one brought up with him, and I was daily his delight, rejoicing always before him. . . . [B]lessed are they who keep my ways. . . . Blessed is the man who hears me, watching daily at my gates, waiting at the posts of my doors. For whoso finds me finds life, and shall obtain favor of the Lord. But he that sins against me wrongs his own soul; all they who hate me love death. (Prov. 8:1, 17, 22-25, 27-30, 32, 34-36)

Here, Wisdom co-exists with God; and pre-existed the Creation. Proverbs 3:19 says, "The Lord by Wisdom has founded the earth; by understanding he has established the heavens." Who is this Wisdom who created the earth and the heavens? Of course, this could be a literary device to convey the importance of Wisdom, but exegetical understanding in Second Temple literature personifies this Wisdom as a para-incarnation. If Wisdom was with God and Wisdom is Yeshua, then Yeshua was with God in the beginning and was the creative force of the heavens and earth. This is the backdrop for the first Jewish disciples of Yeshua, which starts to explain how Yeshua could be deified in their minds without running afoul of the first commandment. The concept already existed. Hence, "In the Beginning was X, and X was with God, and X was God. The same was in the beginning with God." It was only necessary to fill in the unknown X with the One whom the early disciples experienced first-hand.[27]

It also means that this concept of a binitarian nature of God does not break the mold of the first century Jewish understanding of the unity of God. Two Jewish works which would have been available to first century Jews, and from which we can derive a further idea of Jewish thinking and conceptualization, are *Wisdom of Solomon* and the *Book of Enoch*:

> With you [God] is Wisdom, who knows your works and was present when you made the world. (Wisd. Of Sol. 9:9)

> Wisdom went forth to make her dwelling among the children of men, and found no dwelling place. (I Enoch 42)

These certainly support the plain meaning sense of Wisdom as a personage who is an associate in Creation, and who sought to "dwell with man."

Neither is Jewish midrash devoid of the concept of Wisdom being synonymous with Torah, and the creating process:

> The Torah declares: 'I was the working tool of the Holy One, blessed be He.' In human practice, when a mortal king builds a palace, he builds it not with his own skill but with the skill of an architect. The architect moreover does not build it out of his head, but employs plans and diagrams to know how to arrange the chambers and the wicket doors. Thus, God consulted the Torah and created the world, while the Torah declares, IN THE BEGINNING GOD CREATED . . . BEGINNING referring to the Torah, as in the verse, *The Lord made me as the beginning of His way.* (Prov. VIII, 22)[28]

Here, the Torah is the speaker and depicted as a type of incarnation of God. Oskar Skarsaune wisely likens the rhythm of this midrash with the Incarnation of Yeshua:

> 'The Word became flesh and tabernacle among us.' . . . In the Wisdom poem of Sirach 24, Wisdom becomes incarnate as the Torah given at Sinai—and at the center of that Torah is the sacrificial service of the tabernacle (temple). That is probably the meaning

when Wisdom is said to make priestly service in the holy tent on Zion (Sir. 24:10). If Jesus was Wisdom incarnate, this could make us understand that he not only taught the way of life, but that he also had to be the true high priest, bringing the final sacrifice, doing the final priestly service in 'the holy tent.' At the very center of the Mosaic Torah are atoning sacrifices. Jesus, the Torah in person, atoned with his own blood. We see this in the Holy of Holies imagery in Romans 3:25. Hebrews also links the Wisdom Christology of chapter 1 to the theme of Jesus as the high priest in chapters 5-11.[29]

Skarsuane readily identifies the analogy of Wisdom, Torah and Yeshua in relation to Temple service. It is not improbable that such writings afloat in the world of the disciples preconditioned them towards a loftier view of Yeshua than verily man, only.

Memra (Logos)

It is clear from New Testament passages that Yeshua is the Word (e.g., John 1:14). This concept of the Word incarnate is Jewish, referred to in Aramaic as Memra, and in Greek as Logos. Jews of the first century would have been acquainted with this concept through the Hebrew Bible, Apocrypha, and Pseudepigraphic Writings. "He sent forth his *word* and healed them and rescued them from the grave" (Ps. 107:20); "His *word* runs swiftly" (Ps. 147:15); "He sends his word and melts [the hail]" (Ps. 147: 18); and "my *word* that goes out through my mouth . . . shall not return to me void" (Isa. 55:11), all attest to some corporeal entity-ship connected with the Divine in the form of the Word. The Word is an instrument of service that emanates from the Holy One. Hence, the Word was the mediator in a sense between God and Man.

Memra is found in the Targumim time and time again when translating the Hebrew *parshiot* so that they were accessible to an Aramaic-speaking people. The Word was an entity, and not a thing. Here are just a few of the many Targumic parallels with the Hebrew Bible included in Volume Two of Michael Brown's, Answering *Jewish Objections to Jesus*,[30] five volume series.

Scripture	Hebrew Bible	Targum
Genesis 1: 27	God created man.	The Word of the Lord created man.
Genesis 15:6	And Abraham believed in the Lord.	And Abraham believed in the Word of the Lord.
Exodus 20:1	And the Lord spoke all these words	And the Word of the Lord spoke all these words.
Leviticus 26:9	And I will turn to you.	And I will turn through my Word to do good to you.
Numbers 10:36	Return, O Lord!	Return, O Word of the Lord!
Deut. 31:3	The Lord your God will pass before you	The Lord your God, his Word will pass before you.
Judges 11:10	The Lord will be witness between us.	The Word of the Lord will be witness between us.
Isaiah 45:17	Israel will be saved by the Lord.	Israel will be saved by the Word of the Lord.

These Targumim[31] were read in the synagogue weekly. They certainly contributed to pre-conditioning the early believers and mitigating the leap to "[Yeshua] became flesh and dwelt among us." Consider the early disciples' thinking:

> In the beginning was the Memra, and the Memra was with God, and the Memra was God. He was with God in the beginning. Through [the Memra] all things were made and without [the Memra] nothing was made that has been made. In [the Memra] was life and that life was the light of men. (John 1: 1-4)

This was surely more palatable to the first century Jewish mind than to contemporary Jews who have lost the resources exalting the Word. But there is more. As stated, Memra, in Greek, is Logos. Philo, who shared part of the same century with Yeshua, was certainly comfortable in his Greek element with the philosophical concept of Logos as mediator between God and Man; the utterance of God; the divine mind; agent of creation; transcendent power; an intermediary power; and even a secondary deity.[32] He writes:

Why is it that he speaks as if of some other god, saying that he made man after the image of God, and not that he made him after His own image? Very appropriately and without any falsehood was this oracular sentence uttered by God, for no mortal thing could have been formed on the similitude of the supreme father of the universe but only after the pattern of the second deity, who is the Logos of the Supreme Being.

Philo, who is acclaimed in some circles to have laid the foundation for Christianity is also a kind of voice for Jewish thinking during his day. He is obviously wrestling with what the early disciples confronted. He had a desire to maintain Jewish clarity on the monotheistic nature of God; yet, he was troubled by scriptural passages that seemed to lead toward a binitarian axiom. Although Philo comes just short of the deification of the Logos, he does rub up against it and by his logic becomes a silent witness for the embracement of Yeshua as Deity.[33]

Shekhinah (Glory of God)

The *Shekhinah* is the visible manifestation of the presence of God who comes to dwell among the people in the form of the *glory of the Lord* (Hebrew: *k'vod adonai;* Greek: *doxa kurion*). In fact, the origin of the word *Shekhinah* is from the root *shachan* – dwelling. Its Greek equivalent, *Skeini*, takes on the meaning of "tabernacling."[34] The *Shekhinah* shows up on various occasions throughout Biblical history. Arnold Fruchtenbaum does a commendable job tracing the history of the manifestation of "God's glory" as it moved in visible ways synchronously from the beginning in the garden and throughout the journey of the Jewish people. Fruchtenbaum points out that it appears in the form of light, fire and cloud as recorded in the Hebrew Bible, and is associated with the Angel of Jehovah, the Holy Spirit, the cherubim, and thick darkness. Hence, the *K'vod Adonai* makes its presence "east of the garden of Eden;" in the appearance of a "smoking furnace and a flaming torch" when God cut the Abrahamic covenant; in the burning bush; in the pillar by day and the cloud by night throughout the wilderness; at Mount Sinai via the thundering, lightening and a thick cloud; in Moses' observation of the back parts of God; as it reflected from the face of Moses upon his return from the Mount; in the *mishkan* (tabernacle); when authenticating the Priesthood; when rendering judgment for sin and disobedience in the book of Numbers; in the Holy of Holies in Solomon's Temple; and until its departure from Israel and Jewish history as revealed in Ezekiel and by the prophetic name, "Ichabad." The *Shekhinah* had departed from, and did not initially appear in, the Second Temple.[35]

Well, it is a safe assumption that the common and the astute Jew of first century vintage were familiar with the Hebrew Bible and the appearances of the *Shekhinah* throughout Biblical history. The prophet Haggai compares the First Temple and its glory with the Second temple that lacked that "glory" (Hag. 2:3). However, he goes on to say, referring to the Second Temple, "The latter glory of this house shall be greater than the former, saith Jehovah of hosts" (Hag. 2:9). Eventually, the disciples got it. Perhaps it was when the glory returned, and "shone around" the shepherds in the recorded annunciation of the birth of Yeshua (Luke 2:8-9). For others it might have hit when the "brilliance" of the Magi star marked Yeshua's place of nativity; or, in the "transfiguration" when Yeshua's face shone as the sun, and his garments became white as light, and a bright cloud overshadowed him, and a voice bellowed out, "This is my Beloved Son." The *Shekhinah* had returned for the believers, and true to Haggai, Yeshua, upon whom the *Shekhinah* abode, filled the Second Temple with God's glory. Somewhere, sometime, the disciples reflected on these events as they recognized that "the Word became enfleshed, and tabernacled among us and we beheld his glory [the *k'vod adonai*] as the only begotten from the Father, full of grace and truth" (John 1: 14).[36] The memory of the glory of the *Shekhinah* past was a pre-conditioner that supported their awareness of his glorious presence in their midst. They realized that this was the return of the *Shekhinah* of the Hebrew Bible, signaling that there is something new and something Divine about Yeshua.

Malach Adonai (Angel of the Lord)

Theophanies—manifestations of an appearance of God to humans—are recorded in the Hebrew Bible and Jewish literature that preceded Yeshua. God walked in the cool of the day and spoke to Adam and Eve (Gen. 3: 8). He appeared to Abraham (Gen. 17:1; 18:1). Moses, his brother, two nephews, and 70 elders saw the Lord. (Exod.

24:9-11). A common vehicle of the theophany was the appearance of an angel, *malach Adonai*.

Angels who exist in the Hebrew Bible proliferate in post-exilic writings. In most of their roles and manifestations, these angels show up as servants or vehicles of God's power.[37] However, there are a few distinct cases where the *malachi Adonai* (messenger or angel of the Lord) seems to equate with a pre-incarnate manifestation of God. Of course, the early disciples would have been familiar with these texts. Prominent among those biblical texts is when Gideon was called as the judge of Israel in the midst of Midianite oppression. While under an oak tree the *malach Adonai* visited Gideon and spoke with him. When Gideon realized the visitor was no less than the Lord himself, he got scared, saying, "I have seen *Malachi Adonai* face to face." Gideon knew that no person sees God face to face and survives, and thus expressed fear.[38] He believed that he saw God. Still another *malachi adonai* appearance occurs when Manoah, the father of Samson and his wife encounter who they initially believe to be a prophet, who first informs Manoah's wife that she will have a son.[39] The stranger is then recognized as *malach adonai*, and like Jacob, Manoah expresses concern that they have seen the Lord face to face. He exclaims to his wife, "We shall surely die because we have seen God" (Judg. 13:22). Finally, to conclude our trilogy of *malachi adonai* appearances, Jacob, the night before he was to confront his brother, is found wrestling with a "man." Jacob, whose name was changed to Israel, called the place of the occurrence, Peniel, because, "I have seen God face to face and have lived."[40] The Targum translates the relevant portion as "I have seen *malachi adonai* face to face."[41]

Then there is the most famous angel story in the Hebrew Bible as it relates to a pre-incarnate manifestation of God. It occurs when three men visit Abraham and Sarah to inform them that Sarah will have a child. Then two of the men leave and go to Sodom, while one, who is called the Lord, remains and negotiates with Abraham over the destruction of Sodom.[42] Dr. Michael Brown maintains that this is an unequivocal Yeshua pre-incarnation.[43] What is more important for this paper is that the early Yeshua believers had this text available and were no doubt familiar with it. That does not mean that they immediately understood Yeshua to be the enfleshment of God. But it does mean that there was precedent for the possibility. Something still had to trigger the awakening in Yeshua disciples who after his death acted like a defeated rag-tag band of disillusioned lost souls.

VI. WHAT WAS THE PRECIPITATING CAUSE OF THE YESHUA-BELIEVERS' "TURN" FROM A SCATTERED BAND OF SCARED DISCIPLES TO AN UNSHAKABLE COMMUNITY OF UNBENDING FAITH IN THE DIVINITY OF YESHUA?

Although there were para-incarnations of Yeshua through *Hochma*, *Memra*, *Shekhinah*, and *Malach Adonai*, they were not a perfect morphing of the Incarnation to come. There was still a leap that had to be made, though these preconditioning aspects were present, and quite helpful. Larry Hurtado calls the turn—from a band of disappointed to a mobilized army of believers—a "mutation,"[44] precipitated by religious experiences with Jesus.[45] Hurtado presents three causes of the "mutation" with a primary one being the resurrection and post-resurrection appearances.[46] Pinchas Lapide, an orthodox Jewish scholar surprisingly reports that the resurrection is fact:

> Concerning the resurrection of Jesus on Easter Sunday, I was for decades a Sadducee. I am no longer a Sadducee since the following deliberation has caused me to think this through anew. In none of the cases where rabbinic literature speaks of such visions did it result in an essential change in the life of the resuscitated or of those who had experienced the visions. . . .
>
> It is different with the disciples of Jesus on that Easter Sunday. Despite all the legendary embellishments, in the oldest records there remains a recognizable historical kernel that cannot simply be demythologized. When this scared, frightened band of the apostles which was just about to throw away everything in order to flee in despair to Galilee; when these peasants, shepherds, and fishermen, who betrayed and denied their master and then failed him miserably, suddenly could be changed overnight into a confident mission society, convinced of salvation and able to work with much more success after Easter than before Easter, then no vision or hallucination is sufficient to explain such a revolutionary transformation.[47]

Crucifixion was too common for it alone to have been a catalyst of awakening. But resurrection had never occurred; resuscitation, yes, with the Shunnamite woman's son at the hands of Elisha[48] and Lazarus at the hands of Jesus.[49] Yet, resurrection was not new to the Jewish vocabulary of the first century. It is well documented in the New Testament gospels and Josephus that the Pharisees believed in a resurrection of the dead. Israel was to participate in *olam haba* through the resurrection. But that was the future and that was a nation. For the disciples that future was now and that resurrection was Yeshua.

The disciples were convinced of the resurrection and had the best evidence before them. For the disciples, this resurrection undoubtedly triggered "flashbacks," reliving Yeshua encounters, and an epiphany of understanding of the Divine identity of Yeshua. Peter had pronounced him as the Son of the Living God. But it was not until the resurrection and post-resurrection appearances, that we have all the disciples on board, with the consequent realization that the Deity had been in their midst.

Jewish history and experience was not devoid of false pretenders and messiahs. In fact, the New Testament records a number of them.[50] They all had some following and none of them claimed divinity, but only that they were the anointed to fulfill the mission of Jewish destiny: the overthrow of the enemies and the establishment of the Jewish kingdom on earth. Eventually, they all were rejected, killed or disappeared from the scene.[51] Certainly Jesus' disciples were familiar with the stories of at least some of these pretenders who proclaimed to be the Messiah.[52] None of them purported to be the enfleshment of God. None of them had a widespread following. This was to an extent normative Jewish messianism of the day. The messiah would be a human being with some super-human powers. This is in contrast to how the Messiah turned out—God manifest in human flesh. Tens of thousands acclaimed Jesus not just to be Messiah but also Lord. Something triggered the "turn." That trigger was the resurrection as confirmed by post-resurrection appearances. It was the behavior of the early disciples from the time that their "Man" had died on the crucifixion stake to the three days later when he rose, that moved Pinchas Lapide, a twentieth century orthodox Jewish scholar, to change his mind and accept the facticity of the resurrection.[53] This resurrection trigger was dynamite in the hands of the disciples and they changed their direction and moved history by what they did afterwards. And this same trigger undoubtedly contributed to Lapide's refusal to discount the possibility of the Incarnation.[54]

VII. WHAT WERE THE HISTORICAL EVENTS THAT CONTRIBUTED TO THE WIDENING SCHISM BETWEEN THE JEWISH YESHUA-BELIEVERS AND THE JEWISH NON-YESHUA BELIEVERS RELEVANT TO THE DEITY OF YESHUA?

Historical events throughout the ages contributed significantly to the widening of the gap between Jewish Yeshua-believers and the broader Jewish populace in connection with the Deity of Yeshua. The Council of Yavneh and Birkat HaMinim, the Bar Kochba Revolt, Dialogue with Trypho, de-Judaizing of the ecclesia, medieval Jewish persecution and selected writings of Moses ben Maimon, all contributed to the widening of the gap, as related one way or another to the concept of the Deity of Yeshua, embraced by an estranged Church and repudiated by a disenchanted Israel.

Council of Yavneh and Birkat HaMinim

Shortly after the destruction of the Second Temple in 70 CE, and about the time that the Yeshua disciples were gaining influence throughout the land and beyond, Yavneh was established as the "religious center" of Jewry. This "Council" has been credited with saving Jewry by bridging the transition from the Temple to the Talmud. The legend of its formation,"[55] with Yochanon ben Zakkai at the helm with the favor of Rome, lent to the "legislators" the authority that was needed to form a post-Temple Judaism. The classic scholarly thought on Yavneh runs something like this:

> Yavneh, and all that it has come to symbolize, was a "society" that sought to eradicate orthodox dissent, which included all that was contrary to the 'society' at Yavneh's rulings. By such, it cast a wide heresiological net, such that the minim, which included all Yavneh dissenters, were 'outside the camp.'

However, other scholarship paints it as a more tolerant council that incorporated the viewpoints of its contributors, and hence, a broad-based consensus.

Shaye Cohen maintains that the sages of Yavneh held to a principle that "conflicting disputants may each be advancing the words of the living God,"[56] and thus they created a more inclusive theology. Regardless of Yavneh's inclusivity, its rulings were not wide enough to accommodate "Yeshua heresiology" as part of its platform. The sacrifice system as known in the Temple periods was displaced and neither Yeshua, nor his followers, were part of that ecclesial new order. The Deity was simply a deal breaker.

The Temple period, which was replete with sub-religious societies within the whole of Judaism, had a built-in tolerance necessary to maintain a loose sociological unity. Those who believed in the resurrection and those who did not, those who were pro-Rome and those who were not, all lived together. This included the Nazarenes, for a while. However, this unity, broken in part by the destruction of the Temple, was dealt a further blow at Yavneh.

The process of the exclusion of Yeshua believers continued, eventuating in the Birkat HaMinim, a curse against the *minim*, which was incorporated into the *Shemonah Esrei*, and which occurred circa 85 CE.[57] Whether this curse was specifically directed against the Yeshua believers or other sectarians, and heretics, is the subject of continued debate. What is clear is that the curse included the Nazarene sect and it further defined "Jewish heresiology," all steps in the process of barring Yeshua followers from the entrance to the synagogue.

Bar Kokhba Revolt

Jewish Yeshua-believers joined the Bar Kokhba revolt to oust Rome from its sovereign position in the Land. Like all Jews, they were very attached to their homeland. And their attachment was undoubtedly deepened because this was the place where their Messiah revealed himself and from whence he was crucified, buried, resurrected and ascended. Their flight to Pella in 70 CE was apparently because of Yeshua's instructions that "when you see Jerusalem compassed with armies, let them who are in Judaea flee."[58] Their flight would not have been sufficient reason for a complete break with the Jewish community. After all, Yochanon ben Zakkai fled to Yavneh about the same time and that did not cause a breach.[59] Notice that even though they worshiped Yeshua, and treated him as the God-Man, they were still found to be side by side, at least initially, with their brethren in the 132 Bar Kokhba revolt.

It is widely acclaimed that the Yeshua believers eventually withdrew support for Bar Kokhba, the leader of the revolt, because of the competing claim that he was Messiah. This may be wholly or partially true. However, according to the Church Father Justin, Bar Kokhba "gave orders that [Jewish Christians] . . . should be led to cruel punishments, unless they would deny Jesus Christ and utter blasphemy."[60] Apparently, those Yeshua believers who remained to fight were constructively ejected from the army because they could not pass the litmus test—proving their loyalty by blaspheming Yeshua. If Justin is correct, Bar Kokhba knew that they accounted Yeshua as God.[61]

The theology of the Yeshua believers was rejected at Yavneh by the religious authorities. Here a further blow is dealt against them by the larger community, who now treated them as *meshummadim*[62] perhaps due to the combination of the rumor of their disloyalty, and their belief in the Deity of Yeshua. Apparently, what the claims of Yeshua's Deity alone could not do, this coupled with the Yeshua believers' alleged failure to participate in the War for Independence, did. Disloyalty of the community of this sort was sufficient to anathematize the Jewish Yeshua-believers; and the historical memory of animosity toward them remains to this very day. And the schism widened.

Dialogue with Trypho

Dialogue with Trypho was written by Justin Martyr in the 160s and reflects a discursive between him and Trypho, a non-Yeshua believing Jew that occurred in a marketplace perhaps in the 130s. In this dynamic polemical interplay between Martyr and Trypho (whether fictional or not), the concept of Deity arises in a two-dimensional way. First, Trypho disputes the Deity of Jesus by claiming that he is born of a woman:

> Those who affirm Him [Jesus] to have been a man, and to have been *anointed by election*, and then to have become Christ, appear to me to speak more plausibly than you [Christians] who hold those opinions which you express. For we [Jews] all expect that Christ will be a man [born] of men, and that Elijah, when he comes, will anoint him. But if this man appear to be Christ, he must certainly be known as man [born] of men.[63]

Second, Justin argues that Jesus is the Logos and seeks to convince Trypho of this, assuming that Jews do not believe in the Logos.[64] Hence, the widening of the schism continues theologically. And, here we see a further displacement or supersession posture through which Justin, by sleight of hand, engages. He suggests that Jews do not believe in the Logos, when in fact, the origin of the Logos was a very Jewish thing. But if a "parting" must come, and come it would, there must be a clear separation between Jew and Christian, achieved by definition.[65] Christians believe in the Logos. Jews do not. Christians believe that Jesus is Divine. Jews do not. Borderlines were established. The schism was widening. Jews were being defined out of the "new faith" in part, over the Deity of Yeshua.[66]

De-Judaizing of the Ecclesia

The Nicene Creed in 325, and its revision in 381, marked a significant codification of the doctrine of the Son, the Father and Holy Spirit. It defined the Son as "of one substance with the Father," and it characterizes the Holy Spirit, "Who proceeds from the Father, Who with the Father and the Son is together worshipped and together glorified."[67] Although this "doctrine of the Trinity" could be defended on the basis of Jewish theology as understood in the first century, by the fourth century it was foreign to the Jewish mindset. The "three in one" further distanced the Church from the Jews while the rabbis were doing their part by denial, and in some cases disparaging the concept. By this time Logos theology was abandoned by the Rabbis and appropriated by the Church.[68]

The de-Judaization of the Church was the catalyst for greater schism between Christians and Jews. The manner of articulating the theological truths of the Deity of Yeshua became so foreign to the Jewish ear, that it had no resemblance to its original understanding. A gentile Church, which denied the Jewish essence of the faith and thus became the big separator, hijacked the concept of Deity, born of Jewish understanding, in Logos theology. This Jacob/Esau division, which began with Jewish repudiation of the Logos, was a wedge that widened the gap between Judaism and Christianity, and may in fact be considered *Hamakom* (the place) of the "parting of the ways."[69] Before reconciliation there may have to be repentance on each side of the divide—on the Christian side for appropriation of the Logos doctrine and on the Jewish side for repudiation of it.

Not only did Jews become removed from the historical memory and person of Jesus as instructive from the New Testament, but they became distanced from the Hebrew Scriptures as well. They defaulted

61

to the "learned" who had a stake in the claim that Yeshua was not the Jewish Messiah or Lord. They were further dealt blows during their lachrymose history through the most extreme consequences of anti-Jewish sentiment that erupted as early as the Church fathers could breathe venom against them for killing their God. The persecution continued throughout the ages, perpetrated by those whom the Jews perceived to be the Church and the Sovereign in synch with each other. The apex was the systematic extermination of six million Jews under the Nazi enterprise, fueled by some of the "great" German theologians. In the wake of all of this it would be a miracle if the Jews had not rejected Christianity, and its God.

By the end of the fourth century Jewish Yeshua-believers who maintained their Jewish identity, all but disappear from the landscape.[70] Those who were known as Jewish converts became aligned with the Church and its doctrine that was laid out at the Councils. Many Christian groups who broke away from the historical Church, as well, embraced the "council doctrine". Evangelicalism in the 19th century embraced the doctrine of the trinity. The doctrine of the trinity, perceived by many as "three gods," was even harder for the Jewish mind to accept, especially when it was repeatedly shown to be identified with those throughout the Middle Ages, who engaged in the Crusades, the Inquisitions, Expulsions and Exterminations.

Medieval Jewish Persecution

The Middle Ages did not go well for the Jews under Christian sovereign rule. During the height of persecutions Jews were accused of killing "God" (Deicide accusation). And they were depicted as stealing the host ("the body" of God) and gleefully re-enacting the crucifixion by piercing the wafer (Host desecration accusation). These accusations precipitated pogroms, expulsions and mass genocide of the Jews. As can well be understood, this did not endear the Jews to their tormentors. Their reaction was naturally to recoil against any thought of a deification of the One in whose name these atrocities were perpetrated; and to impose upon all Christians the responsibility for the vile deeds of their religious compatriots. The way in which the representatives of the Christian faith taunted, debased, undermined, and slaughtered, only energized the Jewish people to run from "the Christian God."

Additionally, the Christian slander of the Jew, and the widespread supersession position only further alienated Jewish people and enhanced their desire to withdraw from the persecutors and draw a distinction between the Jewish Messiah and Jesus. This persecution of the Jews in the name of Jesus only succeeded in further alienation from the divine side of Yeshua. As the hour grew later in Jewish history, the disconnect with the ancient roots of the pre-conditioning concepts that aided in making the Deity of Messiah palatable for first century Jews, grew wider.

There were certainly Jews throughout the medieval period who embraced Jesus.[71] But because of the de-Judaizing of the "Church," those Jews who became Christians were segregated from their culture, assimilated into the Christian environs, and thus, not identifiably Jewish; consequently, they were not generally in a position from within to "turn on the light" for their brethren. With some exceptions these Jewish believers were not able to satisfactorily explain the Deity of Jesus to a Jewish audience. Although it was not uncommon for Jewish-Christians to be the main advocates in disputations,[72] they did not have a wide appeal for the Jews because of the sharp religious, and cultural disconnect. Moreover, prominent medieval rabbis like Moses ben Maimon contributed to reinforcing the anti-deity notion.

Moses ben Maimon

Moses ben Maimon (Maimonides), 1135-1204, a rabbi/philosopher of the highest order Judaism has produced, wrote with a pen "tainted" by centuries of Christian persecution of Jews. His assertion that God was incorporeal, and does not assume physical form, or possess natural characteristics, has impressed the collective memory of the Jew down to this very day.[73]

His 13 principles of faith went to lengths to deny the Incarnation of God and his humanity. It reacted against a Trinitarian nature of God that was prevalent in the Church (by the fourth century), by a tightening of the Unity of God.[74] These anti-Christian polemical attacks gave further fodder for Yeshua critics. Additionally, Maimonides tended to explain away the supernatural, and sought rational explanations for everything. As concerning the Messiah, in *Mishne Torah*, he laid down a two-tiered test that made the messiah a superhuman hero figure, but not Divine.[75]

> If a king arises from the house of David who studies Torah and pursues the commandments like his ancestor David in accordance with the written and oral law, and he compels all Israel to follow and strengthen it and fights the wars of the Lord—this man enjoys the presumption of being the Messiah. If He proceeds successfully, builds the Temple in its place, gathers the dispersed of Israel, then he is surely the Messiah. He will perfect the entire world so that its inhabitants will serve God together, as it is written, 'For then I will make the peoples pure of speech, so that they all invoke the Lord by name and serve him with one accord.' But if he does not succeed to this extent, or he is killed, it is evident that he is not the one whom Torah promised; he is, rather, like all the complete and righteous kings of Israel who have died.[76]

Hence, Maimonides delivered a two-punch blow against Yeshua's Deity: (1) denying that God could incarnate and (2) maintaining that the Messiah would be human. His influence was great. No rabbi exits training without exposure to the teachings of Maimonides, including his *Mishne Torah* and *Commentary on the Mishna*, containing his articles of faith, which infuse the Siddur.[77] Eight centuries of influence have left a big mark on the rank and file Jew who submits to the opinions of the rabbis and consequently recoils at the sound of Yeshua's Divinity. By Maimonidean days, the rift sharpened by the dispute over claims that Yeshua was Messiah and Deity, was deep and the chasm seemingly unbridgeable.

VIII. WHAT EVENTS ARE HAPPENING TODAY TO IMPROVE RELATIONS BEWTEEN YESHUA BELIEVING JEWS AND NON-YESHUA BELIEVEING JEWS IN SPITE OF THE PRONOUNCED SCHISM CAUSED IN PART BY THE DISPUTE OVER YESHUA'S DEITY?

There is coming a time when all of Israel shall be saved, for there shall come out of Zion the Deliverer, whom they will look upon as one mourns for their first born (Zech. 12:10). In that day there shall be a fountain open for sin and uncleanness (Zech. 13:1). We just do not know the precipitating causes that will move our people to a revelatory understanding that Yeshua is Lord, of the Deity variety. But we can speculate. There are four relatively recent happenings that may facilitate a pre-conditioning of the Jewish people to Yeshua's Deity. They are the growing interest in kabbalah among the Jewish people, the reconciliation movement, the proliferation of Messianic Judaism, and scholarly pursuits.

Popularization of Kabbalah

The conventional view is that Lurianic kabbalah was the cause of the conflagration that raged in the widespread acceptance of the pseudo-Messiah Shabbatei Zevi.[78] Zevi was reputedly the Incarnation of Tifferet (Beauty), one of the sefirah in the Godhead unity.[79] Today, through the popularization of kabbalah, which is flowing down to the rank and file level, there is much exposure to the emanations of God, and their sefirotic interplay. Being exposed to the Zohar is an awakening experience to a variation in common monotheistic thinking. There are ten sefirot who interact with each other, and who play out distinct roles, but all within the indivisible Godhead. Menachem Schneerson, the "Crown Heights messiah," who died in 1992, was seen not only as Messiah by his followers but also as Divine, inasmuch as he was proclaimed to be the incarnation of *Malchut*.[80] Although kabbalism is a stretch for messianic Jews theologically, nevertheless, it just may facilitate a type of preconditioning that harkens back to the first century when monotheism was not an obstacle for faithful Jews to accept Messiah as Deity.

Reconciliation Movement

David Stern characterizes the divide between Christians and Jews as the "worst schism in the history of the world."[81] For some time now Messianic Jews have been very involved in attempts to bridge the gap that has separated Jews and Christians for more than 19 centuries. It seems proper that it is the messianic ecclesial wing of the Body of Messiah that is involved in these endeavors, through prayer, teachings, scholarly and popular writings, public interviews and debates. Beginning in 1996, Toward Jerusalem Council II, a movement for repentance and reconciliation between Christians and Messianic Jews, has been actively engaged in the work of this goal.

Messianic Jews are coming together with like minded-brethren and representatives of the historical Church and other bodies to intercede and pray for reconciliation. They are hopeful that there will be a second Jerusalem Council that will reverse the anti-Semitic creeds the Church embraced throughout the centuries.[82] Through this process Christians are being educated concerning the "sin" of the historical Church's embracement of supersession theology, and its consequent repudiation of the covenant between the Jewish people and God.[83] This process may ultimately help to re-orient Jewish people who tend to commingle those truths in the creeds that are consistent with historical Jewish thought, with the anti-Semitic portions. Further, none of this escapes the throne of God, and it may, in fact, contribute to hastening of the day when the Jewish people as a nation proclaim, "Blessed is He who comes in the *Name* of the *Lord*."

Messianic Jewish Proliferation

The proliferation of Messianic Jews[84] provides real examples that belief in the Deity of Yeshua is not incompatible with being Jewish and living a Jewish life style. Messianic Judaism has risen to a critical mass that cannot be ignored; and every Jewish person knows of at least one Messianic Jew. In the first century the critical mass occurred quickly and then dissolved because it was so effective at reaching out to the Gentile, who then "boasted against the Jew," and displaced the bulk of the Jewish remnant. Messianic Jewish revivalism today appears to be taking a different turn. The gentile ecclesial wing is not unified through a state religion as it was under Roman rule and beyond. Consequently, Messianic Judaism, left to develop without widespread hindrance from the gentile wing of the body, very well may continue to "proliferate" by presenting to its Jewish brethren, the veracity of the Incarnation, while repudiating the anti-scriptural portions formulated by those at Councils who were insensitive to a Jewish audience.

Scholarly Pursuits

Finally, the "parting of the way" discussion in the literature and at conferences is raising awareness of the fallacies historically embraced by both sides of the divide. The "broken shards" are being reconstructed; the lost truths of the overlap contained in these parent-child beliefs and historic theologies are being resurrected. The Church is being called upon to be re-infused with an awareness of the Jewish essence of the faith. These intellectual pursuits may eventually make an impact on the Jewish populace. Oskar Skarsuane,[85] Daniel Boyarin,[86] Israel Yuval,[87] Mark Kinzer[88] and others are on the cutting edge of ground- breaking research that may be prefatory to breaking down the middle wall of partition, in a sort of pre-conditioning for the revelation of the Deity of Yeshua[89] to the Jewish people.

IX. WHAT IS THE CONCLUSION OF THE MATTER?

As the concepts of *Hocham*, *Memra*, *Shekhinah*, and *Malach Adonai* dimmed in Jewish thought and understanding, and were appropriated by the Church, the Jewish people were removed from a very significant part of their "theological" history. Yavneh, Bar Kokhba's Revolt, Justin Martyr's Dialogue, Church Councils, Medieval Persecutions and Moses ben Maimon, all "conspired" to deal further blows to acceptance of Yeshua's Deity among our people. This has unfortunately resulted in a hardening to the concept in the minds of the Jewish masses, which is reinforced daily by consensus validation within the broad-based Church.

The Deity was a mystery not fully embraced until post-resurrection. There was no single prophetic utterance, apocryphal, or pseud-epigraphic writing, that would clearly alert a pre-Yeshua Jew that the Scriptures promised salvation through God manifest in the flesh (a hypostatic union), and that God's enfleshment would be Deity. The general understanding of a Messiah who would be Redeemer was clear. The mosaic was there, but its complex maze was such that there was no uniform thought and interpretation that would yield the exact way it was to play out. Yes, there were the pre-conditioning concepts, but the revelation came to the disciples only *post hoc,* precipitated by an epiphany triggered by the resurrection. God showed up in a surprise body.

This approach was not new to the way in which God worked revelation. No one could have predicted that an Ark would save the world from a flood, though the few who believed in God certainly expected that He would save. Neither were the details clear that a Moses would come out of Egypt and save the Jewish people through the wilderness, although the belief that redemption would happen in a general sense was probably present. The way in which Moses received and delivered the law was not something that God revealed much before the time it happened. That David would be the progenitor of the everlasting kingdom was not clear before Nathan prophetically revealed God's plan for the building of the Temple and the everlasting Davidic throne. No one could have second-guessed some of the "unholy" persons who would be part of the genealogy of the Davidic line for Messiah. These are a sampling of God's revelatory surprises, the manner in which He is prone to work his plan.

Of course, there have always been Jews along the way who have received enlightenment in spite of the dismal past testimony of all the "evil" that Christians represented. Testimonies of that light abound. These are the remnants who continue to be faithful to the covenant, and who hold the truth of the Deity of Messiah Yeshua in mystical reverence. But these are more reminiscent of those comparatively "few" who "did not bow the knee to Baal," during Elijah's time, rather than the first century Jewish revival that witnessed tens of thousands of Jews burst onto the scene and embrace Yeshua as Lord in a very short period of time.

How did the early Jewish Yeshua-believers overcome the hurdle of the first commandment injunction and run headlong into the embrace of Yeshua, not just as an earthly Messiah but also as their heavenly Lord? Since the position of this paper is that a preconditioning of Jewish thought and concepts accommodated the exaltation of Yeshua as Deity, it behooves us to grasp the historical arguments. By replicating the first century environment with the presence of Yeshua as enhanced by New Covenant scripture, and sensitivity to the times in which we live, and the people whom we serve, the environment may be conducive to re-create a response among those who, not unlike the first century disciples, are hearing this news for the first time. Yet, in contrast to a backward-looking approach, some happenings, highlighted in this paper on the current horizon, offer promise: popular kabbalah, reconciliation movement, Messianic Jewish proliferation, and scholarly pursuit. These may combine to effectuate a new turn for the Jewish people.

Finally, when Moses went up the mount to receive the Word, the people rejected the revelation to come. It was only upon his second ascent and advent that Israelite eyes were opened to the revelation that the Mosaic Law came from God. They said, "All that thou say we will do." It is the hope that now is the moment for those who have ascended the mountain to receive the mystery of the hypostasis, to come down from the mount and deliver it to a people who are eagerly waiting at its foot for the news that Yeshua is Lord!

ENDNOTES

1. Oskar Skarsuane, *In the Shadow of the Temple: Jewish Influences on Early Christianity* (Downers Grove, IL: InterVarsity Press, 2002), 335-6 (hereafter referred to as *In the Shadow of the Temple*).

2. Martin Buber, *Two Types of Faith*, Norman Goldhawk, trans. (London: Routledge & Kegan Paul, 1951), 12.

3. See, for example, Amy-Jill Levine, *The Misunderstood Jew: The Church and the Scandal of the Jewish Jesus* (New York: Harper, 2006); David Klinghoffer, *Why the Jews Rejected Jesus* (New York: Doubleday, 2005).

4. Numbers 23: 19. Interestingly, the last four words are ordinarily omitted, which are "that He should lie." The contrast here is between God and Man, and the point is that God, unlike Man, does not lie. This "lifting out of context" is analogous to taking the scripture, "There is no God," and omitting its preface, "The fool has said in his heart . . ."

5. Exodus 20:3. This was clearly referring to the Egyptians and the surrounding foreign peoples who worshiped a plurality of gods.

6. It is beyond this paper to resolve the apparent between Yeshua being God and "no man hath seen God." However, the simple answer is that no one has seen the fullness of the Godhead. Neither have they seen the Father. Yet they have seen God, the Son, manifest in the flesh.

7. There were a number of instances in the first century when the Jewish people were ready to lay down their life rather than submit to deification of a man. Pilate, the governor of Judaea, sought to promote emperor worship by introducing banners bearing the Emperor's image into Jerusalem, and only withdrew when he realized that the Jews were willing to lay down their lives in protest of the idolatry; in still another incident Pilate sought to introduce shields bearing the Emperor's image into Jerusalem. Pilate backed off when the Emperor intervened to abate the crisis. *A History of the Jewish People*, H.H. Ben-Sasson, ed. (Tel Aviv: Dvir, 1976), 252 (hereafter referred to as *A History of the Jewish People)*. The deranged emperor Caligula demanded that his subjects worship him, and he was bent on setting up a statue of himself in the Temple. The masses of Jews demonstrated and evidenced their willingness to give up their lives, rather than tolerate such an abomination. Eventually, Caligula was persuaded by Agrippa to rescind the order, and the crisis totally abated when Caligula was assassinated. Ibid., 254-56.

8. The word gymnasium derives from a Greek word (*gymnos*), meaning nakedness.

9. Richard Baukham takes the position that first century Jewish monotheism was of the "exclusive" variety – that God is transcendently unique and not just the supreme ruler over other beings that share his platform. Richard Bauckham, *Jesus and the God of Israel: God Crucified and other Studies on the New Testament's Christology of Divine Identity* (Grand Rapids, MI: Wm. B. Eerdmans, 2008), 107-26 (hereafter referred to as *Jesus and the God of Israel)*.

10. Larry Hurtado, *Lord Jesus Christ: Devotion to Jesus in Early Christianity* (Grand Rapids: Wm. B. Eerdmans, 2003), 29-50.

11. Oskar Skarsuane takes issue with this, even maintaining that it was just as difficult for pagans to accept Jesus' divinity as it was for Jews to accept such, inasmuch as they did not see their gods intermingling with humans. Oskar Skarsuane, *Incarnation: Myth or Fact?* (St Louis: Concordia, 1991), 15-21(hereafter referred to as *Incarnation: Myth or Fact?*).

12. Gregory A. Boyd and Paul R. Eddy, *The Jesus Legend: A Case For The Historical Reliability of the Synoptic Tradition* (Grand Rapids: Baker Books, 2007), 91-132.

13. Robert M. Bowman, Jr. & J. Ed Komoszewski, *Putting Jesus in His Place: The Case for the Deity of Christ* (Grand Rapids, MI: Kregel, 2007), 267.

14. This is referred to as the acronym, HANDS. For a good summary see the chart at ibid., 281-288. See also Eric Chabot, "The Kingdom of God," *The Messianic Outreach* 27:3 (Spring 2008): 3-21.

15. Bowman & Komoszewski, 29-70, 270-71.

16. John 1: 14; see also Paul Copan, *Loving Wisdom: Christian Philosophy of Religion* (St Louis, MO: Calis, 2007), 154-60.

17. Bowman & Komoszewski, 73-123, 271.

18. Ibid., 127-181, 272-73.

19. See Darrell Bock, *The Son of Man.*
http://www.4truth.net/site/c.hiKXLbPNLrF/b.2902829/k.328F/Jesus_The_Son_of _Man_Apologetics.htm (last visited January 18, 2010);
Ben Witherington, *Did Jesus Believe He was the Son of Man?,*
http://www.4truth.net/site/c.hiKXLbPNLrF/b.2902803/k.D8B7/Did_Jesus_Believ e_He_Was_the_Son_of_Man.htm (last visited January 18, 2010); Michael Brown, *Answering Jewish Objections to Jesus: Theological Objections*, Vol. Two (Grand Rapids, MI: Baker Books, 2000), 216-19 (hereafter referred to as *Answering Jewish Objections*).

20. Bowman & Komoszewski, 185-231, 273.

21. Ibid., 235-66, 273-74.

22. For a full treatment see *Jesus and the God of Israel.*

23. But see *Incarnation: Myth or Fact?* 46-7, where Skarsuane maintains that there was no tension between the disciples' monotheistic concept and a type of "hypostasized agents" who served in the areas of creation and salvation. It was when it came to transferring these concepts to Jesus, a crucified man that the difficulty arose.

24. Larry W. Hurtado, *One God One Lord: Early Christian Devotion and Ancient Jewish Monotheism* (Philadelphia: Fortress Press, 1988), 4 (hereafter referred to as *One God One Lord*).

25. Dialogue with Trypho, 49.1 in *Incarnation: Myth or Fact?* 24.

26. These concepts are not exhaustive, but are the ones that have been most widely accepted by the scholarly audience. "Son of God/Son of Man" could also be added, although wider controversy surrounds the reference of these terms to the Deity of Yeshua. See *supra* note 19.

27. Skarsaune, *In the Shadow of the Temple,* 326. See also, *Incarnation: Myth or Fact?* 24-43, where Skarsuane takes Wisdom found in the Hebrew Bible and other pre-first century Jewish writings and relates it to the "one greater than Solomon," Jesus, and assigns to him the creative powers that are reserved for God and Wisdom.

28. Midrash Rabbah: Genesis, Vol. One, I.1, H. Freedman, trans. (London: Soncino Press, 1983), 1.

29. Skarsaune, *In the Shadow of the Temple,* 337.

30. *Answering Jewish Objections*, Vol. Two, 19-20. Brown also cites the Targum to Genesis 28:20-21, "If the Word of the Lord will be with me . . . then the Word of the Lord will be my God," and Deuteronomy 4:7, "The Memra of Yahweh sits upon his throne high and lifted up and hears our prayer whenever we pray before him and make our petitions." Ibid., 21.

31. For an extensive treatment of the references to the Logos in the Targumim furthering an understanding of Johanine logos theology see John Ronning, The *Jewish Targums and John's Logos Theology* (Peabody, MA: Hendrickson Publishers, 2010); for a later (5th century) discussion of portions of a rabbinic midrash collection, *Shir Hashirim Rabbah*, and some mediatorial and independent aspects of the Word, as a hypostasis see Carl Kinbar, "Israel, Torah, and the Knowledge of God," *Kesher* 24 (Summer 2010): 1-28.

32. Marian Hillar, "The Logos and Its Function in the Writings of Philo of Alexandria: Greek Interpretation of the Hebrew Myth and Foundations of Christianity," *A Journal from The Radical Reformation*, Vol.7:3 (Spring 1998): 22-37; ibid., Vol. 7:4 (Summer 1998): 36-53.

33. Skarsaune, *In the Shadow of the Temple*, 112-16.

34. Arnold Fruchtenbaum, *The Footsteps of the Messiah: A Study of the Sequence of Prophetic Events* (Tustin, AZ: Ariel Press, 1982), 409.

35. Ibid., 409-421

36. Ibid., 421-27.

37. Hurtado, 23-35. Hurtado rejects the view of Bousset that the introduction of angels in the post-exilic literature was due to the need to create intermediaries because God was very distant at this era in history. He also rejects the idea that the doctrine of angels encompassed a system that involved cultic veneration. Ibid.

38. Judg. 6: 11-24.

39. Judg. 13.

40. Gen. 32:24-32.

41. *Answering Jewish* Objections, Vol. Two, 28.

42. Gen. 18 – 19:1.

43. *Answering Jewish Objections*, Vol. Two, 31-34.

44. Hurtado, 93-124. Hurtado lists six features that evidence a significant "mutation" in Jewish monotheism: (1) hymnic practices (2) prayer and related practices (3) use of the name of Christ (4) the Lord's Supper (5) confession of faith in Jesus and (6) prophetic pronouncements of the risen Christ. Ibid., 100.

45. Ibid., 114-123.

46. Ibid. The two other causes he lists are the ministry of Jesus and opposition to the new movement. Ibid., 115-16, 122-23.

47. Pinchas Lapide, *The Resurrection of Jesus: A Jewish Perspective*, Wilhelm C. Linss, trans. (Minneapolis, MN: Augsburg Fortress, 1982), 125.

48. II Kings 4: 8-27.

49. John 11:1-44.

50. Acts 5:36-37.

51. See, for example, Acts 5:36-7.

52. See generally Seth Klayman, "Messianic Expectations 'Messy Antic' Realizations: Evaluating the Influences of Messianisms on Jewish Identity in the Second Temple Period, *Kesher* 12 (Winter 2000): 3-79; for three specific pre-30 CE "messiahs," Judas son of Hezekiah, Simon and Athronges, see ibid., 25.

53. Lapide, 125-6.

54. Skarsaune, *In the Shadow of the Temple*, 335-36.

55. Yochanon ben Zakkai's disciples carried him out of the Temple area in a coffin, on pretense that they needed to bury their master. Instead, he was taken to Vespasian, the general of the Roman forces charged with putting down the Jewish uprising. Ben Zakkai told him that Vespasian would become Emperor, and requested that, upon the fulfillment of the prophecy, Vespasian grant him a place where he and his disciples could continue the study of Judaism. *A History of the Jewish People,* 319

56. Shaye Cohen, "The Significance of Yavneh: Pharisees, Rabbis, and the End of Jewish Sectarianism," *Hebrew Union College Annual* 55(1984): 51. Cohen rejects the view that sectarianism ceased and the uncooperative were ejected. This is what happened at the Council of Nicea a few hundred years later, where "one party triumphs and ousts its competitors." Ibid., 28.

57. However, Daniel Boyarin makes a convincing case that in reality it was not formulated until much later, perhaps the middle of the third century. Daniel Boyarin, *Borderlines: The Partition of Judaeo-Christianity* (Philadelphia: University of Pennsylvania Press, 2004), 69-72.

58. Luke 21:20-21.

59. Boyarin, 91.

60. "Justin, First Apology" 31, in *The Ante-Nicene Fathers*, Vol. 1, Alexander Roberts & James Donaldson, eds. (Grand Rapids, MI: Wm. B. Eerdmans, 1985), 173.

61. One hundred years earlier Yeshua was tried and convicted of blaspheme, purporting to be God. Matthew 26: 64-66; Mark 14: 60-64.

62. See *In the Shadow of the Temple*, 201-02; Hugh Schonfield, *The History of Jewish Christianity: From the First to the Twentieth Century* (London: Duckworth, 1936), 40-41.

63. "Dialogue with Trypho 49.1," in *Incarnation: Myth or Fact?*, 24 (emphasis added).

64. Boyarin, 38.

65. Ibid., 146.

66. For fuller treatments of the Dialogue with Trypho see Boyarin, 28-29, 37-44; *In the Shadow of the Temple,* 269-274.
67. *In the Shadow of the Temple,* 336.
68. Boyarin, 128-147.
69. Ibid. Boyarin maintains that the rabbis rejected Logos hypostasis. Ibid., 139. But see Kinbar, "Israel, Torah, and the Knowledge of God," for a discussion of portions of a rabbinic midrash collection, *Shir Hashirim Rabbah,* and some mediatorial and independent aspects of the Word, as a hypostasis, which takes issue with Boyarin's view. Ibid., 21, 24.
70. Ray A. Pritz, *Nazarene Jewish Christianity: From the End of the New Testatment Period Until its Disappearance in the Fourth Century* (Jerusalem: Manes Press, 1992), 108.
71. For a historical survey of prominent Jewish believers from the 16th century onward see http://messianicassociation.org/profiles.htm
72. See, for example, the disputation between the Ramban and Pablo Christiani in Barcelona, Spain in 126 3 covered in Elliot Klayman, "From Nachmanides to the First Aliyah: The Jewish Community in Jerusalem," *The Messianic Outreach,* Vol. 29:1 (Autumn 2009):3-4.
73. Elliot Klayman, "Maimonides: The Greatest Jewish Thinker of All Time?" *The Messianic Outreach* Vol. 27: 4 (Summer 2008): 11-23. Other Jewish prominent medievalists of the same persuasion as Maimonides included Saadia Gaon, of Babylon and Judah Ha Levi, of Spain.
74. Ibid., 17-18.
75. Ibid., 20-22.
76. Mishneh Torah, Laws of Kings 11:4 *in* David Berger, *The Rebbe, The Messiah and The Scandal of Orthodox Indifference* (Portland: The Littman Library of Jewish Civilization, 2001), 21.
77. Hayim Halevy Donin, *To Pray as a Jew: A Guide to the Prayer Book and the Synagogue Service* (New York: Basic Books, 1980), 200-01; *The Complete Artscroll* Siddur, Nosson Scherman & Meier Zlotowitz, eds. (Brooklyn, NY: Mesorah Publications, 2001), 178-81.
78. See generally, Gershom Scholem, *The Messianic Idea in Judaism: and other Essays on Jewish Spirituality* (New York: Schocken Books, 1971), 36-48, 78-141; Gershom Scholem, *Sabbatai Sevi: The Mystical Messiah* (Princeton, NJ: Princeton University Press, 1973), 1-102, 465-66. But see Matt Goldish, *The Sabbatean Prophets* (Cambridge, MA: Harvard University Press, 2004), for a thesis that prophecy, instead, was the major cause of the spread of Sabbateanism.
79. Elliot Klayman, "Introduction to Kabbalah," *The Messianic Outreach,* Vol. 26:1 (Autumn 2006): 21.
80. Elliot Klayman, "Does the Lubavitcher Rebbe Fit the Festinger Model? Toward a Quantifiable Approach to the Measurement of Failed Prophecy," *Kesher,* Vol. 18 (Winter 2005): 85, 93. In fact, a recent conversation by the author and a Lubavitcher confidentially revealed that at one level or another, most, if not all, Chabad adherents, believe that Rebbe Schneerson is the Divine Messiah and will return. This comports with the fact that they have not made any provision for

a replacement and they do not say *yartzheit* for him. Ibid., 97, 102. This position, in time, may contribute to softening the Jewish people to the claim that Yeshua is Messiah and Deity.

81. David H. Stern, *Messianic Jewish Manifesto* (Jerusalem: Jewish New Testament Publication, 1988), 4.

82. Peter Hocken, *The Challenges of the Pentecostal, Charismatic and Messianic Jewish Movement: The Tensions of the Spirit* (Burlington, VT: Ashgate, 2009).

83. For a discussion of the rift and the healing of the schism see Mark Kinzer, *Postmissionary Messianic Judaism: Redefining Christian Engagement* with the Jewish People (Grand Rapids, MI: Brazos Press, 2005), 210-12, 303-10; see also Gershon Nerel, "*Nostra Aetate*: Between Hebrew Catholics and Messianic Jews," *Mishkan*, Vol. 46 (2006): 47-58.

84. The revival of Jewish believers in Yeshua corresponds to the restoration of Jerusalem in the hands of the Jewish people in 1967. Starting then, a real counter-culture revolution began in the United States and spread throughout the western world. This revolution birthed a Jesus Movement, which included a wave of Jewish youth, who accepted Jesus outside any intentionally organized religious mission. Instead of "converting" and repudiating Jewishness, these youth maintained rudiments of their heritage. The number of Jews coming to Jesus as Jews, and remaining such, triggered the formation and growth of fellowships and congregations of like-minded people. Non-Jewish believers, feeling the cultural call to align themselves with the Jewish believers joined together with them in the messianic congregation. To accommodate the rise of the messianic congregational movement, associations of fellowships arose, beginning in 1979.

The number of messianic Jews and congregations are based on crude estimates and anecdotal guesses since there is no good comprehensive reliable survey of recent vintage. One work copyrighted in 2000 reported a range of 60,000 to 100,000 Jewish believers in North America, of which about 6000 are in about 200 messianic congregations. Jeffrey S. Wasserman, *Messianic Jewish Congregations: Who Sold this Business to the Gentiles?* (Lanham, NY: University Press of America, 2000), 112, n. 59, and accompanying text. In the last decade since that report these numbers have, at least, moderately expanded.

Israel was slower to experience large numbers of Jews coming to Jesus who maintained their distinctiveness. However, that changed with real increases occurring, beginning in the 1980s, and expanding quickly. For a demographic treatment of messianic congregations in Israel see Kai Kjaer-Hansen & Bodil F. Skjott, "Facts & Myths about Messianic Congregations in Israel 1998-1999," *Mishkan*, Vol. 30-31 (1999). From 1948-1999 the number of congregations in Israel increased from 2 to 81, and Jewish believers from fewer than 200 to 2178. Wasserman, ix. There are no reliable surveys of messianic congregations and messianic Jews in Israel since the Kjaaer-Hansen & Skjott survey, although anecdotal reports indicate significant increases over the last ten years.

85. Oskar Skarsuane, *In the Shadow of the Temple*.

86. Daniel Boyarin, *Borderlines*.

87. Israel Jacob Yuval, *Two Nations in Your Womb: Perceptions of Jews and Christians in Late Antiquity and the Middle Ages* (Berkeley, CA: University of California Press, 2006).

88. Mark S. Kinzer, *Postmissionary Messianic Judaism*.

89. For an interesting discussion of the "incarnation of God and his anthropomorphic character see Jacob Neusner, *The Incarnation of God: The Character of Divinity in Formative Judaism* (Binghamton, NY: Global Publications, 2001) where Neusner explains his view of the incarnation of the Torah in the person of the sage. Ibid., 202-210. See also:

Since rabbinical documents repeatedly claim that, if you want to know the law, you should not only listen to what the rabbi says but also copy what he does, it follows that, in his person, the rabbi represents and embodies the Torah. God in the Torah revealed God's will and purpose for the world. So God had said what the human being should be. The rabbi was the human being in God's image. That, to be sure, is why (but merely by the way) what the rabbi said about the meaning of Scripture derived from revelation. Collections of the things he said about Scripture constituted compositions integral to the Torah.

So in the rabbi, the word of God was made flesh. And out of the union of man and Torah, producing the rabbi as Torah incarnate, was born Judaism, the faith of Torah: the ever present revelation, the always open-canon. For fifteen hundred years, from the time of the first collections of scriptural exegeses to our own day, the enduring context for *midrash* remained the same: encounter with the living God. Jacob Neusner, *Midrash in Context: Exegesis in Formative Judaism* (Philadelphia: Fortress Press, 1983), 137.

THE CANON OF SCRIPTURE AND THE DEITY OF CHRIST: IS IT KOSHER TO SUBSTITUTE JESUS INTO GOD'S PLACE?

Darrell L. Bock, Ph.D.
Senior Research Professor on New Testament;
Executive Director of Cultural Engagement, Center for Christian Leadership, and Cultural Engagement; Dallas Theological Seminary

Perhaps one of the most difficult aspects of teaching coming out of the early Jesus community was the extent to which they elevated his status alongside God. For a community rooted in Judaism and accustomed to reciting the *Shema* each Sabbath, such claims seem to stretch the limit of what could or should be believed.[1] How could it be that followers of Judaism could make such a move? The following study serves to indicate how this kind of identification and substitution could take place. It proceeds in three parts. First, we shall look at an incident in Jesus' life that is key to pursuing this question. Second, we shall consider a key speech of Peter, early in the life of the movement, which shows how these events helped the new community see the relationship between God and Jesus. Third, we shall consider a text that likely was a hymn sung in the early church that also addresses this issue. We are asking if it is kosher to substitute Jesus into God's place – and what this means for how we present and talk about Jesus to those for whom this move seems so radical (and even out of place). We are looking at events articulated from within a Jewish matrix by Jewish believers in the earliest period. I make this point because the key to my argument is not that this teaching is in New Covenant texts, but because here are the original messianic Jewish missionaries making their case for Jesus to their unbelieving Jewish neighbors from events tied to God's activity and from texts in the Hebrew canon. These witnesses describe how God has acted, what He has done to show that Jesus is who he claimed to be and why he should be embraced.

A Key Incident on the Road to the Cross: The Confrontation with the Jewish Leadership

The initial incident we consider is Jesus' examination by the Jewish leadership, an interview that ended with the leadership deciding to take Jesus to Pilate and the Romans to ask that he be crucified. In a sense, this is the scene that tells us why Jesus was crucified. Much has brought Jesus to this place. He has had numerous encounters with the leadership over issues related to Jewish practice. He has claimed to forgive sin, something only God can do (Mark 2:1–12). He has acted on the Sabbath in ways the leadership saw as violations of Sabbath rest (Mark 2:23–3:6). Jesus defended these Sabbath actions in two ways: by appeals to the Hebrew Scripture, as well as his more radical appeal that the Son of Man was Lord of the Sabbath. He entered Jerusalem on a donkey, an act suggesting on reflection that Jesus was the awaited king of Zechariah 9 (Mark 11:1–11; John 12:12–16). He had acted against the temple, a direct challenge to the leadership's authority over what Jews saw as the most sacred space on earth (Mark 11:15–18).[2] Such actions evoked hope like that expressed in works like Psalms of Solomon 17:26–31, where the hoped for end time deliverer would purge Jerusalem. It also was like a prayer, the Eighteen Benedictions, where the hope for restored Davidic rule and the restoration of Jerusalem are placed side by side in the fourteenth of these Benedictions. These claims and acts had caused the leadership to ask Jesus about the source of his authority. This seemed a fair question given they, as the Jewish leadership, had not authorized him to act (Mark 11:27–33). Jesus answered this challenge with a question about the authority of John the Baptist, a question the leadership did not answer but one that suggested God is capable of making such appointments without requiring Saducean and Pharisaical approval. These events form a key background to why Jesus found himself in front of the Jewish leadership answering questions about whether he was seeking to destroy the temple or was claiming to be the Messiah, the Son of the Blessed One.

What is under examination is the extent of Jesus' claims and authority. This scene is not a trial in the formal sense.[3] The leadership cannot give a legal verdict that has the force of law in the Roman world. What they are doing is gathering evidence in order to make a case to Pilate, who can make such a judgment. In our legal world, this is like a legal inquiry or a grand jury investigation where the question is whether

Jesus can be charged legally with a crime against the Roman state. The Jewish leadership could bring such a case to Pilate, especially if it came from the High Priest whom Pilate had appointed. So this pre-history of tension that Jesus' ministry generated is important to appreciate as Caiaphas steps forward to ask Jesus a crucial question in Mark 14:61, "Are you Messiah, the Son of the Blessed One?"

In a Jewish context, Caiaphas simply wants to know if Jesus is claiming to be the delivering promised one for Israel. The question about being the son is not asked with later Christian understanding of who the Son is. Rather, the roots are the idea that the king as God's representative is God's son, language that alludes to promises made to David about his dynastic line (2 Sam. 7:12–14), an image that applied to all kings of the line, but which in a context of restoration and call to renewal for Israel would also likely point to a messianic expectation. Since these leaders had wedded their fate to Rome and did not hold to messianic and eschatological expectations like those Jesus appeared to raise, for Jesus to claim such a role would be all they would need to bring him before Pilate. A king that the leadership does not recognize and that Rome did not appoint in their minds would be a candidate to take to Pilate as a threat to the *pax Romana*. Rome appointed the kings of the empire and was responsible for keeping the peace. Rome was to stop anyone who claimed authority Rome did not give. To indicate how serious this question was, Caiaphas asks it and shows respect for God, by not speaking about the Son *of God*. Rather, he shows respect for God by referring to him indirectly as "the Blessed One." In doing so, his question indicates how seriously the leadership takes the uniqueness and glory of God's person.

Jesus' response leads to all that follows, directly triggering a series of core events that stand at the roots of the message of what became a major world religion. What did Jesus say and mean? How was his reply perceived by those who rejected it? Jesus' reply is given variously in the Synoptic Gospels. John does not record this examination, so we are only looking at Matthew, Mark, and Luke. I have defended in detail the historicity of this response in a monograph dedicated to this scene.[4] The core of the reply is a qualified affirmative response with allusions to Psalm 110:1 ("The LORD says to my Lord: 'Sit at my right hand'"), and to Daniel 7:13, an allusion to the Son of Man coming on the clouds. Mark expresses an outright affirmative response ("I am"), with allusions to the Psalm (seated) and to Daniel (coming on the clouds). Matthew has a qualified affirmative response

("You have said it yourself"), with the same allusions to both passages. Luke has a qualified affirmative response ("You say that I am") with allusion to both passages, but with the reference to Daniel 7 only referring to the title Son of Man, not to coming on the clouds. I take these summaries of Jesus' response to indicate he responded positively to the question, but with a qualification that said in effect, "Yes, but not quite in the sense that you asked it." He then elaborates by appealing to God's acceptance of him as Son of Man (Jesus' favorite name for himself) at God's side in heaven (Ps. 110:1 allusion). He also declares that vindication would come in such a way that he would function as judge one day (Daniel 7 as it appears in Mark and Matthew). However, the points I am about to make would be so even if Jesus only used the Son of Man title and alluded to Psalm 110:1 without appealing to coming on the clouds. This more limited appeal is all the gospels affirm in the reply.

This long aside on the nature of the reply is required in order to discuss the saying's significance. Jesus' claim before the Jewish leadership is that God is going to show his support for Jesus' ministry and claims by bringing him into ruling authority with God. This vindication will take place regardless of what is about to happen in terms of a potential crucifixion. Jesus will occupy a regal-executive position in the program of God. The allusion to Psalm 110 points to a text that has regal overtones. The authority Jesus has, however, should not be understood as a strictly earthly authority. The reference from Daniel 7 to the Son of Man, either alone or along with the coming on the clouds, pictures an authority received directly from God to judge and exercise dominion. This is a heavenly and heavenly vindicated authority. What is so controversial is not the intimation of judgment but the idea that Jesus can sit in the presence of God in heaven. He can share God's glory and authority.

Caiaphas is no amateur theologian. He reacts immediately. He tears his robe, indicating that in his view Jesus has uttered blasphemy and is worthy of death. If Jesus is not who he is claiming to be and if God were not to vindicate Jesus or anyone in such a manner, Caiaphas would be right. Some Jews could contemplate such a close relationship between God and another and wrote about it. One need only look at the *Exagoge of Ezekiel* 67–82 or portions of *1 Enoch*, where the Son of Man sits with God, to see the contemplation of this idea as a possibility (applied to Moses in his Exodus authority as a metaphor, or to the future Son of Man seen as Enoch). However, other Jews vehemently denied such a connection. In *3 Enoch*, the angel Metatron is punished for claiming to be a "lesser YHWH" or, at least, for how that can be misunderstood. In Talmudic tradition Rabbi Akiba is rebuked for "profaning the Shekinah" when he says David could sit next to God (*b Hag* 14a). Caiaphas, as a Sadducee, would likely have held a view that did not see any possibility for such a thing.

So Jesus supplies in this remark the testimony that leads the Jewish leadership to take him to Pilate to secure his judgment: that Jesus should be crucified for sedition. They change the blasphemy charge into political terms for Pilate, so he examines Jesus on whether he is "king of the Jews," the title placed on the placard that hung with Jesus on the cross. They "translate" the charge out of its religious significance to make the point that Rome had nothing to do with Jesus' claim to be king, something Rome would read as a threat to their own authority. So in a real way, Jesus supplied the testimony that led to his death, and also produced a challenge that claimed they could see God behind his ministry. If there was a future vindication after the death they were contemplating for Jesus, then they could know God supported Jesus and his claims. It is important to keep an eye on the narrative-theological story line coming out of this scene in the gospels. It is a key element to understanding the early church's preaching about Jesus, as well as the debate between this new movement emerging from within Judaism and other Jews. In effect, this scene says that either Jesus is a figure to be exalted by God or else he was guilty of blaspheming God. Subsequent events are to help us determine which association properly belongs to Jesus.

On the third day, when God empties Jesus' tomb in resurrection, the vindication Jesus predicted took place. With it came a key indication of where Jesus had gone as a result of God's activity. He had gone to God's right hand, to share in God's presence, authority, and glory in heaven. The work of God in salvation became inseparable from the work of Jesus. This connection forms the background for the second passage we wish to consider, part of Peter's speech at Pentecost, and the apostle's appeal to Joel 2 and the coming of God's Spirit. It is to this central early church proclamation that we now turn.

A Central Speech from the Early Church: Peter's Words at Pentecost in Acts 2

Acts 2 summarizes a speech by Peter. This address accompanied the pouring out of God's Spirit on those who had embraced the hope of Jesus and the inauguration of the new covenant brought about by Jesus' death (Acts 2:38–39; Luke 22:20). In fact what is present in this event is part of a key theological theme running through Luke-Acts.

This theme starts with John the Baptist. John called for eschatological renewal in Israel and the coming of God's apocalyptic deliverance in one who was yet to come. In Luke 3:15–16, John notes, amidst speculation that he might be the Christ that he only baptizes with water. However there is one to come who will baptize with the Spirit and fire. This one is so great that even though John is a prophet of God, he as a prophet is not worthy to untie the thong of the coming one's sandal. The act of untying the thong of a sandal was an act no Jew who became a slave was to perform because, according to later Jewish tradition, it was seen as too demeaning a task to perform (*Mekilta de Rabbi Ishmael Nezikin* 1 on Exod. 21:2).[5] However, the difference between the office of eschatological prophet that John occupied and the office of the one to come was so great that such a demeaning task would have been an honor for John to perform. This already indicates that Jesus as the eschatological one to come has a place much greater than a prophet of Israel.

The next strand in the link is Jesus' post-resurrection command to his disciples to wait in Jerusalem for the coming of the "promise" of the Father. This promise will cloth the disciples with power, enabling them to minister effectively on God's behalf (Luke 24:49). Jesus then echoes the remarks of John the Baptist about awaiting the promised baptism of the Spirit in Acts 1:3–5. All of this sets the context for Acts 2. After Peter's Acts 2 speech, the book of Acts again notes how central this event is in Acts 11:15–17, where Peter compares the coming of the Spirit on the family of Cornelius to the Pentecost event. This divine action functions as a sign proving that God accepts Gentiles alongside Jews in this new era of Jesus. In Acts 13:25, the early portion saying of John the Baptist appears again in Paul's speech at Pisidian Antioch. Here the allusion is to the one to come, with the next remark that is not cited being about the Spirit. Finally, in Acts 15:8–9, Peter alludes back to Pentecost in explaining the coming of the Spirit to Cornelius and clan. God has given them "the Holy Spirit just as he did to us" (v. 8, NET). The comparison to how the Spirit was given to us looks back to Pentecost in Acts 2 and pictures the cleansing of their hearts and acceptance into the eschatological program of God that surrounded Jesus (cf. Acts 11:15-17).

That is the context of Peter's remarks in Acts 2. The apostle is explaining the significance of the Spirit's coming for the program of God.[6] He starts out citing Joel 2:28–32 (=3:1–5 Matt.). The promise is of the outpouring of the Spirit in the last days. Peter is proclaiming this text as initially fulfilled by what is taking place. But the key feature I wish to draw attention to comes at the end of the citation. In Acts 2:21, Peter notes that all who call upon the name of the Lord will be saved. Now any Jewish listener of Peter in this scene would immediately think that it is the God of Israel who is to be invoked here. After all, that is the point of the citation in the context of Joel—and it is God who delivers.

However, between making this call and finishing his speech Peter develops the imagery from Joel. He notes the hope of resurrection, appealing to Psalm 16. He then notes the promise made to David of a descendant to sit on the throne and share in rule (Ps. 132:11). Finally he appeals to the very important text, Psalm 110:1, the very text Jesus alluded to at his trial to make the point that Jesus is now seated with God at his right hand, sharing his presence and saving authority. In fact, in Acts 2:33 (NET), Peter says, "So then, exalted to the right hand of God, and having received the promise of the Holy Spirit from the Father, he has poured out both what you see and hear." Now there is something very Jewish about the way this argument is made. It applies an ancient Jewish reading technique known as *Gezerah Shava*. In this technique, the reader of Scripture links two passages, or a passage and an event, together by terms they share. So in Joel 2:28 as cited in Acts 2:17 we have the idea of the Spirit being poured out (*ekcheō*), and in Acts 2:33, we have the verb repeated in a different form to fit the syntax of the sentence that also speaks of the Spirit being poured out (*execheen*). So Peter by *Gezerah Shava* is combining the idea of Psalm 110:1 and Jesus' being seated at God's right hand with what he did when he got there, namely, to distribute the promised Spirit that had been announced as far back as John the Baptist.[7] Salvation is being mediated through Jesus who shares God's presence, a place on his throne, and the execution of salvation.

Because of this sequence of connections, Peter is able to say in Acts 2:36 that God has shown Jesus to be Lord and Christ to Israel, in the same manner John announced in Luke 3 that the Messiah could be identified. In fact, Israel can know this is who Jesus is because of what God has done through Jesus. There is another, complicated *Gezerah Shava* here, as the term Lord (*kyrion*) appears in verse 36, invoking the presence of the second use of the term Lord from Psalm 110:1 in verse 34 (*kyriō*), and recalling verse 32 from Joel 2, where one is to call upon "the Lord" (*kyriou*).[8] The significance of this becomes evident when Peter calls on the crowd to be baptized "in the name of Jesus Christ for the forgiveness of sins" in Acts 2:38. Salvation is now taking place in his name and authority, including the forgiveness of sins. Jesus is equated in his activity and responsibilities with the actions of the God of Israel. To invoke him as Lord and Christ is to invoke the authority of God. To call on Jesus' name as Lord is the same as calling on the God of Israel. As Jesus says in John 10:30, "I and the Father are one" (NET). What Jesus does in mediating the blessing of God's Spirit is to save and forgive, undertaking the prerogatives of God and showing divine authority from the very side of God in heaven. As such to call on him is to call on God. Thus, through the exposition of the speech, on reflection Peter is saying in Acts 2:21 that anyone who calls on the name of the Lord (Jesus) will be saved.

This teaching invoking the Lord Jesus is not unique to Peter. In Romans 10:9–13, Paul also appeals to Joel 2:32 (=3:5 Matt.). In verse 9, Paul treats the idea of confessing with one's lips that Jesus is Lord and believing that God raised him from the dead. At the end of this exposition in verse 13, he says, "Everyone who calls on the name of the Lord will be saved." *Gezerah Shava* tells us the Lord that Paul is referring to here is Jesus. Jesus is referred to in a text that originally invoked the God of Israel, and the substitution is entirely kosher because of what Jesus is doing, how God is working through Jesus, and the way the Scriptures are linked in a very Jewish manner.

One of the great difficulties in sharing Jesus in a Jewish context is explaining how Jesus can receive the unequivocal honor believers in Jesus give to him. The two scenes we have examined are a key explanation as to why and how that honor came to be so central to the emerging faith. Here we have Jesus at the hub of the execution of divine activity and authority, associated with both forgiveness and the establishing of a new covenant. Here the promised Spirit, the sign of the arrival of God's promise for his people, is shown to have arrived. Mediating all of this from God's side is Jesus, sharing in the divine presence, rule, and authority. Everything comes together in what God does through Jesus. Jesus even shares the title of Lord, and can be invoked for this salvation because it came through him. So Peter can speak of God and Jesus in one breath, even to the point of sharing a reference in passages that invoke God for salvation.

It is easy to see how crucial a text Acts 2 is for the question we have raised. I also have suggested that Paul and Peter agree on this point. However, there is one more passage to examine, because it appears in what was likely originally an early Christian hymn, showing what early Christians were singing in praise to God in the first century. It is to this hymn of praise that we now turn to show that Peter's view was not unique to him.

A Central Hymn from the Early Church— Philippians 2:5–11

Our final text is generally regarded as a hymn, sung by the early church and providing a summation of the career of Jesus. This hymn originates at a fairly early point in the theological development of the Jesus movement. What makes the text important is that it predates the letter in which it appears, Philippians, written from prison in about 62. So we are within three decades of the end of Jesus' ministry. As a hymn, it is likely older and reflects what communities were told about Jesus as they engaged in corporate praise for what God had done through Jesus. It is the crisp nature of the contrasts and the balance of the lines that cause people to see a hymn here. Here is the text:

> [6]who although he existed in the form of God did not regard equality with God as something to be grasped,
> [7]but emptied himself by taking on the form of a slave, becoming in the likeness of other men, and being found in form as a human.
> [8]He humbled himself, by becoming obedient to the point of death—even death on a cross.
> [9]Therefore God exalted him and gave him the name that is above every name,
> [10]so that at the name of Jesus every knee will bow—in heaven and on earth and under the earth—
> [11]and every tongue confess that Jesus Christ is Lord to the glory of God the Father. (Phil. 2:6–11, author's translation)

There is much in the hymn that is debated. Is its key portrait rooted in a strong sense of the pre-existence of Jesus, as one sent from heaven, or is it rooted in imagery related to his being the second Adam, representative of humanity?[9] Is the hymn present in the letter to make an ethical point about being like Jesus (because of the call to have a mind like that in Jesus Christ), or is it more directed at a presentation of who Jesus is? Might both those ideas be at work in Paul's letter? The career of Jesus is seen as a reverse parabola, which has him coming and sent from heaven, dipping down to take on humanity and death, and ascending again to greatness by receiving the name of Lord. All these are important questions about the passage that have led to no loss in the expression of opinions on one side or the other. In other words, the literature on this text is vast. But I am not interested in the hymn as a whole or in these specific debates that overview the career of Jesus. Our concern is how the hymn ends in verses 10–11.

The twin themes of every knee bowing and every tongue confessing have precedent in the Hebrew Scripture. Again, we need the full context to get the force of the point. In Isaiah 45:20–25, God is calling all to account for denying the Creator and choosing to engage in idolatry rather than give God the honor due to him. So he calls the nations to court and says this,

> [20]Gather together and come! Approach together, you refugees from the nations! Those who carry wooden idols know nothing, those who pray to a god that cannot deliver. [21]Tell me! Present the evidence! Let them consult with one another! Who predicted this in the past? Who announced it beforehand? Was it not I, the LORD? I have no peer, there is no God but me, a God who vindicates and delivers; there is none but me. [22]Turn to me so you can be delivered, all you who live in the earth's remote regions! For I am God, and I have no peer. [23]I solemnly make this oath—what I say is true and reliable: "Surely every knee will bow to me, every tongue will solemnly affirm; [24]they will say about me, 'Yes, the LORD is a powerful deliverer.'" All who are angry at him will cower before him. [25]All the descendants of Israel will be vindicated by the LORD and will boast in him. (Isa. 45:20–25 NET)

This text is one of the clearest declarations of God's uniqueness and sovereignty in the Hebrew Bible. God declares that allegiance will be uniquely his one day. There is no other God, nor is there any other savior or judge. The indication of this divine position is the fact that one day everyone will acknowledge this. Every knee will bow and every tongue will confess that God is the Lord and a powerful deliverer. The name given above every name is that which affirms the sovereignty of the Creator God over those whom he rules. There is no other place to go. There is no other one to whom to turn. One day all creation will know and affirm this. That is Isaiah's teaching.

Now Paul was a rabbi. He surely knows this background as he cites this hymn with its intentional allusion to Isaiah 45. In the hymn, the bowing of the knee and the confessing of the tongue include giving such honor to the Lord Jesus. His work of emptying and death is so in conjunction with the Father, and so rooted in a heavenly origin, that the honor due the God of Israel will come to be given to the one through whom God worked. Once again we see that substituting Jesus in the place of the God of Israel is kosher, justified by the calling and activity of Jesus at God's behest. Note how the hymn makes it clear that God is the one gifting Jesus with this name and role. Jesus does not act, nor does he claim to act, independently of the Father. But they are like a double helix in a piece of DNA, a package deal, operating as an inseparable team to deliver and save with a mighty hand stretched out, ironically, through the death of a frail human who once had been in the presence of God and who afterward was vindicated back to that original position. To see and speak of one is inevitably to speak of and see the other.

It is this kind of identification that has always been at the core of the teaching of the early Jesus community. It is what led to the kind of technical philosophical articulation of the relationship between God and Jesus in later creeds. Those creeds seek to translate the kosher connections we have traced in our three passages, and to express them in terms of implications for the kind of person Jesus had to be in order to be in this role and share such glory without division from the Father. The result meant that God was affirmed as One, even though the divine also took on flesh (John 1:1-14).

The *Shema* Revisited in the New Community: 1 Corinthians 8:4-6

Three ideas controlled the affirmation of monotheism in Second Temple Judaism. They were the idea of only worshipping God (monolatry), the idea of God's universal sovereignty, and the idea that God is the one Creator.[10] To affirm Jesus as divine while affirming the unity of God were two things the early Jesus community did. Nothing shows this more powerfully than the way Paul plays with the idea of Creation and the confession of the *Shema* in 1 Corinthians 8:4-6. Here is the text laid out in parallel structure in English:

> But for us [there is] one God, the Father,
> From whom [are] all things and we for him,
> And one Lord, Jesus Christ,
> Through whom [are] all things and we through him.

The context of this remark is the many gods of the Greco-Roman world. The text affirms the oneness of God in the face of that polytheism, but does so noting that there is one God and One Lord. Both God and Lord in the context of being Creator look to describe who God is and what God does, since in Judaism only God creates (Isa. 44:24; 4 Ezra 3:4; Josephus, *Contra Apion* 2.192). The fact that "all things" are created through Jesus shows he is in the category of Creator, not creature. As Bauckham says, "No more unequivocal way of including Jesus in the unique divine identity is conceivable, within the framework of Second Temple Jewish monotheism."[11]

To show the connection to the *Shema*, one need only look at how the LXX: "The Lord (*kurios*) our God (*ho theos*), the Lord (*kurios*), is one." There is one God and one Lord who participates in the creation as the Creator is Paul's point. This affirms a divine activity and status for Jesus as the Christ. Here it is kosher not to substitute Jesus for God but to place him alongside God to show their equality. So Jesus shares God's glory by his exaltation to God's throne as Jesus' examination by the Jewish leadership shows. He also shares the divine task of creating the world as the one through whom creation the creation of all things took place. Such a handling of the *Shema* helps us see how the earliest community rooted in the writings of believers emerging from Judaism presented Jesus. They did so affirming the oneness of God and the deity of Jesus as Creator and one who sits on the throne of heaven.

Conclusion

We have traversed into great mysteries of the Jesus movement by examining one aspect of the use of the sacred Hebrew Scripture in the early years of this new, Jewish-rooted movement that came with Jesus. These Jewish believers did not just proclaim Jesus; they explained what they believed. They did so by appealing to a combination of the affirming actions of God and teaching from their Scripture. In linking Jesus, and substituting him in places where that Scripture had spoken of the God of Israel, they were expressing a core element of their faith. God had demonstrated to the world, both inside and outside Israel, who this Jesus was. John the Baptist pointed to it when he spoke of the coming of God's Spirit through Jesus. Jesus pointed to it when he predicted a vindication that expressed itself in a tomb emptied three days after a horrific death. The Jesus movement preached it when they substituted Jesus and proclaimed him as Lord in those very places where the uniqueness of God was being affirmed in their Scripture. It all reflected the very activity of Israel's own God, who also was affirmed as the Creator of all life. This God was the Savior of that same precious world. The story of that deliverance came through an invitation to enter into life God extended through Jesus and pictured in him. Delivering the message this way was explanatory and clarifying. It disclosed the mystery of how God had made the choice and taken the action to work through Jesus, to present Jesus from the earth up to heaven. Through this means one could begin to grasp Jesus' own uniqueness: a one of a kind person, bringing God's promised kingdom as God's uniquely anointed deliverer, the Messiah of Israel who also could fully represent God. And, best of all in their view, it was all completely kosher.

ENDNOTES

1. A couple of texts that tell us this are from the Mishnah, *Megilllah* 4.5 and *Aboth* 2.13.

2. I treat these texts and others that lead into this scene in *Jesus According to Scripture* (Grand Rapids: Baker, 2002), 605–23.

3. Darrell L. Bock, Blasphemy and Exaltation in Judaism: The Charge against Jesus in Mark 14:53–65 (Grand Rapids: Baker, 2000), originally Blasphemy and Exaltation In Judaism and the Final Examination of Jesus (Tübingen: Mohr/Siebeck, 1998). This is a detailed study of this scene and the Jewish background that informs it.

4. Darrell L. Bock, *Blasphemy and Exaltation In Judaism and the Final Examination of Jesus*, 184–237; updated in "Blasphemy and the Jewish Examination of Jesus," *BBR* 17 (2007): 53–114.

5. Jacob Z. Lauterbach, *Mekilta de-Rabbi Ishmael* (1933; repr., Philadelphia: Jewish Publication Society, 2004), 2:358. The remark appears in a section discussing the six years one can serve. He should not wash the feet of his master, put shoes on him, carry things for him to a bathhouse, lift him by the hips as he goes up stairs, or carry him in a chair or sedan chair.

6. This is another text I have discussed in detail in two places: *Proclamation from Prophecy and Pattern: Lucan Old Testament Christology* (Sheffield: Sheffield Academic Press, 1987), 153–87; *Acts* (Grand Rapids: Baker, 2007), 108–48.

7. This text is about kingship, rooted in the divine promise that the king would be as a son to the father from 1 Samuel 7:14. This starts with Solomon, as the following remark about sin and accountability indicates. That such promises and hope extend to the dynasty is shown by (1) Psalm 18:50 and 1 Samuel 22:51 where God's faithfulness to the David and the Davidic covenant seed as a dynasty is affirmed and (2) from the evidence the location of the temple with reference to the City of David in Old Jerusalem, where the palace was at the right hand of the temple as one looked out from the Shekinah. Of course, the Messiah is included in such promises made to the dynastic line.

8. These are the same words. The forms differ because of the syntactical difference between an object and a genitive in Greek, which points to their syntactical role.

9. The classic study of this text is from Ralph Martin, *Carmen Christi: Philippians 2.5–11 in Recent Interpretation and in the Setting of Early Christian Worship* (Cambridge: Cambridge University Press, 1967). For a defense of Adam Christology being present here, see James D. G. Dunn, *Christology in the Making*, 2nd ed. (Grand Rapids: Eerdmans, 1996), 114–21. Adam Christology roots the text in man made in God's image, from Genesis 1–3. We prefer the interpretation pointing to divine pre-existence, in part because grasping at or holding onto divinity does not make as much sense in a model that only sees this Adamic background in play. Our exposition assumes this larger christological

backdrop, but the point I will make about the use of Isaiah works no matter which background is operating in the hymn.

10. These three themes are developed in detail in a series of important essays by Richard Bauckham, *Jesus and the God of Israel: God Crucified and Other Essays on the New Testament's Christology of Divine Identity* (Grand Rapids: Eerdmans, 2008).

11. Bauckham, Jesus and the God of Israel, 102.

JEWISH TRADITION AND THE DEITY OF YESHUA

Joseph Shulam, M.A.

Director of Netivyah Bible Instruction Ministry in Jerusalem
Elder of Congregation Roeh Israel, Jerusalem
Former adjunct professor at Abilene Christian University (ACU)

Introduction:

The title of this paper ought to be: "Jewish Tradition and the Deity of the Messiah." It is a little presumptuous to think, "Jewish Tradition has anything to say about the Deity of the Yeshua." However, on the other hand Jewish Tradition has no little to say about the Deity of the Messiah. There is a principle that I hold to that might be a surprise to some of you, but upon your examination it will prove itself to be true i.e. "anything that is contradictory to the Torah that the good Lord gave us in Mt. Sinai must not be true." I do hold and believe in progressive revelation, but only in respect to a direct mandate give by God's Spirit and expressly written in the Bible. Like in the words of Jeremiah and Ezekiel (18), *"'What mean ye, that ye use this proverb in the land of Israel, saying: The fathers have eaten sour grapes, and the children's teeth are set on edge? As I live, saith the Lord GOD, ye shall not have occasion any more to use this proverb in Israel. Behold, all souls are Mine; as the soul of the father, so also the soul of the son is Mine; the soul that sinneth, it shall die."* At one time in Israel they used to say that Fathers will pay for the sins of their children and children will pay for the sins of their fathers, but this will no longer be so, said God to Ezekiel and to Jeremiah too. The principle is clear, the New Covenant is standing on the shoulders of the Torah and the Prophets and anything that contradicts the truth of God's Word in the Torah and the Prophets is to be considered as outside of the divine truths that were given by God to Israel, i.e. the Bible.

On the other hand it should be made clear that Rabbinical Judaism is not in any way an authority for all those who believe that the Bible, and the Word of God alone is the ultimate and true revelation of God for mankind. We can use, compare, learn from judicially, and respect Rabbinical tradition and hold it at a very high esteem as an historical record with reflections of times past that might shed some light on how better understand the Word of God, and no more than that.

The above is a general introduction to my own attitude and hermeneutics. The New Testament is the last and ultimate revelation of God's will, but it is based on the Torah and the prophets.

The question of the divinity of the Messiah is a Jewish question not a Christian issue at all. The Christian World since the time of the Emperor Constantine has had no problem with idolatry or a multiplication of gods. They inherited this attitude from their pre-Christian Greco-Roman culture and religions. It is true that over the centuries Christianity has struggled with this issue and many good people have been burned and killed by the Church for holding to a strict monotheistic ideology. However, the general attitude of the Christian church has been muddled and not so clear since the second counsel of Nicaea in 333 C.E. It is my conviction that the most central truth in God's Word is that there is ONE GOD. The New Covenant states more than 50 times that there is ONE GOD and One Father of us all, and ONE Messiah and Savior. There is not even one time in the New Covenant that states or even hints that there is more than one God, and not one place that states that there is tree Gods independent of each other and self standing on their own authority.

Now that I have made the above statement as an introduction here is a list of my personal convictions:

1. The idea that the Messiah is divine is an Old Testament concept.[1] I don't need to relay on what Christianity and the Counsels that the Church made in the fourth century to know that the Messiah is divine and that HE can be called "the L-rd our Righteousness" or "A mighty God." When I read prayers like "Shir HaKavod" "שיר הכבוד" in the Siddur I have a very clear representation of the divinity and the humanity of the Messiah in a totally Jewish setting.

2. The idea that God has a Son is also an Old Testament concept.[2] Here too if we did not have a O.T. and a Jewish concept the idea would be preposterous, but fortunately we do have clear biblical texts that speak of the Son of God in a way that is not open to misunderstanding. With this issue too I am very comfortable with the idea that God has a Son and that

there is total equality between the Father and the Son, but at the same time there is no reason for me to understand the Son of God in a pagan context when I have such rich material in the Hebrew Scriptures.

3. The idea that the Messiah will suffer and die for our transgressions is an Old Testament concept. There is no doubt that the idea of vicarious atonement is found in Isaiah 53 and in several other examples and texts in the Torah and in the prophets, like in the death of the High Priest and the release of the captives of the cities of refuge. On the other hand in the New Testament there are different paradigms of atonement than just vicarious atonement. An example of this last point can be seen in Hebrews 5:8-10, *"Although He was a Son, He learned obedience from the things which He suffered. And having been made perfect, He became to all those who obey Him the source of eternal salvation, being designated by God as a high priest according to the order of Melchizedek."* In this text there are actually two different paradigms of salvation or of the role that Yeshua as the Messiah plays in the plan of God to save us human beings with our weaknesses and bring us to a fellowship with the Almighty God Himself.

Taking into consideration all of the above, even long before looking into Jewish Rabbinical literature, no Jew ought to have a problem with the concept that the Messiah is divine if the Messiah is presented in Jewish colors and not embedded in the colors and smell of Paganism and with the décor of a Pagan church.[3] If we can look objectively and define modern Christianity with measurable sociological elements we would surly see that Christianity is essentially still pagan in relationship to the Word of God and also in relationship to the attitudes toward Monotheism, Torah, Judaism, and especially to the basic teachings of the Gospel. I realize that this is a generalization and like all generalizations there are many exceptions in both the past and the present, but as a generalization I stand by this statements. I also realize that some would say that modern Judaism falls in a close category of basically pagan, and I could easily agree with such a judgment with one caveat that we still have the Torah and we are still basically a Monotheistic nation. If we are interested in bringing Yeshua back home into the heart and consciences of the Jewish Nation we must as Jewish Disciples of Yeshua review and examine the product and train the messengers to bring to the people of Israel a true Jewish Messiah the King of the Jews and replace the presentation of Yeshua as the God of the Goim. I fear that this is the way that Yeshua is perceived and presented in much of what is called "Jewish Evangelism." I am a witness of what has and is going on in Israel where the first note of evangelism is "you need to know the true God, Yeshua." Understanding the Messiah as divine and as deity is one of the most complicated theological ideas that even the whole New Testament only hints at it and speaks around it, but does not come out and shouts it from the rooftops. WE have to present the divinity of the Messiah in Jewish context and with Jewish Biblical colors and that is not so hard or impossible and much more biblical than the confused views of modern Christianity and Trinitarian formulas that in the end come to the conclusion that it is all a mystery anyway and we will not be able to explain it.

The Biblical understand of the divinity of the Messiah.

Even according to some of the traditional Jewish commentaries written by well respected Rabbis Isaiah 9:5-7 is attributed to King Hezekiah and there is a total circumvention of the issue of such divine names given to a child that is born unto us. Rashi, Radak, and others actually don't deal with the issue and just attribute the "Prince of Peace" to Hezekiah. Malbi"m does bring the possibility that these attributes given to this child could be the Messiah.[4] How is it possible for a child that is born unto us to be called such names as "a mighty God" or "an everlasting Father" or like in Jeremiah 23, someone from the seed of David be called "YHWH our righteousness?"

These very fine and wise Rabbinical commentaries of the Tanach lived in Christian Europe and they actually either ignored or on purpose distorted their own understanding in order not to give ammunition to the Christians to convert Jews to Christianity.

On the passage of Jeremiah 23:5-6, Radak actually states very clearly that this text is about the Messiah.

I must note that there is no place in the New Covenant that is as clear an expression of the idea that the Messiah is divine as these passages from Isaiah, Jeremiah, and Proverbs. The New Covenant has hints and innuendoes about the divinity of the Messiah but never as clear as these passages of the Tanach that God gave to Israel. Therefore by any rule of hermeneutics we must put the greater stress on understanding the divinity of the Messiah on a better understanding of the clearer passages in Jeremiah, and Isaiah, and only than turn to understand the New Covenant ideas of the divine Messiah.

In conclusion of this first point the Messiah is divine because the Jewish Scriptures attributes to Him divine character, divine mission, and divine names. He is equal to the God who sent Him in all aspects of His person, soul, desire, mission, nature, purpose, but there are areas that this equality does not cover like the knowledge of the day and the hour of His return.[5]

I must at this point make it clear that I use the word divine here as equal to "deity" and not as anything less than the full revelation of the God of Abraham, Isaac, and Jacob to the children of Israel.

The New Covenant writers make an effort to present Yeshua as equal to God without compromising the Oneness of God and that is the reason why the Gospel of John actually opens speaking of the "Word of God" that was from the beginning and the "Word of God" that is God. This kind of convoluted language is actually a sign of the desire to say that the Messiah is divine without actually coming out and saying it in a direct and clear statement, "Yeshua is God." John actually had the language ability to make direct statements. He did not choose to make such a direct statement because of the danger of misunderstanding and encouraging people to believe in more than ONE God. The Gospel of John puts great emphasis on the fact that Yeshua was SENT and the Father SENT Him. Being SENT by the Father is a clearly a position of subordination as Yeshua Himself said: "the Father is greater than the Son."[6] The messenger is equal to his sender is a well-known legal principle that is applied in all-legal systems. When the discussion is of the Messiah or the First Adam the principles is taken even one point further and it is a clear indication of the divine / deity nature of the Messiah.[7] This is a very Jewish way to say, that the Messiah is divine and human at the same time, it is the classic "Yes" and "No" answer. Without the basic tools of Midrash and the way that second temple Jews interpreted Scripture the non-Jewish readers of the Gospels in the second and third century could not really understand what was being said in the Jewish text even though they could read it in Greek.

When Constantine convened to Christianity and setup the counsel of Nicaea in the early part of the fourth century there were no Jewish believers or Jewish Bishops invited to participate in this counsel. The newly appointed leadership of the church after the official declaration of the Byzantine Empire as Christian the leadership of the church was essentially pagan and did not have the basic intellectual and spiritual tools to understanding the Semitic background and basic premises that the New Testament writers had when the text was written. These leaders were "converted" by a royal decree and not by study and conviction of faith and commitment to God's Word or truth. The most important counsel of Christian History met twice in the forth century, 325 and 333 AD, and in both times there were no Jewish Disciples of Yeshua invited to participate. The commitment that Evangelical Christians to the Christian creeds is out of place in any case, but it is especially repulsive because of the anti-Semitic nature of this Counsel. I don't believe in any of the Creeds that the Christian Churches have created for themselves and I have no obligation to defend these Creeds. As a Jew I am obligated to the Word of God and only to the Word of God as authority over my faith and my life. I don't even understand why so many Messianic Jews are so argumentative about the teachings of the Creeds and are willing to vilify each other over what a bunch of pagan "galachs" (Yiddish for Pagan Priests) decided. As Jews our commitment should never be to the denominations and churches but always to the God of Abraham, Isaac, and Jacob, and to Yeshua the Messiah who is on God's right hand.

The language of equality I the Gospel of John:

The language of the Gospel of John makes it clear that Yeshua is 100% equal to the Father who sent Him to this World.[8] It makes it clear that whoever has seen the Son has seen the Father. Statements like, "so that all will honor the Son even as they honor the Father. He who does not honor the Son does not honor the Father who sent Him." (John 5:23) are abundantly clear to be able to write an equal sign in the formula of the Son = the Father. However, in Christian theology there is a deafening silence on the issue of hierarchy between the Father and the Son. In **John 14:28** we read that Yeshua Himself said, "The Father is greater than the Son." In **1 Corinthians 11:3-4**, we read that the God is the head of the Messiah and the Messiah is the head of man and man is the head of woman. There is a very clear hierarchical order in this passage and only when we can understand the paradigm of equality and hierarchy at same time can we understand the real issue that is posed before us on this question.

It is interesting that not only the New Covenant is struggling with these questions, but also the Jewish Rabbis in the Talmudic and even the Mechanic period are struggling with the issue.

The issue of hierarchy is very crucial for the ability to have Yeshua as a deity and at the same time to maintain a strict monotheistic position. The issue of monotheism is not an arbitrarily chosen issue for Jewish Disciples of Yeshua and in fact for all Christians. Monotheism is the main message of the whole Bible. It is the clearest truth from Genesis to Revelation. In the New Testament I find 25 times that the express phrase, ONE GOD or ONE LORD is found. In the Tanach we find near 400 times an affirmation of the ONENESS of God. It is of prime importance that Monotheism be the clearest message that all of us, and especially those of us who are Jews need to have etched into our lives and witness. Yeshua's deity is clear to us as His Disciples, but it can not and most not be the main message because the Scriptures does not make this issue even clear and it is only clear to us by reason of theological deductions and not by chapter and verse clear statements.

I often use parables to explain the relationship that the Father has with the Son and the Son with the Father and their equality and uniqueness at the very same time.

The Greek paradigm for relationships: a=b=c ▲ a

The Hebrew paradigm for relationships: a=b=c ▲ a>c

THE EXAMPLES FOR THIS PARADIMA are actually in every relationship that we find in the Word of God and also in true life.

The first and clearest of such relationships is the basic family unit. Man and Woman are equal, as we see the passage in Galatians 3:28 states: "There is neither Jew nor Greek, there is neither slave nor free, there is neither male nor female; for you are all one in Christ Jesus." But at the same time the woman is to be submitted to the man and she has limitations imposed on her by both God and her husband.[9] The same principle is between Landlords and Slaves as we see: "Therefore submit yourselves to every ordinance of man for the Lord's sake, whether to the king as supreme. . . . Servants, be submissive to your masters with all fear, not only to the good and gentle, but also to the harsh" (1 Pet. 2:13, 18 NKJV). The same principle works in the relationship between Yeshua and the Father. There is equality and hierarchy at the same time. The Word of God says it very clearly: "I and My Father are one" (John 10:30). And, "For there are three that bear witness in heaven: the Father, the Word, and the Holy Spirit; and these three are one" (1 John 5:7 NKJV). At the same time we find Yeshua say it very clearly: "My Father, who has given them to Me, is greater than all; and no one is able to snatch them out of My Father's hand," (John 10:29 NKJV) + "You have heard Me say to you, 'I am going away and coming back to you.' If you loved Me, you would rejoice because I said, 'I am going to the Father,' for My Father is greater than I'" (John 14:28 NKJV).

There is no text in the Bible that makes this equality and hierarchy clearer than: "But I want you to know that the head of every man is Christ, the head of woman is man, and the head of Christ is God" (1 Cor. 11:3 NKJV). I repeat this idea here at the end of this paper because it is a little hard to digest for people with a Western education.

The special relationship of Yeshua to the Father—and the relationship of ONE who sends and ONE that is being sent give us a clue of how to interpret and understand the deity of the Messiah and at the same time be totally faithful to the ONE GOD—the God of Abraham, Isaac, and Jacob.

Conclusion

Rabbinic Judaism has no problem with the issue of the deity of the Messiah, the problem is with the explanation that Christianity has given to this deity and has created a situation that it is impossible to explain biblically the deity of the Messiah and Monotheism without resorting to non-biblical materials. The explanation of the Watermelon and the Egg and other such examples give a partial picture but none actually satisfies the problem fully.

ENDNOTES

1. See: Isaiah 9:5-7 & Jeremiah 23:5-6 – in both of these text there is a clear messianic reference made by the prophet and the name given to the child / plant of David is a divine name. The biblical names are always much more than just names they have intrinsic relationship between the person and his destiny and role.

2. See: Proverbs 30:4 – a wisdom passage dealing poetically with the creation story and acknowledging that the Creator has a name and His Son has a name.

3. The post Constantinian church was pagan because it was first and foremost a political decision made by the emperor Constantine a short period after the Diocletian persecution and the leadership was essentially the same pagan leadership that conducted the imperial cult and the pagan temples. They did not have the tools nor the understanding nor did they have any respect for the Jewishness of the Bible or the New Testament. For the Post Constantinian church the Jews were negligible and the Bible was only a tool for the accomplishment of their political agenda. This can be seen clearly in Collins' book, "Constantine's Sword" and on the pages of the more modern church histories.

4. All the Jewish commentaries have a great deal of difficulty with Isaiah 9:5-7, some just ignore the "EL-Gibor" (God Almighty) passage, others try to circumvent it. The Malbi"m says that the three titles are titles of God and that only "Sar-Shalom" is in reference to King Hezekiah. Most of the Rabbinical commentaries actually attributed this passage to King Hezekiah and in fact had to retract their attribution because it is clear that Hezekiah did not fulfill any of the expectations that these name give. The malbi"m also states that "Avi-Ad" is the one who created time and renews it. There can be no mistake that the Malbi"m considers this figure of a child born to us as divine.

5. Matt. 24:36, "But of that day and hour no one knows, not even the angels of heaven, nor the Son, but the Father alone."

6. See: John 14:27-28

7. R. Hoshaya said: When the Holy One, blessed by He, created Adam, the ministering angels mistook him [for a divine being] and wished to exclaim 'Holy' before him. What does this resemble? A king and a governor who sat in a chariot, and his subjects wished to say to the king, 'Domine! (Sovereign)!' but they did not know which it was. What did the king do? He pushed the governor out of the chariot, and so they knew who was the king.

   Similarly, when the Lord created Adam, the angels mistook him [for a divine being]. What did the Holy One, blessed be He, do? He caused sleep to fall upon him, and so all knew that he was [but mortal] man; thus it is written, Cease ye from man, in whose nostrils is a breath, for how little is he to be accounted (Isa. N, 22)! This Midrash has some very interesting elements that need to be developed in the lecture.

8. John 14:9, Jesus *said to him, "Have I been so long with you, and yet you have not come to know Me, Philip? He who has seen Me has seen the Father; how can you say, 'Show us the Father'? John 10:30, "I and the Father are one." John 17:22, "The glory which You have given Me I have given to them, that they may be one, just as We are one;

9. "Wives, submit to your own husbands, as to the Lord. For the husband is head of the wife, as also Christ is head of the church; and He is the Savior of the body. Therefore, just as the church is subject to Christ, so let the wives be to their own husbands in everything" (Eph. 5:22-24 NKJV).

    "Wives, likewise, be submissive to your own husbands, that even if some do not obey the word, they, without a word, may be won by the conduct of their wives" (1 Pet. 3:1 NKJV).

COMMUNICATING THE DEITY OF YESHUA TO THE JEWISH PEOPLE

Daniel F.J. Nessim, B.Th., MCS

Executive Director of Chosen People Ministries U.K.
Leader of Messianic Congregation Beth Sar Shalom
Trustee of the British Messianic Jewish Alliance Introduction

Introduction

אחד אלוהינו, גדול אדוננו, קדוש שמו

No doctrine is closer to the heart of Judaism than the Unity of God. Whether on the core or on the periphery, we Jews understand that God is One and that there is no Unity like His Unity. In the context of our absolute commitment to monotheism then, how do we communicate the deity of Yeshua to our community?

To communicate the deity of Yeshua to Jewish people, we must not only understand the doctrine, but we must understand ourselves.

No theology comes out of a vacuum, but for Messianic Jews the past is problematic. 2,000 years of dogmatic formulation that lack a Jewish sensitivity and reading of the scriptures, a theological tradition seen as hostile and other, have made communication of the 'fullness of the Godhead dwelling bodily in Yeshua' nigh on impossible to communicate. 2,000 years of structural supersessions, anti-Judaism, and persecution of our people have not given us a ready audience. Nevertheless, as Jewish believers in Yeshua we have never shrugged from the impossible. Even as the mission of Yeshua can be seen as failure – a despised, rejected leader, abandoned by his closest followers, dying the death of a common criminal – and yet ending not in tragedy but in ultimate triumph, vindication and overwhelming victory—so we too cannot shrink from the task of joyful proclamation of a message which is both the savor of victory and the stench of defeat.

Messianic Jewish theology is still in its infancy. As yet there have been few systematic expositions of the Messianic Jewish faith. Most major Messianic organizations subscribe to creeds and bases of faith that are acceptable and similar in content to that of Evangelical organizations and churches. Few have articulated a rounded doctrinal position that deals systematically with the person, life, work and nature of Yeshua. Nevertheless, much heat (and a little less light) has been generated by an apologetically driven attempt to re-examine our Christology in Jewish terms.

This paper is to form part of a dialogical presentation by Richard Harvey and myself as to how we might communicate the deity of Yeshua within our community. Drawing on Richard's strength as an academic with a practitioner's background and my strength as a practitioner with academic aspirations, we show how and why the Messianic movement should develop its understanding of the plurality of views expressed in the Messianic community today, and how to take ownership of them. A sampling of current theological positions will be discussed and evaluated, with a view to their advantages and disadvantages in terms of communicability.

In presenting Yeshua's deity to others we cannot avoid the missiological implications of our theology. Historically, the Church's creeds have been given a sympathetic endorsement by the vast majority of Jewish believers in Yeshua. These creeds were, of course, the best attempts of Christians in the past to portray revealed truth. Words are words, but they are also far more. Our actual theology is closely tied to our articulation of it, in a somewhat symbiotic relationship. We cannot separate the two. Thus our missiological momentum impels us to examine the ways in which we express our theology. We are faced with momentous questions.

We have to ask—what are the salient features of the message to be conveyed? What exactly is to be conveyed? Is it dogma? Doctrine? Or is it possibly an appreciation of the man from Nazareth? And is it possible to appreciate him, to come face to face with him, without an appreciation for his divine nature?

We must also ask—who are the 'we' who are communicating? Is the 'we' the combined body of Messiah—Jew and Gentile, standing on the basis of the Word of God, as interpreted by the Church Fathers and the historic creeds? Is the 'we' that of our contemporary Messianic Judaism in the process of re-examining its relationship to church history and the historic articulations of Christian faith? On whose shoulders are we standing—those of the Apostle Paul, the fourth century church or evangelical Christianity? Or are we just beginning to seek a footing on the shoulders of the first generation of Messianic theologians now documented in Richard's monograph *Mapping Messianic Jewish Theology*?

If the Jewish community has resisted our presentation of Yeshua's deity in centuries past, how much of the resistance is due to the *content* of our beliefs concerning Him, and how much is due to the platform, the perspective, or the framework from which we propound those beliefs? We cannot act in a reactionary manner decrying Jewish 'blindness'[1] if we hope that Jewish people might themselves refrain from being reactionary and consider our case fairly and honestly.

Defining the Message

In seeking to communicate Yeshua's deity, it is important for us to be clear as to what it means to say that Yeshua is both God and man.

A. Creedal Formulas

The biblical formulations of divine truth are not enough for us. As in the days of the Judges, the prophets and Ezra's day, so today we need those who interpret the Scriptures to our generation. We need to be aware of the doctrine of the Church, as it has sought to express biblical truth. We should not abhor availing ourselves of the great creedal statements of the past.

We have no need to be ashamed to use the creedal formulas that have been accepted by the Church and stand the test of Scripture. In contrast to our amateur and ad-hoc attempts to gather, collate and interpret Scriptural arguments for Yeshua's deity, such creeds have been carefully crafted, in many cases hammered out against a background of controversy. While limited in themselves, and certainly not 'inspired' they generally convey truth in a much better and precise way than we ever could. We are then able to work backwards from the creeds and show how they actually do express biblical truth. It is no accident that the earliest creeds are themselves found in Scripture. As we read from Paul himself:

For I handed on to you as of first importance what I in turn had received:
That Messiah died for our sins in accordance with the scriptures,

And that he was buried,
And that he was raised on the third day in accordance with the
scriptures,
And that he appeared to Cephas, then to the twelve.
Then he appeared to more than five hundred brothers and sisters
at one time, (most of whom are still alive, though some have died).
Then he appeared to James, then to all the apostles.
Last of all, as to one untimely born, he appeared also to me.[2]

In 2001 Oskar Skarsaune reviewed some of the early Christian creeds in *Mishkan*, from 1 Corinthians, Justin Martyr and Irenaeus. He observed that 'In this type of summary the focus is not on the nature, the essence of Messiah's person, but on the Messianic *task*'.[3] In describing Yeshua's Person in terms of the tasks he performed, it seems that language is quite adequate, and it can be said that his divinity is implicit in these early creeds. Where language fails is in its inability to describe Yeshua in ontological terms.

The very use of the word logos for Yeshua is a creedal attempt to portray Yeshua's divinity in human terms. As we seek to address the issue of the self-manifestation of God Tillich argues that 'Logos doctrine is required in any Christian doctrine of God' and 'He who sacrifices the Logos principle sacrifices the idea of a living God, and he who rejects the application of this principle to Jesus as the Christ rejects his character as Christ.'[4]

The Church Fathers were themselves aware of the limitations of human language, and in a very Hellenistic fashion pontificated long on the meanings of the terms they used to convey Scriptural truth. Gregory of Nyssa (c 335-394) wrote that 'every term either invented by the custom of men, or handed down to us by the Scriptures is indeed explanatory of our conceptions of the Divine Nature, but does not include the signification of that nature itself . . . Hence it is clear that by any of the terms we use the Divine nature itself is not signified, but some one of its surroundings is made known.'[5]

Are we bound to the creeds? Kinzer correctly pointed to the deity of Yeshua as an issue that defines a boundary of the Christian Church, demarcating its unique character.[6] To ignore the creeds would be to poke the Church in the eye—its most sensitive spot. On the Jewish side however, there is a corresponding boundary marker that says '"You shall not believe that Jesus is the Son of God."'[7]

In communicating the deity of Yeshua among Jewish people we are always aware of this boundary. Darrell Bock has argued that as Messianic Jews we must accept the Church's boundary if we intend to maintain our solidarity with the church.[8] I think this is correct, but I also think we must develop a way of living with understanding with Jewish people who confess Yeshua as the Messiah but have controversial or even negative views concerning his deity. The boundary is certainly one that demarcates correct doctrine, but it should not prevent us from remaining in dialogue or even fellowship with 'heretical' Jewish 'believers'. To disallow this would keep us from the very task we are about—communicating the deity of Yeshua among the Jewish people.

B. Biblical Formulas

Sola Scriptura as commonly (and over simplistically) understood belies the need for theology and creed. Creeds and formulas interpret Scripture in relation to our contemporary mindsets, sociological and theological issues. Furthermore, it must be understood that while Scripture conveys to us the truth that we need to know for a life of faith, it can by no means convey to us all that there is to know about G-d. Indeed, no man has even seen him![9] As Calvin put it, "If we regard the Spirit of God as the sole fountain of truth, we shall neither reject the truth itself, nor despise it wherever it shall appear, unless we wish to dishonour the Spirit of God."[10]

In fact, *Sola Scriptura* demands that Scripture itself measure every theology, formula or creed. It makes it clear that the source of all true doctrine is in the Word of God. Therefore we can require of no person any more than an acceptance of what the Word says. It is too much to say 'if the Word says such and such, it means this and that' and force an acceptance of the 'this and that.'

For example, it has often been noted that in the Septuagint the word κύριος is used of God. Since the same word is used of Yeshua in the New Testament it is argued that this is a title of divinity. The New Testament passages that speak of Yeshua as *God* using θεός however are relatively few. I believe this is because to do so would confuse Yeshua's Person with that of the Father. In John 20:28 Thomas cries out. In this statement as elsewhere, while the divinity of Yeshua is attested, it is not confused with θεός, who is the Father.[11] Therefore, one will search in vain for the statement 'Jesus is God' in the New Testament.

The word κύριος was used both of Yeshua and the Father, so it doubtless conveys Yeshua's divinity—but the word θεός is a different matter. How is it then that we started to call Jesus 'God'? The statement that Yeshua is Lord was likely the 'terminological bridge' to the attribution of the title 'God' to Jesus in the early church[12] but is that a bridge that we need to cross today? I would argue that if we are to stick to Biblical terminology we are on safe ground. If we believe it is essential to use the terminology of the Church, which undoubtedly reflects Scripture but can also distort it, we must tread very carefully.

In the Tenach, the Son is progressively revealed. The same is true in the New Testament, although we move rather rapidly from 'The book of the generations of Yeshua Messiah' to 'come, Lord (κύριε) Yeshua'. At the pinnacle of revelation, Yeshua's divinity is clearly revealed and expressed. There is little need to go beyond the use of biblical formulae and expressions in our communication of Yeshua's deity.

C. Sins of Omission

Judaism has no limit on its reverence for the Name of God. The very paper on which God's Name is written is to be treated with great respect. We read daily. Jewish creed says there is 'no Unity like His Unity'. Just as Christian creed portrays the truth but potentially distorts it in the mind of the reader, so does the Jewish. Such statements are true but are not the whole picture. Statements such as 'Yeshua is God' without qualification are as inaccurate and misleading as the statement 'Yeshua is man' without qualification. No creed can suffice. While needed, creeds necessarily involve us in a sin of omission.

Putting the Message in Context

D. Centrality

Is Yeshua's deity a central salient fact? Is it a necessary part of the proclamation of Yeshua?

A few years ago a friend of mine sent me a picture of himself evangelizing the Jewish community in Philadelphia with a large sign that stated 'Jesus is God'. I was appalled. This is the wrong way in which to bring people face to face with Yeshua. While it may provoke some conversations with some Jewish people, in the big picture I believe it 'poisons the well' for future discourse.

'The Gospel is the joyous proclamation of God's redemptive activity in Christ Jesus on behalf of man enslaved by sin.'[13] By this definition the deity of Yeshua is not *central* to the *presentation* of the Gospel. This is not to deny that it is central to the efficacy of the Atonement. Nor is it to deny that Yeshua's deity is implicit in the Gospel. But keeping it simple, Yeshua told his disciples to go and 'make disciples'.[14] Paul, the supposed 'inventor' of Yeshua's deity focuses primarily on the crucifixion and resurrection of Yeshua.[15] The saying goes that 'the main thing is keeping the main thing the main thing.'

Not everyone who comes to faith in Yeshua is fully aware of his divinity at the start. Did Peter have a mature understanding of the deity of Yeshua when he proclaimed 'you are the Anointed One, the Son of the Living God'?[16] I would argue not, based on his subsequent actions. The periscope was included in the Gospels, as were all of their contents, after time and by the author's deliberate choice when the importance of the event was better understood.

When the Gospel is presented in the Brit Chadasha Yeshua's deity is not presented as the initial salient fact. It is at the conclusion of Peter's speech on Shavuot that he says 'God has made this Yeshua, whom you crucified, both Lord and Messiah'.[17] Significantly, it comes *after* Peter's declaration that Yeshua sits at the Lord's right hand. This is the normal order of things in the New Testament. The central facts are the historical facts. That is what cuts Peter's audience to the heart, and knowing what Yeshua has done, his deity is no longer an obstacle to faith in him. As time goes on, one can see the New Testament's authors developing awareness of the full implications of Yeshua's deity. Thus, for example, it is in John's Gospel that Yeshua's deity is most clearly set forth. But one must also remember that in John's Gospel more than any other, the bulk of space is devoted to the time of Yeshua's 'passion'. Thus while we assert that Yeshua's deity is essential to the Gospel, it is not central to our proclamation of it.

E. Necessity

It is out of our scope to discuss whether a conscious knowledge of and recognition of Jesus and Savior is required for salvation. But is a conscious understanding and acceptance of the divinity of Yeshua required to ensure a place in the '*Olam Haba*? To what extent is it essential that we stress the fact of his deity to those who are becoming smitten with Person of Yeshua?

I do not think we should shy away from declaring our faith in Yeshua as the Son of God; neither should we hinder people from placing their faith in Yeshua as Messiah and *Go'el*—their personal *Go'el*—If they are not yet sure about the implications of accepting his full divinity. 1 John 2:23 states 'no one who denies the Son has the Father.'[18] 2 John 9 tells us 'anyone who . . . does not abide in the doctrine of Messiah does not have God.'[19] The point of both texts is that we must recognize the Son-ship of the Son, and that we must remain in this belief, to have the Father. But how much of this needs to be fully accepted at the point of conversion? It has been my experience that it is more common for Jewish people to accept Yeshua as the Messiah than to accept him as their personal *Go'el* and/or the divine Son of God.

Certain truths are spiritually discerned over time. It is fair to say that few who have gone forward to major evangelistic events in the last century have had a sufficient presentation of the deity of Yeshua. It is the Ruach HaKodesh who guides us into all truth (John 16:13). Things of God's Spirit are spiritually discerned (1 Cor. 2:14). We are all expected to progress from 'milk' to 'meat' in our walk with God (Heb. 5:12). Augustine wrote long ago that ''we desire to understand the eternity, and equality, and unity of the Trinity, as much as is permitted us, but ought to believe *before* (emphasis by DJN) we understand.'[20]

F. Accuracy

Beyond the centrality and necessity of communicating the deity of Yeshua among the Jewish people, it is necessary to have a clear and accurate message to convey. It is after dealing with this consideration that this paper will discuss some of the common theological *approaches* to Yeshua's divinity in the Messianic movement.

One cannot conflate the doctrine of Yeshua's deity down to one simplistic statement such as 'Jesus is God'.[21] If it were possible to do this, Church creeds would be much shorter than they are! Certainly there is truth in the statement that 'Jesus is God', but it is inadequate as a creedal proposition or as a theological test of orthodoxy. Other terminology, such as reference to Yeshua as the 'God-man' in an attempt to express the hypostatic union is also open to misinterpretation and can be a barrier to effective communication in the Jewish context—or any context. It brings us to the first question many Jewish people have about our Messiah – how can a Jew believe that a man could be God? On the other hand, while we may eschew simple answers, we must also eschew the complex. A dissertation on the Hypostatic Union is no more helpful.

Trinitarian terminology also hampers the accuracy of our communication. Already in Augustine's writings there is a tendency to talk about the Trinity in a way that almost gives it a life of its own, as if the Godhead were a fourth person! No one would seriously lay this charge at the feet of Augustine, but seminars on 'the Trinity and the Gospel' or church names such as 'Trinity Worship' or Catholic prayers 'to the one God, Father, Son, and Holy Spirit' on Trinity Sunday all threaten to personify the Trinity in a way that takes Augustinian thinking a little bit too far.[22] As theologians we might understand what is meant—but the person in the pew? The Jew in the Messianic Synagogue? We must be clear not just in what we might mean when we use language, but what we might be perceived and meaning. I would suggest that in this instance it is important for us to be clear on the procession from the Father to the Son to the Spirit as enunciated in the Chalcedonian creed.

In communicating the Gospel and the deity of Yeshua simply, we must be well informed ourselves. A lack of clear theological understanding on the part of many Christians, pastors and presumable Messianic Rabbis as well results in a confused communication that leaves our faith open to refutation. Our message must be simple and clear, and it will not be so unless we understand the deity of Yeshua in greater depth. Once again, the use of Biblical terminology is our ally in communicating effectively.

G. Identity

Years ago, Marshall McLuhan coined the phrase 'the medium is the message.' The 'medium' is any projection of ourselves—our thought, for example, expressed in words. The 'message' is the change that the message effects.[23] It may not be an entirely appropriate adaptation of McLuhan's phrase, but I think it is fair to say that our medium—be it a Christian, Messianic, or Jewish, has a profound effect on the message—on the results we see as it changes the world. I think you'll agree with me that the platform from which we speak greatly changes the way in which the message is perceived.

If we speak from the Christian platform, we can speak with the authority of two millennia of Christian scholarship and interpretation of the sacred texts. We can speak for a sound tradition that is highly credible in its own way. Most of us speak from this platform. Whether we like it or not, the Jewish community views us as 'Christian' and therefore in the 'other camp.' The very 'to' in the title of this paper illustrates the difficulty—it is a position of seeking to reach out *to* a community of which we are not part. We don't help matters because our thought patterns, our theological training and almost invariably induction to the faith have been through the Christian world and its institutions. There are times when we must just accept this. It is a position that has both positive and negative ramifications.

On the other hand, we may well seek to place ourselves thoroughly within the Jewish camp. Messianic Jews are still on a journey seeking to return to the Jewish world. Nevertheless, we are still greatly hindered by our Christian programming. Sometimes even in our efforts to shake it off, we prove its existence. We don't always know even which Jewish world we most readily identify with. Nevertheless, this is my choice for the way forward. Our Jewish community is fractured, with many different strands and movements, most at odds with each other. The hindrance is primarily in our own minds.

As we come to realize that we are Jews, not 'Christians' in the Jewish understanding of the term,[24] when our primary community becomes the Jewish community and the Messianic Jewish community within it, then we are able to convey the deity of Yeshua in a Jewish context. This goes beyond our use or non-use of Jewish 'proofs' of multiplicity in God's Person. It transcends our commonalities with various movements within the Jewish community, whether we feel most akin to Reform or Orthodox Judaism. Once we are comfortable within our own skin as Jews—authentic Jews—then we are able to speak as Jews to other Jews. Then we can actually demand to be heard.

The difficulty with taking a Jewish stance in communicating Yeshua's deity is the credibility gap from which we suffer. Unfortunately we are often inauthentic. When we endorse congregations with only one—or no—Jews in attendance we cannot claim to be Messianic *Jews* or a Judaism. When we misuse Jewish traditions and symbols we understandably open ourselves up to the charge of deception. A lack of scholarship has also rendered some of our literature a laughing stock of anti-missionaries. We have sometimes failed to be honest about exactly *who* and *what* we are. Inauthenticity is worse than attempting to speak from a platform we may feel uncomfortable with. It destroys credibility.

In seeking to communicate the deity of Yeshua, of course we are justified in looking for common ground. Sometimes in our eagerness to prove the deity of Yeshua – or the tri-unity of God, we tend to carelessly argue from the existence of semi-divine or intermediary figures such as the *Memra, Metatron* or the *Logos*. Richard Bauckham issues the caution that 'some of these figures are unambiguously depicted as intrinsic to the unique identity of God, while others are unambiguously excluded from it.'[25] His point is that such figures do not blur the 'firm line of distinction' between God and all other reality

We are right, however, in supposing that since modern Judaism is very much in continuity with that of the second Temple, that there are lessons to be learned. On the one hand the exaltation of Yeshua by early believers opened them to the charge of blasphemy (e.g. Acts 7:56ff). On the other, they in no way saw themselves as idolaters and rejected idolatry (1 Cor. 10:14; 1 Pet. 4:3). In the New Testament we have examples both of how they thought of Yeshua's deity and also how they communicated that to those who were not his disciples. As far as they were concerned, Bauckham is right to stress 'That Jewish monotheism and high Christology were in some way in tension is one of the prevalent illusions . . . that we must allow the texts to dispel.'[26]

Until we are able to speak from a credible, authentic Jewish position, we are thrown upon the last and best alternative. We need to be able to speak from the perspective of the Scripture. From this platform we need offer no apology. Using the *Tenach* carefully, without trying to make it say more than it does, we can indeed show the unique unity that is God's Person.[27] From the New Testament, even if Jewish people don't respect it highly we can assert with Paul that idolatry is to be absolutely shunned.[28]

Communicating the Message

There is no one answer as to how one might communicate the deity of Yeshua to a Jewish person as each transmitter and each receiver have to find their own 'wave length' on which to converse.

The following are a few solutions, or 'wave lengths' as to how one might converse, with some evaluation.

H. Traditional Proclamation

Some Messianic, or Jewish Christian theologians, as Baruch Maoz might describe himself, are committed to doctrinal frameworks developed from outside the Messianic community. From this position, they have yet been able to make a significant contribution to the Messianic world and Messianic Jewish theology. Indeed, none of us are in a position to 'reinvent the wheel' and discard two millennia of often-profound Christian thought regarding our Scriptures. Such teachers have also been invaluable to the Church, as they bring a fresh perspective to these theological perspectives.

Some could be framed as providing no translation into a Jewish frame of reference. In fact, in the early days of 1985 Fruchtenbaum remarked that 'there is no difference' between a Messianic theology and a Gentile theology. But he went on to clarify that 'Messianic theology is an attempt to maintain and to accommodate Jewishness in the face of a Gentile majority' and 'it can also correct Gentile theology by separating that which is biblical from that which is merely Gentile.'[29] This substantiates my assertion that there are no Jewish-Christian or Messianic theologians who have remained in the Jewish world who can be framed as absolutely not contextualizing the Gospel (and in this case the deity of Yeshua) to the Jewish context.

Theologians such as Baruch Maoz and Arnold Fruchtenbaum are tremendous anchors and bridges between the Messianic community and the Church. As Jews they are able to understand both perspectives and mediate between them. While coming down on the side of traditional Christian expressions of Scriptural doctrine, they yet are aware of how these doctrines are received in the Jewish context.

I. An Accommodative Approach

On the other end of the spectrum from the Traditional approach is the Accommodative. This approach to communicating the deity of Yeshua is that of *not* communicating it. This perspective would say (at the least) that Yeshua is not God in the sense that HaShem is God. Such an approach rules in favor of a Maimonidean singularity and Aristotelian perfectionism which rules out the divisibility of God into parts. Theologians such as Uri Marcus or Hugh Schonfield have been named in this category.

In this category we have assertions such as that of Schonfield who stated that Yeshua had to be seen as 'an embodiment of Deity' in order to be seen as 'superior to the Divine Caesar.'[30] In just the same way in which Schonfield believed that early Christians invented the deity of Yeshua to accommodate themselves to the Roman Empire, so it seems to me that some Jewish followers of Yeshua have denied his deity.

This approach does not therefore communicate Yeshua's deity or the esteem in which He is to be held.

J. A Jewish Approach

The 'Jewish' approach to communicating Yeshua's deity relies on knowing who we are. It opens the door to many possibilities as we view Yeshua's deity from our Jewish mindset(s).

There is much work still to be done in this field, not only in terms of ancient texts but also modern Jewish streams such as Chassidism and contemporary Kabbalah. One interesting development is that of a Jewish form of panentheism. Panentheism is be belief that all that exists is within God, in contrast to Pantheism that holds that all that is, is God. Noted authors such as Abraham Heschel have been described as having such an outlook. Fritz Rothschild writes of him 'Gods' glory ubiquitously sensed in and behind all things leads to a pantheistic outlook.'[31]

From such a perspective, scriptures such as 1 Corinthians 15:28 where we read about God as 'All in All' provide grist for the mill. Is it possible that Paul infers that everything that exists is *in* God? His Word upholds everything (ῥήματι – Heb. 1:3). As such we worship our Messiah.

1 Corinthians 8:6 states 'yet for us there is one God, the Father, from whom all things come and for whom we exist; and one Lord, Yeshua the Messiah, through whom were created all things and through whom we have our being.' Some scholars such as Bauckham even see this as an early statement that echoes the Shema. It is clearly a model statement concerning Yeshua's divine nature in a way that clearly identifies him and differentiates him from the Father. This is the kind of approach that we need to take as Jewish followers of Yeshua. Such terminology is relatively clear and unambiguous. By using Biblical terminology we are freed from the Evangelical

straitjacket that we might not even be aware that we are wearing. We may be liberated to relative sanity in the eyes of the Jewish people all the while not compromising the truth of the Word because we are standing upon it.

This approach relies on Messianic Jews being aware of Jewish thought. There are many ways in which we are encumbered unaware by our non-Jewish conceptual underpinnings. One of those is highlighted by someone who is not Jewish himself. Bauckham notes that we are conceptually tied to issues of the past—those that focused on the divine *nature* of Messiah and have largely missed that the Jewish concern and that of the Scriptures is more one to do with the *identity* of Messiah. He writes, 'once we have rid ourselves of the prejudice that high Christology must speak of Christ's divine nature, we can see the obvious fact that the Christology of divine identity common to the whole New Testament is the highest Christology of all. It identifies Jesus as intrinsic to who God is.'[32] When we see that Yeshua is intrinsic to whom God is, we may recall Dan Juster's words in *Jewish Roots*: 'The divinity of the Messiah is not idolatry, but reflects the fullest revelation of God.'[33]

Where our knowledge of Jewish thought is not sufficient, the Messianic Jew can take comfort in his or her commitment to Scripture and the knowledge that as Jews we have an advantage over other cultural groups. Our Jewish culture retains a substantial continuity with the culture and mentality of the writers of the *Tenach* and *Brit Hadashah*. We would be foolish not to avail ourselves of this benefit. Both knowledge of Jewish thought and the Scriptures are required. Richard Harvey quotes Dan Juster in MMJT as writing 'Jewish ways of expression are needed, ways more consistent to the New Testament, if Jews are to penetrate Christian rhetoric to see the truth of Yeshua's divine nature.'[34]

A Way Forward

Finally, it must be said that our biggest problem in communicating Yeshua's deity is not just our language but our altered frame of reference as well. We have become habituated to a community outside the Jewish world. Surely, for the sake of eternal life it has been a trade worth making, but it is not a necessary trade, and we must struggle to re-contextualize ourselves to the Jewish world.

Should we do so, our language and terminology will inexorably re-contextualize itself as well.

True, there are different theological positions within the Messianic movement. Messianic Jews can scarcely be accused of a lack of creativity with which the issues surrounding Yeshua's deity and communicating that doctrine are concerned. Defining where the movement as a whole stands on these issues is part of communicating the deity of Yeshua to the Jewish people. Being able to compellingly state our case regarding Yeshua's deity is not only important for the sake of those outside the Movement but also some who are within. In this case, we need to make a case to Jewish people who are captivated by the figure of Yeshua the Nazarene, but ambivalent to his claims to equality with HaShem. To a degree, the amount of heterodoxy—or even heresy—among those who self-identify as Messianic Jews presents us a test case or a pilot study in how we might present Yeshua's deity to the wider Jewish world.

However we might formulate, express and communicate Yeshua's identity as the Son of God to other Jewish people, it is part and parcel of our worship of Him.

We have a great truth to communicate. Yeshua's deity is Who He Is, and is part and parcel of the miracle of God reaching down to man. His sacrifice on the cross, and the efficacy of that sacrifice, depends directly upon his divine Identity. We are brought to the foot of the cross and to the statement of the Centurion guarding him who said 'Truly this was the Son of God!'[35] Yochanan Muffs, in the context of God reaching out to Israel: 'There are two choices: to love or to die. One can hardly conceive of a death more tragic than that caused by a love that does not find its destined partner.'[36]

Bibliography

Augustine, 'On the Trinity' Nicene and Post-Nicene Fathers: First Series, Philip Schaff and Henry Wace, eds. Peabody, Mass: Hendricksen, 1994.

Bauckham, Richard Jesus and the God of Israel: 'God crucified and other studies on the New Testament's Christology of Divine identity. Milton Keynes: Paternoster, 2008.

Bock, Darrell. 'Response to Mark Kinzer's Finding our Way Through Nicaea.' Los Angeles: Hashivenu Forum, 2010.

Calvin, Jean. Institutes. Book 2, 2:15.

Cohn, Leopold. To an Ancient People. Charlotte: Chosen People Ministries, 1996.

Federman, Mark. 'What is the Meaning of the Medium is the Message?' McLuhan Program in Culture and Technology. http://individual.utoronto.ca/markfederman/article_mediumisthemessage.htm, viewed 19 February 2010.

Fruchtenbaum, Arnold. 'The Quest for a Messianic Theology', Mishkan, Issue 2, Winter 1985.

Gregory of Nyssa, 'On "Not Three Gods"' Nicene and Post-Nicene Fathers: Second Series. Philip Schaff and Henry Wace, eds. Peabody, Mass: Hendricksen, 1994. Vol. 5.

Harvey, Richard. 'Jesus the Messiah in Messianic Jewish Thought', Mishkan. Issue 39 2003.

Harvey, Richard S. Mapping Messianic Jewish Theology. Milton Keynes: Paternoster, 2009.

Johnson, Boaz. 'Toward a Theology of God.' Mishkan. Issue 38, 2003.

Juster, Dan. Jewish Roots: A Foundation of Biblical Theology. Shippensburg, Penn: Destiny, 1995.

Kac, Arthur. *The Messiahship of Jesus, Revised Edition.* Grand Rapids: Baker, 1986.

Kinzer, Mark. 'Finding our Way through Nicaea: The Deity of Yeshua, Bilateral Ecclesiology, and Redemptive Encounter with the Living God.' Los Angeles: Hashivenu Forum, 2010.

Longenecker, Richard N. The Christology of Early Christianity. Grand Rapids: Baker, 1981.

Mounce, Robert H. 'Gospel' Evangelical Dictionary of Theology, ed. Walter Elwell. Grand Rapids: Baker, 1984.

Muffs, Yochanan. The Personhood of God: Biblical Theology, Human Faith, and the Divine Image. Woodstock, Vermont: Jewish Lights, 2005.

Patai, Raphael. The Messiah Texts. New York: Avon, 1979.

Riesner, Rainer. 'Christology in the Early Jerusalem Community.' Mishkan. Issue 24, 1996.

Schonfield, Hugh. For Christ's Sake: A Discussion of the Jesus Enigma. London: MacDonald and Janes's, 1975.

Skarsaune, Oskar. 'The Making of Creeds.' Mishkan. Issue 34, 2001.

Strong, Augustus H. Systematic Theology. Judson Press: Valley Forge, PA, 1979.

Tillich, Paul. Systematic Theology: Three volumes in one. Chicago: University of Chicago, 1967.

Skarsaune, Oskar 'the Making of the Creeds' Mishkan Issue 34 (2001).

ENDNOTES

1. Rom. 11:25.
2. 1 Cor. 15:3-5.
3. Oskar Skarsaune 'The Making of the Creeds' *Mishkan,* Issue 34 (2001), 24-25, quotes 1 Corinthians 15:3-5, Justin Martyr 1. *Apologia.* 31:7f, and Irenaeus *Against Heresies* I:10:1.
4. Paul Tillich *Systematic Theology: Three volumes in one* (Chicago: University of Chicago, 1967), vol. 3, 288.
5. Gregory of Nyssa, 'On "Not Three Gods"' *Nicene and Post-Nicene Fathers: Second Series*, Philip Schaff and Henry Wace, eds. (Peabody, Mass: Hendricksen, 1994), Vol. 5, 332.
6. Mark Kinzer 'Finding our Way through Nicaea: The Deity of Yeshua, Bilateral Ecclesiology, and Redemptive Encounter with the Living God' (Los Angeles: Hashivenu Forum, 2010), 2.
7. Ibid., 3.
8. Darrell Bock 'Response to Mark Kinzer's Finding our Way Through Nicaea' (Los Angeles: Hashivenu Forum, 2010), 7-8.
9. 1 Tim. 6:16.
10. Calvin, *Institutes* Book 2, 2:15.
11. Richard N. Longenecker *The Christology of Early Christianity* (Grand Rapids: Baker, 1981), 137.
12. Longenecker, 136.
13. Robert H. Mounce 'Gospel' *Evangelical Dictionary of Theology*, ed. Walter Elwell (Grand Rapids: Baker, 1984), 472.
14. Matt. 28:19.
15. 1 Cor. 1:23-24; 2:2; 15:3-5.
16. Matt. 16:16.
17. Acts 2:36.
18. πᾶς ὁ ἀρνούμενος τὸν υἱὸν οὐδὲ τὸν πατέρα ἔχει. (WH)
19. πᾶς ὁ προάγων καὶ μὴ μένων ἐν τῇ διδαχῇ τοῦ Χριστοῦ θεὸν οὐκ ἔχει. (WH)
20. Augustine, 'On the Trinity' *Nicene and Post-Nicene Fathers: First Series*, Philip Schaff and Henry Wace, eds. (Peabody, Mass: Hendricksen, 1994), Vol. 3, 119.
21. Augustus H. Strong *Systematic Theology* (Judson Press: Valley Forge, PA, 1979), 334. 'The Son is not God as such; for God is not only Son, but also Father and Holy Spirit.' Elsewhere Strong reminds us regarding the two natures of Messiah 'orthodox doctrine forbids us either to divide the person or to confound the natures' p. 673. Tillich, *Systematic Theology*, vol. 3, 142 also writes 'The two dangers which threaten every Christological statement are immediate consequences of the assertion that Jesus is the Christ. The attempt to interpret this assertion conceptually can lead to an actual denial of the Christ-character of Jesus

as the Christ; or it can lead to an actual denial of the Jesus-character of Jesus as the Christ.'

22. I take it to be a flaw in the Athanasian Creed that 'the Unity in Trinity and the Trinity in Unity is to be worshipped' and a misinterpretation of the Nicene Creed. Augustine writes 'we say and believe that there is a Trinity, we know what a Trinity is, because we know what three are; but this is not what we love.' Augustine, 'On the Trinity' *Nicene and Post-Nicene Fathers: First Series*, Philip Schaff and Henry Wace, eds. (Peabody, Mass: Hendricksen, 1994), Vol. 3, 119.

23. Mark Federman, 'What is the Meaning of the Medium is the Message?'McLuhan Program in Culture and Technology, http://individual.utoronto.ca/markfederman/article_mediumisthemessage.htm, viewed 19 February 2010.

24. It is worth noting that as far back as Rabbi Leopold Cohn's day there was a reluctance to use the word 'Christian' when describing his faith to his wife. Leopold Cohn, *To an Ancient People* (Charlotte: Chosen People Ministries, 1996), 23.

25. Richard Bauckham *Jesus and the God of Israel: 'God crucified and other studies on the New Testament's Christology of Divine identity* (Milton Keynes: Paternoster, 2008), 13-14.

26. Bauckham, 19.

27. John Fischer, 'Yeshua: The Deity Debate,' *Mishkan*, Issue 39, 2003, 28 addresses Rambam's 'unique unity' as a 'quintessential' description of God.'

28. 1 Cor. 10:14; Gal. 5:18-21.

29. Arnold Fruchtenbaum, 'The Quest for a Messianic Theology', *Mishkan*, Issue 2, Winter 1985, 1-3.

30. Hugh Schonfield, *For Christ's Sake: A Discussion of the Jesus Enigma* (London: MacDonald and Janes's, 1975), 97.

31. Fritz Rothschild, 'Introduction,' *Between God and Man: An interpretation of Judaism from the Writings of Abraham J. Heschel.* New York: The Free Press, revised edition, 1975.

32. Bauckham, 31.

33. Dan Juster, *Jewish Roots: A Foundation of Biblical Theology* (Shippensburg, Penn: Destiny, 1995), 189.

34. Ibid., 188.

35. Matt. 27:54.

36. Yochanan Muffs, *The Personhood of God* (Woodstock, Vermont: Jewish Lights, 2005), 16.

WORSHIP AND WITNESS TO THE DEITY OF YESHUA

Richard Harvey, Ph.D.

Member of the Lausanne Consultation on Jewish Evangelism
European Board Member, Jews for Jesus
Board of Reference, Caspari Centre, Jerusalem
Editorial Board, *Mishkan* (Academic Journal on Jewish Evangelism
and Messianic Judaism) Jerusalem

Introduction

Some fifty years ago Jacob Jocz wrote:

> At the centre of the controversy between Church and
> Synagogue stands the Christological question. This is
> not a question whether Jesus is the Messiah, but
> whether the Christian understanding of the Messiah is
> admissible in view of the Jewish concept of God. Here
> lies the dividing line between Judaism and Church. On
> this point neither can afford to compromise.[1]

But as Messianic Jews we challenge the reality of this dividing
line. In constructing the boundaries of Messianic Jewish identity we
claim to be members of both Christian and Jewish communities.[2] Does
this mean that we present an unacceptable compromise on the deity of
Christ? Or does our understanding of the nature of the Messiah and the
being of God clash with the fundamental tenets of Jewish
monotheism? If our belief in Jesus as Messiah is acceptable within a
Jewish frame of reference, how is the Christian community to react
when it appears that the key doctrine of the Triune nature of God is
being challenged?

And if we worship Yeshua as only God deserves to be
worshipped, how do we witness to our people that we have not
abandoned the central tenet of Judaism, the oneness, uniqueness and
indivisibility of God?

The two aspects of worship and witness, unless held together, result in a dangerous separation between apologetics, our giving of a reasoned defense of our faith, and systematics, our ability to articulate authentically, coherently, contemporaneously and with communal acceptance, what we believe. The Messianic movement ends up being a two-headed monster, with one half speaking the language of the Christian church, mouthing the creedal formulations of doctrinal orthodoxy, whilst at the same time living in Jewish social space where discussion of Trinitarian formulae is irrelevant at best and offensive at worst. How can we resolve this impasse?

My proposal is that we find ways of articulating the divinity of Yeshua which allow both our witness and worship to cohere, to define an authentic theological position which is sensitive to the publics we address, but even more sensitive to the truths of scripture and tradition (both Jewish and Christian) which we affirm. Before suggesting how this is to be done, we want to evaluate five strategies already being attempted by Messianic Jews. These five Christologies represent the breadth of thought on this topic in the movement, and each has its own strengths and weaknesses from which we may learn. Each answers a particular question we have about our witness to and worship of Yeshua, and we will state the question and summarize the response briefly, ranging from the least to the most acceptable.

The five questions I am using to structure our discussion are:

> *Can we have witness to Yeshua as Messiah without worshipping him as the embodiment of God?*

> *Can we articulate our Christology without recourse to a Jewish frame of reference?*

> *How much can we use the Jewish mystical tradition to express and illustrate the divinity of Yeshua?*

> *How can we recontextualise Nicene Christology?*

> *Is it kosher to affirm a trinitarian and incarnational theology whilst recognising the hiddenness of the Messiah?*

Can We Have Witness to Yeshua as Messiah Without Worshipping Him as the Embodiment of God?

I know that all of us here affirm the deity of Yeshua, but the debate within our movement is broader than the creedal affirmation we make here today. It is important to listen to and engage with the views of those who deny the deity but affirm the Messiahship of Yeshua, even if we disagree.

Uri Marcus is representative of those who pose the question "Isn't it enough to affirm Yeshua as Messiah?" He states his position clearly and adamantly:

> Myself as well as our entire congregation of Believers in Ma'aleh Adumim, completely reject the Trinitarian notions of plural unity, and will not acquiesce to any theology which challenges the ONEness of HaShem in any fashion. . . . Yeshua is the Son of the living G-d, never G-d the Son, in our view.[3]

David Tel-Tzur and Emanuel Gazit, also leaders in the same group, indicate a clear denial of Yeshua's pre-existence and deity.

> John (the Evangelist) is not teaching that the Son (of God) was living prior to his birth. The Son appeared for the first time as an entity when he was miraculously created as the 'Second Man' in his mother's womb. The 'Word' (Logos) in Scripture never appears in the meaning of an entity or a person . . . The Trinity is paganism, contrasted with 'Hear (Sh'ma) O Israel our God is One'. Yeshua is not the creator of the world, but the world was created for him.[4]

Marcus argues against the Deity of Jesus on the grounds that the Hebrew Scriptures and Jewish tradition forbid idolatry; the Christian understanding of the Incarnation is idolatrous, and Trinitarian doctrine is a Hellenistic misreading of the biblical data. He defends this with a Unitarian critique of NT passages that suggest the divinity of Christ, claiming that this is a misreading of scripture without the necessary understanding of the Jewish background and frame of reference. This is given by rabbinic tradition, which Marcus sees as providing the authoritative understanding of the nature of God, the meaning of idolatry and the nature of the Messiah. Only with the use of this interpretive tradition can the Early Church's excessive reliance on an anti-Semitic Hellenistic influence be avoided.[5]

Marcus is clear about his assumptions:

> I love discussing theology. It can be lots of fun, if people follow basic rules, like: "What the Scripture presents as a mystery should not be made into Dogma." [6]

However, Marcus is quite dogmatic about the nature of idolatry, assuming that any representation of the deity or suggestion of a plural nature should be seen as idolatrous. He uses the Maimonides' *Thirteen Principles of Faith* to affirm the in-corporeality of God.

> In addition to his law code, Maimonides penned the famous "Thirteen Articles of Faith" whose words speak about the attributes of G-d and the beliefs that were intended to map out the borders between Judaism and other then acceptable belief systems (such as Christianity and Islam). Why was this necessary?

> In the 12th century, Jews had already suffered a significant amount of persecution by the "min," a term used in the *Talmud* to refer to early Christians, which meant "heretic." A need arose for Jews exiled in Christian Europe, to set forth a definitive basis, upon which a person might know if he or she was diverging from the basic tenets of the Torah.

> Already, a plethora of polytheists, deists, atheists, those who believe one should worship demigods (middle-men), and those who say that G-d has a body, were vying for social and religious supremacy.

> Rambam took the challenge seriously. To him, putting G-d in a body was tantamount to polytheism, since it was just a verbal difference between talking about a god who has parts and a pantheon of multiple gods. After all, pantheism is belief that G-d, or a group of gods, is identical with the whole natural world.

> Anyone who wants to find out how the Jewish People, to whom were committed the oracles of G-d for the past 4000 years, are going to define who G-d is, and consequently who He is NOT, should study this prayer. Regardless of the failure of our people to remain faithful to HaShem, and to His Torah, as history records, it in no way invalidates the primary revelation that the Jewish People received at Sinai and held onto, which we later transmitted to the rest of the world.[7]

Marcus here equates Maimonides' rationalist and Aristotelian formulation of the divinity with Sinaitic revelation, allowing the authority of later Jewish tradition to set the terms of the debate on how the divine nature should be conceptualized. He does not refer to the more fundamental issues that motivated Maimonides, who aimed to harmonize Judaism with the philosophy of his day, and reconcile the *Tanach* and *Talmud* with Aristotelian thought. For him the anti-incarnational emphasis is valid. This particular reading of the intent of the 13 Principles fits Marcus' overall position of denying at all costs the possibility of plurality within the Godhead.

Marcus rightly understands that the *Yigdal*, a prayer reflecting the *Thirteen Principles*, implies that "HaShem is indivisible, unlike humans, who have many different body parts" but does not acknowledge that this position reflects the same Hellenistic currents of thought which Marcus opposes. For Maimonides, in seeking to introduce Aristotelian thought into Jewish understanding, could do no other than deny the possibility of pre-existent parts in an uncreated Creator. For Maimonides belief that God might have corporeality or is liable to suffer affection is worse than idolatry.[8]

Marcus looks to rabbinic tradition to define the nature of the Messiah, appearing to give it greater authority than the New Testament scriptures. On the pre-existence of the Messiah he quotes the well-known passage from the talmudic Tractate *Pesachim* 54a on the seven things that were created before the world was created, including the name of the Messiah. He argues that because tradition ascribes this teaching to the period of Hillel and Shammai (c. 10 CE), its origins can be traced back perhaps even earlier, "to Moses and David', and that the New Testament writers would have used this as the basis for their own teaching. He then goes on to say that the Church Fathers refused to consider

> anything about what the Jewish mind had to say, the same which birthed the concepts of the Messiah, redemption and the belief in ethical monotheism, as they (the Church Fathers) formulated their wording of the creeds which the Church to this day stands upon, and enforces with furious intolerance. . . .

> I don't think they considered any of this. I think rather, that these Church Fathers did everything possible to avoid any contact with "Hebraic Thinking" or "Hebraic Thinkers" and instead embraced the common Greco/Roman Hellenistic philosophical understandings of who G-d was in the world, as they set out to determine what defined Christian beliefs. After that, it was just a simple matter of superimposing those ideas onto the Gospel accounts, in order to arrive at a palatable form of Christianity for the Gentiles.

> Seventeen hundred years later, the Church is now at a point where it must ask itself if it is at all serious about restoring the vibrancy of the message carried to the world long ago by its earliest members? If they ever hope to attract the Jew to hear that message, they are going to have to relate to us differently, not simply as another ethnic group that enters the Church, but as a people chosen by G-d and upon whose well-being the rest of humanity's well-being rests.

> So, with our agendas clearly exposed, and our two approaches to tackle the text in front of us, as a fork before us in the road, I'll tell you what I've told you in the past . . . I'm taking the road to Jerusalem, rather than that which leads to Rome.

Ultimately Marcus' position lapses into a Unitarian view of God, and an adoptionist or Arian Christology. Without the reality of the incarnation there can be know true atonement, not dynamic relationship between the Creator and his creatures, and no harmony of Father, Son and Spirit within the Godhead. Such a view does not allow us to affirm the true nature of Yeshua's Messiahship, but limits us to the framework set by Jewish orthodoxy.

Can We Articulate our Christology Without Recourse to a Jewish Frame of Reference? Do we Need to Translate our Christology into Dynamic Equivalent Terms?

Baruch Maoz, whose work reflects the Protestant Reformed Christology of the Creeds, is reluctant to express the divinity of Yeshua in terms not directly from scripture, and without recourse to rabbinic tradition.

Baruch Maoz argues for an orthodox Christology within a systematic theology framed by Reformed Dogmatics. His exposition of the divine and human nature of Christ, and his Trinitarian understanding of the nature of God, are clear and unequivocal. His material, in the form of lectures and his recent book[9] is both challenging, provocative and uplifting, but leaves little room for flexibility when it comes to expressing the nature of the Messiah or God outside the biblical frame of reference.

Maoz is critical of the Messianic movement for failing to focus on the Trinity:

> The Messianic Movement has been far too tolerant of deviant views on central doctrinal issues . . . it is important to take note of the Unitarian tendency that finds acceptance among many non-Unitarian Messianics as expressed in a growing embarrassment with the Trinity and the deity of Christ.[10]

In response to this trend he is one of the organizers of the recent "Jewish Christian Conference"[11], an "effort to promote a courageous Gospel witness to the Jewish people that refuses to kowtow to rabbinic standards or place cultural matters where Christ should be." Sessions on the topics such as the Deity and Centrality of Christ; the Trinity and Jewish Evangelism; Nicea and Chalcedon all show the clear emphasis of Maoz and others in this stream. Whilst labeling himself "Jewish Christian" rather than "Messianic Jewish" Maoz is clearly engaged in dialogue with the main positions within the Messianic movement.

Maoz is open about his presuppositions. As to his theological assumptions, Baruch acknowledges his debt to the theological tradition of Reformed Protestantism in which he has been nurtured.

I know nothing but what I have been taught. I lay claim to no originality, so all you can read from me has been better said by others before me and can be found in all the major books on theology, particularly in this case on Christology. I see little wisdom in attempting to reinvent the wheel.[12]

His exposition of the nature and being of God echoes that of Christian Reformed Dogmatics:

When I refer to "God" (*Elohim*) I mean that one and only self-existent, holy, perfect and gracious spirit who created all things, apart from himself, and that has neither beginning nor end. God is, as I learn from the Bible, unchangeable, immeasurable, beyond human comprehension. There are no limits to his power, wisdom or knowledge. He is the source of all life, of all existences, free from any dependencies. All creatures owe him worship and loving obedience. He revealed himself to mankind in scripture as the creator of all worlds, the covenant God of Abraham, Isaac and Jacob, and as the Father of our Lord Jesus Christ.

Divinity (*elohut*) is that mass of attributes that make God what he is and distinguishes him from all and any other beings. By definition, divinity is indivisible and cannot be imparted, earned or taken because it includes the attribute of self-existence that neither began nor can end.[13]

Christianity stands or falls with regard to the identity, nature and accomplishments of Jesus. It has to do with his pre-existence, his birth, life, suffering, teachings, deeds, death, resurrection, ascension, reign and return. It is as dependent on him as is life on the existence of oxygen. Jesus is not the primary apostle in a long list of devoted servants of God. He is not the founder of a new religion. If he is, to the slightest extent, less than all the scriptures declare him to be, then the message of the Gospel has no objective, binding validity in our lives because it has been robbed of its power to save (Rom. 1:16). If Jesus is not both God and man, and

God and man in the fullest sense possible – equal to the Father in his deity, in all things but sin like us in our humanity—the Gospel is a vanity of vanities, a pursuit after the wind.[14]

Maoz explains the dual natures of Christ from his exposition of scripture.

Before Jesus was man, he was God. He had the very nature of God, that sum of essential, inherent characteristics that distinguishes God from all other beings. Whatever could be said of God could be said of Jesus. He was eternal, self-existent, perfectly holy, and glorious beyond description. He knew all things, was present everywhere, and could do all that was in his holy will.

He is *equal to* God—yet God has no equal. Please note: Paul does not think or speak in terms of graduations of divinity—a greater, a lesser and a still lesser God. To do so is to believe in many gods of different divine stature. We know that there is but one God, but we have repeatedly discovered that in the one God there is a mystery of the divine nature, so that God is at the same time both one and more than one. Here is the difference: not that there are two or three gods, but that God is more than one. Not that there are two or three divine essences, but that the one divine essence is more than one.[15]

There is no lower grade of deity. *Hear O Israel, the Lord our God the Lord is one.* Jesus is either very God of very God, the only begotten of the Father— begotten and not made—of the same and equal essence of the Father, or he is not our Saviour. Nor may he be considered divine in any sense. Only by distancing ourselves from Jesus as he appears in the scripture, only to the extent that we allow human grids and human interests to determine our understanding of who Jesus is, only then can we find cause to deny his utter deity. Only then dare we speak of him as in some sense divine yet not God, unequal to the Father in his deity.[16]

Baruch's Doctrine of Christ is theologically *kosher*, yet this is at the expense of any substantial engagement with Jewish thought or expression that goes beyond the biblical data. His matrix of interpretation leaves little room new articulation of Trinitarian concepts or discussion of the divine and human natures of Christ, and stays deliberately within the mode of Chalcedonian thought, as interpreted through the Reformed tradition. For Baruch, the distinction between "Judaism" and "Jewishness" is crucial to his theological method. Religious Judaism, as continued by the Rabbis, is a false path away from the New Testament revelation, and no use should be made of it in the attempt to articulate or legitimate Christian truth about the Messiah. Jewish identity has ethnic, cultural and national value, but should not be linked to a religious component. For Baruch, the error of the Messianic movement is the blurring of these two categories, at the expense of biblical revelation and a proper focus on the supremacy of Christ.[17]

> It is very dangerous for us to choose to think of Jesus in terms that we might find more comfortable, or more understandable. We need to listen intently to what scripture says, submit to its superior authority, and obey. This, it must be admitted, is an act of faith. But *without faith it is impossible to please* God (Heb. 11:16).

> It is wrong to give ourselves over to the rabbis, to allow them to wrest from our hearts increasing portions of our Faith, until they take us wholly captive, to do their will. We ought never to forget that precisely denials of Jesus such as are common to rabbinic Judaism today brought about the rejection and crucifixion of our Lord.[18]

There is much in this argument that is helpful for a rediscovery of the significance of Jesus within the Messianic movement, although the central premise of Maoz's argument, that the "Judaism" of the rabbis is not properly "Jewish" will not convince all. On theological grounds the position is arguable, but if cultural factors are taken into account on how Jewish identity is constructed, and how faith in Christ might affect this, the argument oversimplifies the complex interaction between religious, ethnic, cultural and other factors that make up Jewish identity and peoplehood as a present-day witness to the electing purposes of God. Furthermore, it is unlikely that the Messianic Jewish movement will fully accept the norms and criteria of Maoz's own theological system, with its own particular perspective on the relationship between the Gospel and Culture. Nevertheless the emphasis on the centrality of Christ, and a right understanding of his divine and human nature, is a much needed one within the Messianic movement, and Maoz is surely right to re-emphasize this.

How Much Can We Use the Jewish Mystical Tradition to Express and Illustrate the Divinity of Yeshua?

From the time of Pico della Mirandola (1463-94) it has been proposed that the *Kabbalah* confirmed the truth of Christian teaching, especially on the nature of the Trinity. Pico was the first of many Christian students of the *Zohar* who believed that he could prove the dogmas of the Trinity and the Incarnation on the basis of kabbalistic axioms. In his 900 theses he claimed

No science can better convince us of the divinity of Jesus Christ than magic and the *Kabbalah*.[19]

Christian *Kabbalah* came from two sources, Christological speculations of Jewish Christians such as Abner of Burgos, Paul de Heredia and Petrus Alphonsi (1062-c.1110), and Christian speculation that developed around the Platonic Academy sponsored by the Medicis in Florence, which developed alongside more general Renaissance discoveries and new learning.

Under Pico's influence Johannes Reuchlin, a non-Jew, linked the doctrine of the Incarnation to kabbalistic speculation on the names of God. He argued that history could be divided into three periods, corresponding to the ages of Chaos, Torah and the Messiah.[20]

In the first period, that of the patriarchs, God revealed himself as the three-lettered Shaddai (שדי). In the period of the Torah he revealed himself to Moses through the four letters of the Tetragrammaton (יהוה), and in the period of redemption and grace He revealed himself in the five letters of Yehoshua (Jesus) (יהושע). This miraculous name contained the unpronounceable name of God with the addition of shin (ש).

This Trinitarian view of history was later adopted by the Christian Joachim de Fiore into that of three reigns, that of the Father, the Son and the Holy Spirit.

The Christian Kabbalists continued to develop their views throughout the Renaissance and Reformation periods, and the 19th century missions used their findings as apologetic resources. A particularly noteworthy attempt at Christianizing the mystical tradition was that of Johann Christian Jakob Kemper of Uppsala.

Kemper, whose Hebrew name was Moses Ben Aaron Kohen of Cracov, was a 17th century Jewish Christian whose primary goal was to establish the truths of Christianity on the basis of Jewish sources, particularly the *Zohar*, to show that the messianic faith of the Christians was in fact the truly ancient *Kabbalah* of Judaism.[21]

In his commentary on the *Zohar* published in 1711 he begins with three initial chapters, on the Trinity, the divinity of the Messiah, and on *Metatron*, the embodiment of the Messiah. To this is added a series of defenses of the Christian faith, and finally a translation into Hebrew and commentary on the Gospel of Matthew.[22]

Kemper shared the same strategy as other Christian Kabbalists of the Renaissance, and foreshadows that of later authors such as Pauli, and the modern generation of apologists. They had two related aims, the use of Jewish esoteric teachings to confirm Christian truth, and the Christian application of kabbalistic methods to construct new ideas and symbols. The work of the Christian Kabbalists is to be set in the overall context of the Christian attempt, as Wolfson describes it, "to subvert Judaism by means of appropriating it".

Kemper's attempt to re-orientate the Jewish mystical tradition to prove the truths of Orthodox Trinitarian Christianity is noteworthy for his dexterity in handling the Jewish sources, the creativity of his exegetical methods and the awareness he shows of the Jewish context into which he is bringing a Christological interpretation of the tradition. He distinguishes sharply between the false Oral Torah of the rabbinic tradition and what is for him the true Oral Torah, the Sayings of Jesus as recorded in the Gospels. Rabbinic tradition is used to confirm the truth of the Gospel presentation of the Messiahship, pre-existence and divinity of Jesus, and of his membership of the Trinity.

Wolfson sees Kemper's Approach as Naturally Reflecting

The split consciousness of his own existential situation. He cannot divest himself completely of his rabbinic upbringing even though he is a fully committed Christian. On the contrary, the veracity of his Christian affiliation is confirmed most precisely by the rabbinic and kabbalistic sources with which he is so intimately familiar.[23]

Kemper uses Jewish sources not just to prove the truth of Christianity, but also to legitimize a Jewish Christian approach as the most authentic way of elucidating biblical and traditional texts, and one of which non-Christian Jews and non-Jewish Christians should take note. Only a Jewish Christian approach can bring out the true significance of the *Zohar* and other mystical texts. Only a Jewish Christian approach can rightly relate Christianity to its Jewish roots.

I have chosen the example of Kemper because he illustrates the strengths and weaknesses of this approach, which is gaining ground in the Messianic movement today. In Jewish mission this approach was used by Joseph Christian Frey, the son of a Rabbi from Posen who was instrumental in the setting up of the *London Society for the Promotion of Christianity amongst the Jews* (CMJ) in 1809. In *Joseph and Benjamin*,[24] a series of letters on the nature and divinity of the Messiah, Frey uses material from the *Talmud* and *Kabbalah* to demonstrate the divinity of the Messiah, in addition to the material from the scriptures pointing to the plurality of God.

The most familiar example of the Christian Kabbalist approach, which avoids some the dangers that will be noted later, is Rev. C. W. H. Pauli's *How Can Three Be One?*[25]

The title of Pauli's book is taken from the passage in the *Zohar*, which suggests the Trinity, and has been used in many other works of Apologetics.[26] Pauli's aim to prove that "our sages of blessed memory, long before the Christian era, held that there was a plurality in the deity." Whilst quoting from rabbinic literature, he asks the reader to bear in mind the fact that

> the Holy Scriptures, and nothing but the Holy Scriptures, are the foundation to which he holds, and upon which he claims that the Holy One, Blessed be He, is a divine and wonderful Tri-unity. Quotations from human writings, however old, venerable and reliable, are only presented in order to show my beloved brethren of Israel how inconsistent they are to reject such a thought regarding our great God and Saviour, while professing—as they do—to follow

closely after their forefather who, it is here proved, believed this wholeheartedly.[27]

Pauli uses Jewish tradition to explore the three-fold nature of God: the identity of the *Memra,* Angel of the Covenant and *Metatron* as descriptions of the Son of God, "who is an eternal emanation from God, therefore called Jehovah";[28] and the Divinity of the Holy Spirit. Pauli concludes by appealing to his readers:

> Whether I am not right in maintaining that the Jewish church before the Christian era, and in the first two centuries of the same, held רזא דשלושא, the Doctrine of the Trinity, as a fundamental and cardinal article of the true faith?[29]

Pauli's method is not without its critics. His dating of the *Zohar* to the second century is now generally rejected in favor of a twelfth century origin, and his examples of rabbinic hermeneutics including *gematria*[30] as proofs for the Messiahship of Jesus "bring no honor to Christianity and reflect badly against the one who uses them as well as the one convinced by them."[31] William Varner decries such attempts as deeply flawed:

> Although their motives may have been sincere, their hermeneutical methodology was so defective that they did more harm than good in its implementation. Their writings serve to warn Christians today about how *not* to conduct the Jewish-Christian discussion.[32]

Yet this approach, whilst "straying from a grammatical-historical hermeneutic", continues to have its proponents.

A contemporary example of this approach is that of Tsvi Sadan, whose views have been quoted in recent debate on the Divinity of Jesus. Sadan seeks to articulate a Messianic Jewish Christology by developing a "high Christology" which can take in issues such as the Incarnation and Tri-unity of the Godhead, whilst being accessible to a Jewish realm of discourse. Although this has not always been clearly communicated or understood, he represents a significant concern within the Messianic movement.

Sadan says:

> In Judaism, the search for God's unity is not shaped through precise definitions. Instead, it is framed as a

midrash, that is, imbedded in a story and therefore subject to an ongoing interpretation. .... On the other hand, to understand God's unity by Attempting to strictly define his essence leads to a rigid and Uncompromising Dogma.

Sadan's method is to remain within the Jewish understanding of God.

If I can sum up my methodological assumption it will be this: anything a Jew needs to know about the Messiah (Yeshua) can be found within the Jewish tradition. This is a bold assumption but nevertheless, one that can be substantiated without violating this very tradition that stresses its incompatibility with Jesus. In "Hundred Names of Messiah" I am trying to demonstrate how this is possible. One of the more difficult things to do is my attempt to "talk Jewish" rather than bring disguised Christian concepts.[33]

Sadan recognizes the difficulty of this, not only in the misunderstanding that it can cause, but also the fact that the "Jewish tradition" is not monolithic and could rightly include the Christian Jewish tradition of the New Testament and later Christianity. Yet Sadan's method, like that of Kemper and other Christian Kabbalists, is to explore and express the Messiahship and Divinity of Christ in mystical terms, whilst being aware of the need for controls on interpretation and the dangers involved in handling esoteric materials with occult, Gnostic and pantheist influences:

One of the more complex issues is that of mystical tradition. Beside the point that it is unaccepted in the Protestant world from which we Messianic Jews are so heavily influenced, it is an abused field since the very nature of mysticism is that of very loose boundaries. Nevertheless, I think it is possible to discern where valid interpretation ends. Characteristically the sign is when the text is aimed at the possibility to manipulate either divine or occult powers. I am not saying it is easy and one needs to approach it with extreme caution. All I am saying is that it is usable and valuable, and by the way, to lesser degree, you can find elements of gnosticism, occult and you name it in almost any Jewish source, including *Talmud*, midrashim and what not. I don't think we need to respond to it but simply put it aside. No human source is a pure source. After all, don't we need to exercise discernment also when dealing with Christian material? The doctrine of the *sefirot* should be particularly intriguing for us since it deals with the very concept of the Trinity but instead of three godheads they have ten.[34]

Sadan does not wish his attempt to be understood as a denial of the Deity of Messiah, but rather addresses the Jewish objections to the plural nature of God from within the tradition itself. He recognizes that Judaism presents an "outward face" which rejects the possibility of the Trinity, whilst in internal debate allows for the plural unity of God to be expressed in at times controversial ways:

Among the Jews, the Trinity is bound to raise the question whether idolatry is in fact a feature of Christianity. In the Jewish discourse that is directed outside, toward Jewish unbelievers and Christians, it is clear that the doctrine of the Trinity provokes a strong negative reaction. In this discourse, Judaism presents a united front: Christianity (not to be confused with the New Testament) is an idolatrous religion because it teaches that Jesus and the Holy Spirit are gods on their own merit. The Christian theory of three entities—God the Father, God the Son and God the Holy Spirit—violates the command not to worship any other god. As such, the doctrine of the Trinity in its popular understanding—three gods who are one—violates one of only three commandments a Jew must die for and not transgress.[35] This explains the strong Jewish reaction to it and why it presents an obstacle for any Jew who is willing to think seriously about his or her relationship to Jesus and the New Testament.

Within the internal Jewish discourse, matters are a little more complicated. Two examples will suffice to illustrate it. In his book *Aderet Elijahu*, the Gaon of

Vilna, one of the greatest Jewish sages of all time, writes the following: "The tabernacle was one. . . . One is something that encloses things in unity within itself, and such is with 'Hear O Israel [our God is one Lord].'" The Vilna Gaon had no problem to see even in the most important declaration "the Lord is one," an indication to God's unity. And regarding the divinity of the Redeemer, in a discussion in the *Talmud* on the meaning of the term *Man of God*, the following was said: "If it were not written, I would not be able to say it.'" Here the difficulty inherent in the term *Man of God*, is acknowledged but not explained. Yet in the same *midrash* (story) Rabbi Abin explains the difficulty: "When he [Moses] went up, and did not eat or drink, he was called God, and when he came down, and ate and drank, he was called man. From halfway upwards he was God, and from halfway downwards he was man." Moses, who is referred to in other places as "the first redeemer," is called both man and God hence *man of God*; albeit, nowhere does it say Moses is God! These few examples show that, in Judaism, the search for God's unity is not shaped through precise definitions. Instead, it is framed as a *Midrash* that is, imbedded in a story and therefore subject to an ongoing interpretation. As a result, the discussion on a sensitive topic of this kind produces a dynamic and tolerant understanding. On the other hand, to understand God's unity through attempts to figure out God's essence through strict definitions leads to a rigid and uncompromising dogma.[36]

Sadan seeks to avoid the confusion of the contemporary debate, which to him is a result not of the doctrine of the Trinity itself, but "because a man-made doctrine was turned into the very living word of God." He proposes that "if the Messianic Jews will decide to speak about the unity of God within the boundaries set by the Bible, they would not only be able to promote unity among themselves, but also improve their relationship with the Jewish community."

In his "Hundred Names of the Messiah" Sadan elaborates on this method, showing how more evidence is found in Jewish sources for

Jesus' assertion that Moses and the prophets explained things concerning himself.[37]

Not all will agree with this approach to Christology in the Messianic movement, but it is an exploratory one, which deserves consideration.

How Can We Recontextualise Nicene Christology?

Louis Goldberg recognized the problems inherent in formulating a Messianic approach to Christology, and warned:

Some Messianic Jews have sought to ingratiate themselves with the Jewish community and have spoken of God as simply a Unity. However, to this writer, this accommodates too much to the Jewish position of how to understand God as interpreted by the rabbis and therefore gives away what the Scriptures would assert. We must give a strong positive witness that God be considered as a composite unity thereby allowing for the possibility of the persons within the Godhead but yet at the same time, insisting that God is one. In that way, we have re-contextualized the doctrine of God from that of Nicea and dealt primarily with what the Hebrew texts have to say, and at the same time, also considering what the Messianic Jews of the first century asserted regarding who God is.[38]

Several have made preliminary attempts to re-contextualize Nicaea, by explaining the difficulties raised for Jewish and Messianic Jewish thought, yet engaging with the context and content of the Nicaea formulation, and finding ways to express this within a Jewish frame of reference.[39]

Daniel Juster recognizes that

> to raise the question of Yeshua's divinity is to open one of the greatest debates between Jews and Christians. This question leads to the whole debate about the Trinity, since the Messiah is said to be divine as one part of the Triune God.[40]

Juster, as we have seen, rejects the "widely held conclusion of modern scholarship" that sharply differentiates between Hebraic and Hellenistic modes of thought as functional and ontological. For him the real question is rather . . . how a metaphysic that is implied by biblical teaching compares and contrasts with a Greek metaphysic. Because all human beings are created in the image of God, communication and evaluation with regard to metaphysical views is cross-culturally possible.[41]

For Juster this realization places the debate on Christology on a less simplistic and more fruitful foundation. The Nicene statement in the light of all of this is neither totally Greek and unacceptable nor an accurate metaphysical statement of biblically implied truth. Those dimensions of Nicea implied by the Bible, in Juster's view, still are "Son of God," "only begotten from the Father," "begotten not made (created)" and "light from light." Other dimensions of the Nicene formula are biblically defensible, if properly defined, but are unhelpful in a Jewish context because they lend themselves to connotative misunderstanding. "God from God" and "true God from true God" are phrases that too easily lend themselves to misconception. These statements emphasize divinity to such a degree that the humanity of the Son and His submission to the Father are eclipsed (e.g., a danger of Docetism). New Testament Christology, at least with regard to the relationship of the incarnate Messiah to the Father, in all biblical language and in all apocalyptic pictures of the Father and the Lamb in heaven, reflect subordination overtones. "One substance" language is difficult philosophically even if there are reasons for its use. He is in His divine nature everlastingly one in being with the Father. Perhaps other language such as "one in essence" or "one in His divine being" could be more helpful.[42]

For Juster there is a need to reformulate the same truths safeguarded by Nicea in order to better communicate to the modern Jewish mind. He urges Messianic Jews to look to the very Jewish roots that influenced the Nicene creed and from these roots speak afresh to our day.

The basic question addressed to Jew and Gentile from the Messiah is "Whom do you say that I am?" That the New Testament Scriptures reveal Him as the risen Messiah is at the centre of Christological controversy. The supernatural risen Messiah transcends the issues of Hebraic and Greek categories because His work was not conceived by the mind of man.[43]

In *Jewish Roots* Juster defends of the plural nature of God in the Tenach, and follows this with discussion of the Angel of the LORD, the superhuman nature of the Messiah (Isa. 9:6-7) and discussion of New Testament passages that show the divinity of Yeshua. He then gives his own view of the nature of Yeshua.

He is one person or aspect of that plural manifestation of God (from the Tenach) who became a human being. He, therefore, is a man who depends on the Spirit, prays to the Father, gets weary and dies. His divine nature never dies, but he is human as well as divine. As such, prayer in the New Testament is not primarily addressed to Yeshua but to "Our Father" in the Name of Yeshua. For Yeshua is the human revelation of the Father.[44]

Juster warns against the Christo-monism of losing sight of God the Father, calling for full recognition of Yeshua's divinity whilst recognizing that God is more than just Yeshua. He then calls for a deeper expression of the Trinity in Jewish terms.

Jewish ways of expression are needed, ways more consistent to the New Testament, if Jews are to penetrate Christian rhetoric to see the Truth of Yeshua's divine nature.[45]

Juster gives several reasons why it is important to accept the uni-plurality of God and the divine nature of Yeshua. Only a perfect man could bring a full revelation of God, as man is made in the image of God. A revelation of God's love in the form of a human being is the greatest way possible to show God's love. Such a revelation has a unique redemptive significance, as the Messiah's suffering is the revelation of the suffering love of God himself. As the divine Messiah Yeshua's suffering has infinite redemptive value.

So for Juster "the divinity of the Messiah is not idolatry, but reflects the fullest revelation of God." "The scriptures thus communicate to us the impression of one great divine reality of three inseparable manifestations of God. The relationship of love and accord blends the three into eternal oneness beyond human comprehension. ... The reciprocal *giving relationship* of love is eternally existent within the plural unity of God."[46]

Elazar Brandt also advocates the freedom to develop this line of thinking, whilst being sensitive to the classical Trinitarian position. His presuppositions are as follows:

For several years now I have been asking myself whether I accepted the "trinity" concept because I was taught it in the church, or because I found it in the scriptures. I have been thinking that what I always thought I knew from the scripture may have been only proof texts for what I was fed in church as unassailable truth. This is putting the cart before the horse. So I've been trying to get my thinking built more from the ground up, the "ground" being the Torah and Tenakh, and the NT doctrines standing on that foundation.[47]

Brandt's method is based on the need to ... process the revelation of G-d in the order he gave it to us. That is, Creation, Redemption, Torah, Sacred worship - place and procedures, prophets, Kingship, and ultimately, NT, with focus on the Gospels and the historical person and sayings and deeds of Yeshua first, and only then on the writings of Paul and others. All this should be carried out under the assumptions that:

1) Later covenants are built on previous ones and do NOT cancel them.

2) Conclusions of church councils far removed in time and distance from the events of the revelation (need) not be taken as *a priori* incontestable truth. Rather, we must carefully examine whether the revelation itself leads to such conclusions without being forced into a pre- (or actually, "post") conceived form.

3) Those who question the deity of Yeshua but serve him faithfully ought not to be labeled as heretics or unsaved for their ideas alone; likewise, Trinitarians ought not be labeled idolaters by non-Trinitarians if their intent is to worship and serve one G-d. If we cannot grant each other some room for fresh thought, we will never advance beyond Nicaea in our concept of G-d.

Brandt here reflects the views of Jacob Jocz, who stated:

> (The Synagogue) has a right and an obligation to ask ... "How is Jesus of Nazareth God?" The Christian answer cannot be evasive. It must not fall back upon the authority of Church Councils. To refer a Jew back to the Council of Nicaea is an admission of our own helplessness and lack of conviction. It is the task of theology to attempt a *contemporary* answer, but with a view to the past. The Jewish questioner to-day is not edified by the historical information what Christians in the fourth century thought about Jesus; he wants to know what we think about him in the intellectual context of our own time.[48]

David Stern views the present debate on the Divinity of Yeshua as significant, but wishes it to be understood properly in context, rather than misconstrued. Referring to the *Israel Today* article that reported the debate in Israel, Stern stressed:

More importantly, whilst most of the twelve are concerned not to become "Gentilized," few have theological training; and this combination can distort theologizing. In such cases the statements should be evaluated less as theology than as a heart cry to preserve Jewish identity. I think all twelve of the Messianic Jews quoted are believers who love God and his Messiah Yeshua with all their heart, even if some of their words about Yeshua deviate from what most Christians consider acceptable."

Stern uses the concept of antinomies[49] because the Biblical data underlying the theology of Yeshua's deity are too complex to be discussed in short magazine articles or debated in the form of slogans. The Deity of Yeshua is a topic which refuses to "submit to law", and is one of the "paradoxes, mysteries, phenomena in which "A" and "not-A" both hold."[50]

In the *Jewish New Testament* and *Jewish New Testament Commentary* Stern addresses such questions as "Is Yeshua God?" and "Is God a Trinity?" but tries to push past the reflex responses of "Absolutely" (Christian) and "Absolutely not" (Jewish) in order to discuss the substance of the matter—what positive and negative answers might mean, and whether both Christian and Jewish contexts might admit of "less confrontational formulations without compromising the scriptural data".[51]

Michael Schiffman has gone further than most in engaging and re-expressing Chalcedonian orthodoxy in Jewish terms. In discussing the background to the Councils of the church fathers he recalls how in the post-Nicean period Jews were expected to renounce all things Jewish when they became believers. This policy of renunciation deepened the separation between Jewish Christians and the Jewish community.[52]

Recognizing that the terminology of the debate "sounds very Catholic, and hence, very non-Jewish" he suggests that there may never be a suitable answer to the semantic issue because there will always be a tension between finding a word that is Jewish palatable and one that is theologically precise. The Trinity is a theological word based on a biblical concept that does not occur in scripture. If it were a biblical term, or if there were a Jewish equivalent, it would be more acceptable.

Schiffman sees a theological development between the HB revelation of God, plurality notwithstanding, and the doctrine of the Trinity.

The reason a formal Trinitarian concept does not exist in the Old Testament is not because it is borrowed from Hellenism, as some suggest, but because as the revelation of God is progressive, so as with the nature of the Messiah himself, a full enough revelation did not exist in Jewish scripture until the New Covenant.[53]

Whilst the conclusions of Nicaea were "looked upon by some as having a distinctively anti-Jewish bias" such as the changing of the day of worship from Sabbath to Sunday, and the discouragement to celebrate Jewish festivals, Schiffman recognizes the good that was achieved in the facing of theological challenges affecting the *Ekklesia*, and the articulation of truth in the light of error.

Schiffman also challenges the notion that the Nicaean Trinitarian formula is incompatible with the Jewish view of monotheism, showing this to be an anachronistic reading of the nature of early Jewish monotheism, which was far more flexibly interpreted than that of today, in the light of later Maimonidean rationalism and anti-Christian polemic.

Joseph Shulam of *Netivyah* in Jerusalem is concerned at the level of heat generated by the controversy on the divinity of Christ.

The question . . . is one of the hottest in all of Christianity and especially among the brothers and sisters in Israel. There have been inquisitive actions taken here by some brothers as if they were Savonarola or Torquemada during the darkest periods of Christian history, but with God's help we shall overcome this wave of tyrannical leadership with the love of the Lord and the Grace of the Cross.

In his own statement of faith Shulam is emphatic in his belief in the deity of Jesus:

1. I believe that Yeshua is the Messiah the Son of the Living God.

2. I believe that Yeshua is 100% man and 100% God by virtue of his commission and by virtue of His very nature.

3. I believe that God sent His unique Son to the World because He loves mankind and wants to see all men saved from the judgment day of the Lord.

4. I believe that the New Testament is a Jewish book and that we must understand it from a first century Jewish context and not allow the Protestant worldview and a Hellenistic Christianity to color our views of God, the Bible, and the Messiah, but restore the Jewishness of our faith both as Jews and as non-Jewish Christians.

He adds:

> One thing I do want to state clearly—I have never
> even one time denied the deity of the Messiah.[54]

Is it Kosher to Affirm a Trinitarian and Incarnational Theology whilst Recognizing the Hiddenness of the Messiah to Our People?

As the question here is with specific reference to our friend Mark Kinzer, I want to engage with his discussion in *Postmissionary Messianic Judaism* (*PMJ*) and other writings. Let me say at the outset that I find Kinzer's thinking refreshing, challenging and orthodox in Christian terms. I also find it Conservative in Jewish terms, and challenging the paradigms of Jewish and Christian tradition. But I have several questions, and do not agree with some of his assumptions.

Mark Kinzer's *PMJ* presents the potential for a programmatic theological system. Combating supersession readings of Scripture to argue for the ongoing election of Israel and the legitimacy of a Torah-observant Messianic Judaism, Kinzer employs post-liberal[55] and post-critical Jewish and Christian theological resources. His understanding of the revelation of God through the Scriptures and Jewish tradition acknowledges the significance of the Jewish and Christian faith communities through which such revelation is mediated. Ecclesiology and soteriology cohere around his bi-lateral understanding (reflecting Karl Barth) of the community of God made up of both 'unbelieving' Israel, and the Church, with Jesus present in both, visible to the *ekklesia* but only partially recognized by Israel.

It is clear that Kinzer's influences and assumptions place him outside the mainstream of Protestant evangelicalism, especially the conservative variety often found within previous forms of Messianic Judaism. His view of the authority and inspiration of Scripture is tempered by respect for Jewish traditions of interpretation, and the influence of critical and post-critical biblical scholarship, and post-liberal theology.

Judaism' arises as one way of negotiating the tension between proclamation of Jesus as Messiah, and the preservation of Jewish belief, practice and identity. Such concerns reflect the challenges facing the Messianic movement worldwide as it grows in theological, spiritual, communal and personal maturity. Kinzer's response is a

Messianic Judaism that echoes Conservative Judaism in its liturgy and practice, and integrates belief in Yeshua in the context of loyalties and identity to 'Jewish space.'

Kinzer sees Jesus as divine, but within a Judaism not inhospitable to the possibility of the divinity and incarnation of the Son of God. The historic Christian formulations of the Trinity are inadequate in Jewish contexts because they are steeped in Hellenism. New post-critical formulations are required that emerge from Jewish tradition and are recognized as possible understandings of the nature of God. The Scriptures of Judaism and Christianity are both inspired, and to be interpreted within a non-supersession appreciation of the canonical and communal contexts in which they arose.

Mark Kinzer's *Postmissionary Messianic Judaism* proposes that the Jesus the Messiah is hidden in the midst of the Jewish people. Kinzer proposes a 'bilateral ecclesiology' made up of two distinct but united communal entities:

(1) The community of Jewish Yeshua-believers, maintaining their participation in the wider Jewish community and their faithful observance of traditional Jewish practice, and (2) The community of Gentile Yeshua-believers, free from Jewish Torah-observance yet bound to Israel through union with Israel's Messiah, and through union with the Jewish ekklesia (Kinzer 2007:iv).

Kinzer's stresses on the inherent 'twofold nature' of the *ekklesia* preserves 'in communal form the distinction between Jew and Gentile while removing the mistrust and hostility that turned the distinction into a wall'. Kinzer argues that a bilateral ecclesiology is required if the Gentile ekklesia is to claim rightfully a share in Israel's inheritance without compromising Israel's integrity or Yeshua's centrality.

In Chapter Six Kinzer turns to the Jewish people's apparent "no" to its own Messiah. Kinzer argues that Paul sees this rejection as 'in part providential, an act of divine hardening effected for the sake of the Gentiles'. Paul, according to Kinzer, even implies that this hardening involves Israel's mysterious participation in the suffering and death of the Messiah.

In the light of Christian anti-Semitism and supersession, the Church's message of the Gospel comes to the Jewish people accompanied by the demand to renounce Jewish identity, and thereby violate the ancestral covenant. From this point onward the apparent Jewish "no" to Yeshua expresses Israel's passionate "yes" to God—a "yes" which eventually leads many Jews on the way of martyrdom.

Jews thus found themselves imitating Yeshua through denying Jesus! If the Church's actual rejection of Israel did not nullify her standing nor invalidate her spiritual riches, how much more should this be the case with Israel's apparent rejection of Yeshua! (Kinzer 2004:5).

The Jewish people's apparent 'no' to Jesus does not rule them out of God's salvation purposes, any more than the Church's *actual* 'no' to the election of Israel. Both are within the one people of God, although there is a schism between them. The New Testament 'affirms the validity of what we would today call Judaism' (Kinzer 2005:215).

Kinzer recognizes that the presence of Yeshua is necessary in order to affirm Judaism.

Those who embrace the faith taught by the disciples will be justifiably reluctant to acknowledge the legitimacy of a religion from which Yeshua, the incarnate Word, is absent (Kinzer 2005:217).

Judaism's validity can not demonstrated if Jewish people have a way to God that 'bypasses Yeshua.' However, Kinzer argues that in some mysterious and hidden way 'Yeshua abides in the midst of the Jewish people and its religious tradition, despite that tradition's apparent refusal to accept his claims' (Kinzer 2005: 217). This divinely willed 'disharmony between the order of knowing and the order of being' means that Yeshua is present with his people without being recognized. The *ontic* is to be distinguished from the *noetic*, what exists from what is known. The New Testament affirms that Yeshua is the representative and individual embodiment of the entire people of Israel, even if Israel does not recognize Yeshua and repudiates his claims. Even this rejection testifies to his status as the despised and rejected servant. Echoing Karl Barth's doctrine of the Church in relation to Israel, Israel's 'no' is answered by the Church's 'yes' to Jesus, and in Jesus himself both 'yes' and 'no' are brought together, just as Jesus is both divine and human, and accepted and rejected.

Both church and Israel are 'bound indissolubly to the person of the Messiah', one in belief, the other in unbelief. Therefore 'Israel's no *to* Yeshua can be properly viewed as a form of participation *in* Yeshua!' (Kinzer 2005:223).

If the obedience of Yeshua that led him to death on the cross is rightly interpreted as the perfect embodiment and realization of Israel's covenant fidelity, then Jewish rejection of the church's message in the second century and afterward can rightly be seen as a hidden participation in the obedience of Israel's Messiah (Kinzer 2005:225).

This sounds decidedly paradoxical. How are we to understand and respond to it? Kinzer's argument draws from earlier thinkers like Lev Gillet, the friend of Paul Levertoff.

His entire notion of "communion in the Messiah" presumes that faithful Jews and faithful Christians can have communion together in the one Messiah. In fact, he seems to hold that the Messiah is also hidden for Christians to the extent that they fail to understand or acknowledge the ongoing significance of the Jewish people in the divine purpose (Kinzer 2007:1).

Gillet views the Jewish people as a '*corpus mysticum*—a mystical body, like the church.' (Kinzer 2005: 280). The suffering of the Jewish people is to be understood in the light of Isaiah 53, as both 'prophetic and redemptive,' but Gillet does not, according to Kinzer, lose 'his Christological bearings' (2005: 281). Gillet's aim is to build a 'bridge theology' that links the mystical body of Christ with that of the mystical body of Israel.

The *corpus mysticum Christi* is not a metaphor; it is an organic and invisible reality. But the theology of the Body of Christ should be linked with a theology of the mystical body of Israel. This is one of the deepest and most beautiful tasks of a 'bridge theology' between Judaism and Christianity (Gillet 1942:215 in Kinzer 2005: 281).

Gillet aims to heal the schism between Israel and the Church, showing that both Christian and Jew are united in the Messiah.

The idea of our membership in Israel has an immediate application in al the modern questions concerning Jewry. If we seriously admit the mystical bond which ties us, as Christians, to the community of Israel, if we feel ourselves true Israelites, our whole outlook may be modified, and our lives of practical action as well (Gillet 1942: 215).

However, Gillet's argument relies on a 'the mystery of the [future] restoration of Israel, who are still, in Paul's words, experiencing 'Blindness in part' (ibid). The Messiah is hidden from them, because of the blindness of unbelief. Whilst He is hidden within His people, he is also hidden from them by their partial hardening.

Kinzer's concept of the 'hidden Messiah' derives not from the anonymous Christianity of the Roman Catholic theologian Karl Rahner, but from Karl Barth and Franz Rosenzweig, and later Jewish-Christian relations thinkers such as Paul van Buren. Kinzer also refers to Edith Stein, the Jewish philosopher who became a Carmelite nun, who saw the sufferings of the Jewish people as 'participating in the sufferings of their unrecognized Messiah' (Kinzer 2005: 227).

Thomas Torrance lends support to this Christological understanding of the suffering of Israel as participation in the suffering of the Messiah, albeit unconsciously.

Certainly, the fearful holocaust of six million Jews in the concentration camps of Europe, in which Israel seems to have been made a burnt-offering laden with the guilt of humanity, has begun to open Christian eyes to a new appreciation of the vicarious role of Israel in the mediation of God's reconciling purpose in the dark underground of conflicting forces within the human race. Now we see Israel, however, not just as the scapegoat, thrust out of sight into the despised ghettos of the nations, bearing in diaspora the reproach of the Messiah, but Israel drawn into the very heart and centre of Calvary as never before since the crucifixion of Jesus. (Thomas Torrance, *The Mediation of Christ* (Colorado Springs: Helmers and Howard, 1992, 38-39, in Kinzer 227).

Kinzer echoes Protestant theologian Bruce Marshall in arguing that the Jewishness of Jesus implies his continuing membership of and participation in the Jewish people. God's incarnate presence in Yeshua thus 'resembles Gods presence among Yeshua's flesh-and-blood brothers and sisters' (Kinzer 2005:231). Quoting Bruce Marshall, the doctrine of the incarnation of God in Christ is analogous to the doctrine of God indwelling Carnal Israel, as articulated by Michael Wyschogrod, the Jewish thinker.

The Christian doctrine of the incarnation is an intensification, not a repudiation, of traditional Jewish teaching about the dwelling of the divine presence in the midst of Israel (Marshall 2000:178 in Kinzer 2005:231).

If God is 'present in Israel, Yeshua is also present there', and according to Robert Jenson, the 'church is the body of Christ only in association with the Jewish people.'

Can there be a present body of the risen Jew, Jesus of Nazareth, in which the lineage of Abraham and Sarah so vanishes into a congregation of gentiles as it does in the church? My final—and perhaps most radical – suggestion to Christian theology . . . is that . . . the embodiment of the risen Christ is whole only in the form of the church *and* an identifiable community of Abraham and Sarah's descendants. The church and the synagogue are together and only together the present availability to the world of the risen Jesus Christ. (Jenson 2003:13 in Kinzer 2005:232).

Kinzer is covering much new ground here, painting in broad brushstrokes an ecclesiology developed by post-liberal Christian theologians in dialogue with contemporary Jewish thinkers. Much of the discussion draws from Karl Barth's Christological doctrine of the election of the one 'community of God' as Church and Israel, and the doctrine runs the same risks of universalism on the one hand, and a continuing supersession on the other. Whilst Karl Barth withdrew from participation in Rosenzweig's 'Patmos group' because of its perceived Gnosticism, there is also a danger of Gnosticism in this doctrine of the Hidden Messiah incarnate in his people Israel (Lindsay 2007:28).

Kinzer relies on a 'divinely willed disharmony between the ontic and the noetic, following Bruce Marshall.

For most Jews, Paul seems to say, there is at this point a divinely willed disharmony between the order of knowing and the order of being which will only be overcome at the end of time (Kinzer 2007:1).

But if the mystery of God's dwelling in Christ is known to the Church, it can not be equally true that Israel can know that the opposite is the case, and that Jesus is not the risen Messiah. Whilst Christians recognize a continuing election of Israel (the Jewish people) and thus a continuing commitment of Jesus *to* His people, they will be reluctant to admit that this commitment in itself is salvific, or that the hidden presence of the Messiah *with* His people is the means by which he is revealed to them. The Hidden Messiah of PMJ owes more to a Christian re-orientation of perspective on Jesus and the election of Israel than on a Jewish recognition of a hidden Messiah. The hidden Messiah of PMJ is more a Christian re-evaluation of the presence of Christ within the Jewish people than a Jewish recognition of the Messianic claims of Jesus.

Conclusion

Each of the above options has its attractions—but the adoptionist Christology of Marcus cannot be accepted, as it breaches the fundamental understanding of the divine unity of the Trinity.

In terms of communication of the deity of Yeshua, several options exist within the Messianic movement, from Maoz's theocentric Christology to Kinzer's hidden but nevertheless divine Messiah. As will all communication, our situating of ourselves in different contexts, and our understanding of our audience, will result in different strategies of communication. Let us not cease from using every means at our disposal, in proclaiming the Good News that the Messiah has come, and his name is Yeshua—to God be the glory!

BIBLIOGRAPHY

Bauckham, Richard, *Jesus and the God of Israel: 'God crucified and other studies on the New Testament's Christology of Divine identity.* Milton Keynes: Paternoster, 2008.

Bernstein, A. *Some Jewish Witnesses for Christ.* London: Operative Jewish Converts Institution, 1909.

Feher, Shoshanah. *Passing over Easter: Constructing the Boundaries of Messianic Judaism.* Walnut Creek, CA: AltaMira Press, 1998.

Fischer, John. 'Yeshua: The Deity Debate.' *Mishkan.* Issue 39, 2003.

Frey, Joseph C.F. *The Divinity of the Messiah.* Israel: Keren Ahavah Meshichit, 2002.

Fruchtenbaum, Arnold. 'The Quest for a Messianic Theology', *Mishkan*, Issue 2, Winter 1985.

Fruchtenbaum, Arnold. 'The Quest for a Messianic Theology.' *Mishkan*, Issue 2, Winter 1985, pp. 1-3.

Gillet, Lev. Communion in the Messiah: Studies in the Relationship between Judaism and Christianity. London: Lutterworth Press, 1942.

Goldberg, Louis. 'Recontextualizing the Doctrine of the Trinity as Formulated by the Council of Nicaea.' LCJE-NA Regional Conference, Chicago: 1996,

Harvey, Richard. 'Jesus the Messiah in Messianic Jewish Thought', *Mishkan.* Issue 39 2003.

Harvey, Richard S. *Mapping Messianic Jewish Theology.* Milton Keynes: Paternoster, 2009.

Jenson, Robert W. 'Towards a Christian Theology of Judaism.' in *Jews and Christians*, edited by Carl El Braaten and Robert W. Jenson, 9-11. Grand Rapids: Eerdmans, 2003.

Jocz, Jacob. 'The Invisibility of God and the Incarnation.' in *The Messiahship of Jesus* edited by Arthur Kac, 189-196, Rev. ed. Grand Rapids: Baker, 1986.

Johnson, Boaz. 'Toward a Theology of God.' *Mishkan.* Issue 38, 2003.

Juster, Dan. *Jewish Roots: A Foundation of Biblical Theology.* Shippensburg, Penn: Destiny, 1995.

Kac, Arthur. *The Messiahship of Jesus, Revised Edition.* Grand Rapids: Baker, 1986.

Kinzer, Mark. 'Finding our Way through Nicaea: The Deity of Yeshua, Bilateral Ecclesiology, and Redemptive Encounter with the Living God.' Los Angeles: Hashivenu Forum, 2010.

Lapide, Pinhas. *Hebrew in the Church.* Grand Rapids: Eerdmans, 1984.

Lindsay, Mark R. Barth, Israel and Jesus: Karl Barth's Theology of Israel. Aldershot: Ashgate, 2007.

Longenecker, Richard N. *The Christology of Early Christianity.* Grand Rapids: Baker, 1981.

Maoz, Baruch. *Judaism is not Jewish.* Fearn, Scotland: Mentor, 2003.

Maoz, Baruch. *Lectures on the Person of Christ.* Unpublished.

Mounce, Robert H. 'Gospel' *Evangelical Dictionary of Theology, ed. Walter Elwell.* Grand Rapids: Baker, 1984.

Muffs, Yochanan. *The Personhood of God: Biblical Theology, Human Faith, and the Divine Image.* Woodstock, Vermont: Jewish Lights, 2005.

Nerel, Gershon. *(1967-1917)* :יהודים משיחיים בארץ ישראל. Hebrew U.: Jerusalem, 2003.

Patai, Raphael. *The Messiah Texts.* New York: Avon, 1979.

Pauli, C.W.H. (Zevi Nasi/Hirsch Prinz). *The Great Mystery: or, How Can Three Be One?* Amsterdam: Pauli, 1899.

Riesner, Rainer. 'Christology in the Early Jerusalem Community.' *Mishkan.* Issue 24, 1996.

Schiffman, Michael. The Return of the Remnant: The Rebirth of Messianic Judaism Baltimore: Lederer, 1992.

Schonfield, Hugh. *For Christ's Sake: A Discussion of the Jesus Enigma.* London: MacDonald and Janes's, 1975.

Skarsaune, Oskar. 'The Making of Creeds.' *Mishkan.* Issue 34, 2001.

Stern, David. *The Jewish New Testament Commentary.* Jerusalem: Jerusalem New Testament Publications, 1992.

Stern, David. 'Israel's Messianic Jews and the Deity of Yeshua: An Update.' *Israel Today* (July 2002).
http://mayimhayim.org/Academic%Stuff/David%Stern/Article.htm (accessed 24th May 2007).

Strong, Augustus H. *Systematic Theology.* Judson Press: Valley Forge, PA, 1979.

Tillich, Paul. *Systematic Theology: Three volumes in one.* Chicago: University of Chicago, 1967

Scholem, Gershom. *Kabbalah.* New York: Quadrangle, 1974.

Skarsaune, Oskar 'the Making of the Creeds' *Mishkan* Issue 34 (2001).

Tillich, Paul. *Systematic Theology.* Chicago: U. of Chicago, 1967.

Torrance, Thomas Forsyth. *The Mediation of Christ.* Colorado Springs: Multnomah, 1992.

Varner, William. 'The Christian Use of Jewish Numerology.' *The Masters Seminary Journal* 8, No. 1 (Spring 1997): 47-59.

Wolfson, Elliot R. 'Messianism in the Christian Kabbalah of Johann Kemper.' In *Millenarianism and Messianism in Early Modern European Culture: Jewish Messianism in the Early Modern World,* edited by Matthew D. Goldish and Richard H. Popkin, 139-187. The Netherlands: Kluwer Academic Publishers, 2001.

ENDNOTES

1. Jocz (1958) in Kac 1986:189. See my "Mapping Messianic Jewish Theology" (Paternoster, 2008) for full references.
2. Feher 1998:20.
3. Email correspondence, 3/2003.
4. Letters to the Editor, *Kivun* no. 30, quoted in Nerel 2003.
5. Marcus strongly rejects this interpretation of his position: "You stated that I see Rabbinic tradition as the authoritative understanding of the nature of G-d, and that I employ an interpretive tradition in my reading of the Tanach . . . All I can do is deny your allegations. I do not accept Rabbinic Tradition as authoritative interpretations, when I read my Bible! I find them useful. I find them helpful. I find them in many cases wise. But I also find them stupid, and ridiculous and completely false, in many other cases." (email 6/2003). I have given quotations at some length, to allow the reader to decide whether my interpretation is fair.
6. Marcus' views are to be found at *Adonai Echad: Deity of Yeshua Debate: Why Yeshua is NOT G-d . . . An Internet Course from a Jewish Perspective* (http://groups.yahoo.com/group/AdonaiEchad/). The group has 161 members.
7. Lesson 3 — I'll take ONE please . . . (http://groups.yahoo.com/group/AdonaiEchad/message/16)
8. "For the idolater does not deny the existence of God; he merely makes the mistake of supposing that the image of his own construction resembles a being which mediates between him and God . . . How much more serious is the error of him who thinks God is body! He entertains an error regarding the nature of God directly, and surely causes the anger of God to burn." (Guide to the Perplexed Bk. II, ch.36, summarised in *A History of Medieval Jewish Philosophy* by Isaak Husik, 1916, 1969, New York: Temple, 261)
9. Maoz 2003.
10. Maoz 2003:252-254
11. May 22-24, 2003 in Vienna, Virginia, USA.
12. Maoz email, 1/2003.
13. "Lectures on The Person of Christ – Part One –Introduction," 5. (pre-publication copy)
14. "The Person of Christ" (Annual Lecture of the Israel College of the Bible in Jerusalem, March 2002), reprinted in abbreviated form in *Maoz News*, May 10, 2002 (Volume 4.69), 1.
15. "Lectures on The Person of Christ – Part Four (Philippians 2:1-11)", 5 (pre-publication copy)
16. "Lectures on The Person of Christ – Part Six - Other NT Texts and a Systematic Summary", 9 (pre-publication copy)
17. See Maoz 2003, and my review in CWI Herald, Summer, 2003.
18. "Lectures on The Person of Christ – Part Six - Other NT Texts and a Systematic Summary", pre-publication copy, 11.

19. Scholem 1974:197.
20. cf. Sanhedrin 97b "There are three ages: two thousand years of chaos; two thousand years of the law beginning with the revelation on mount Sinai; two thousand years of the Messianic kingdom; and then finally the world with is only Sabbath, rest in eternal life." When the "days of the Messiah come", the "days of the Torah" come to an end. (Moltmann 1991:104)
21. Wolfson 2001:1.
22. On Kemper's translation see Lapide, Pinchas, *Hebrew in the Church*, (Grand Rapids, MI: Eerdmans, 1984), 76.
23. Wolfson 2001:3.
24. Reprinted as *The Divinity of the Messiah,* (Israel: Keren Ahavah Meshichit, 2002). Frey argues in vol. 2 Part II-IV (122-252) on "The Divinity of the Messiah", that although the doctrine of the plurality in unity is a stumbling block, the Rabbis acknowledge the divine plurality of *Elohim,* give testimony to the divinity of the Messiah, equating the Angel of the Lord (*Malak YHWH*) with God himself, and accept the Divinity of the Holy Spirit as the third person of the Trinity.
25. Rev. C. W. H. Pauli was born in Breslau in 1800, named Zevi Nasi (Hirsch Prinz). He was educated as a rabbi by his father, was given a New Testament by the London Society missionary C.G.Petri, and became a believer. He studied at Cambridge, and went on to become Lecturer in Hebrew at Oxford. He served as a missionary in Berlin and Amsterdam from 1840 to 1874, then retired to the UK where he died in 1877, with the words on his lips: "Into Thy hands, O God, I commend my spirit. My Saviour is near." (Bernstein 1909: 210-211).
26. *Zoha*r, Exodus 34b, vol. 3, 134 (Soncino ed.), referred to frequently in apologetic literature.
27. Pauli 1970: preface.
28. Pauli 1970:70.
29. Pauli 1970:89.
30. Mathematical computations involving the numerical values of the Hebrew letters.
31. Varner 1997:53.
32. Varner 1997:59.
33. Email correspondence, 6th March 2003.
34. Ibid.
35. Idolatry, incest and murder.
36. Ibid.
37. For example, on the letter *vav,* Sadan explores the letters of the Tetragrammaton: "A name of the Messiah that begins with *vav,* the sixth letter in the Hebrew alphabet is of great mystery. In Jewish mysticism, letters possess great importance since it is assumed that if God created the world by words and the words were spoken in Hebrew, each of the letters – its sound, shape and positions within the word – is significant. The letter *vav* thus is especially important since from it the name of God – the Tetragrammaton, is made. This fact makes the *vav* unique in that, along with *ha* (ה) and *yod* (י) it is not part of creation but of letters that create, as is befitting the name of God. Knowing this, the sages noted that the

vav is positioned between two *ha* like so (יהוה). In other words, since *ha* is also the name of God, the positioning of the *vav* in the midst of God, in Hebrew: *bein elohim* (אלוהים בין) means a great deal because, due to the nature of the Hebrew language, where the vowel letters are not always pronounced, *bein elohim* can be easily read as *ben elohim* and in English, Son of God. Having learned this, the sages have reached the same conclusion John has reached, that *Vav*, the Son of God, creates and is not created."

38. Goldberg 1996:26.
39. Space does not permit consideration of Yellin, Frydland, Rosenthal, Harvey and many others.
40. Juster 1986:181.
41. Ibid.
42. Ibid.
43. Ibid.
44. Juster 1986:187.
45. Juster 1986:188.
46. Juster 1986:189-190.
47. Brandt email, 3/2003.
48. Jocz 1958:62.
49. He ascribes this term to "Philosophical Issues in Religious Thought" (Boston: Houghton Mifflin, 1973) by Geddes MacGregor (email 3/2003).
50. Stern 2002:23.
51. Stern 1992:xiii.
52. Schiffman 1992:25.
53. Schiffman 1992:12.
54. Shulam email, 3/2003.
55. Postliberalism began as a reaction to theological liberalism. Karl Barth's reaction against Protestant liberal theology of the 19th and early 20th centuries was taken up by some of his followers in the USA to produce a new engagement with the Bible, Church tradition and contemporary culture. This sat in between the 'liberal' and 'conservative' labels. Key postliberal theologians include George Lindbeck, Hans Frei and Stanley Hauerwas, and the academic journals *First Things* and *Pro Ecclesia* are representative of postliberal thought. Postliberalism reacts against the relativism and rationalism of theological liberalism, with a more sympathetic reading of the Bible and Church tradition, but with an openness to theological ecumenism, the existence and impact of other faiths, and engagement with contemporary culture. Cf. Richard Harvey, 'Shaping the Aims and Aspirations of Jewish Believers (Review of Mark Kinzer's *Postmissionary Messianic Judaism*)' *Mishkan* 48 (2006): 18-21.

HOW TO EFFECTIVELY COMMUNICATE THE DEITY OF MESSIAH TO A JEWISH POST-MODERN COMMUNITY

Jhan Moskowitz, D. Min.
North American Director of Jews for Jesus
Co-founder of the New Jerusalem Players

I have been invited to address the question of the "Deity of Messiah and the Mystery of God," and to specifically communicate these eternal truths to a post-modern Jewish community. The letter of invitation asked specifically *how* to effectively move beyond Jesus as the first century Rabbi and to show that "He needs to be something more than a teacher."

This paper will focus on the missiological challenge of communicating to the post-modern Jewish community. The paper will not focus on what to say, but how to say it.

Speaking in post-modern terms, I am located in my worldview. That worldview accepts a metanarrative, and that metanarrative is Creation, The Fall, Redemption, and Consummation. Within that narrative, Creation implies a Creator, and Redemption encompasses the place of Israel in history. I start out with certain presuppositions. The received text we have of the Scriptures is authoritative in doctrine and practice.

I believe that a thorough understanding of that text will bring readers to the conclusion that those who wrote the texts under the inspiration of the Holy Spirit wanted their readers to come to specific conclusions about the topics they wrote on, including the deity of Messiah. The deity of Messiah is an integral part of the metanarrative mentioned above.

The question before us is communicating a propositional truth to a community that, by definition, 1) has a problem with the very idea of propositional truth, and 2) whose very identity in some way is connected to the rejection of that particular propositional statement.

I suggest that before we make recommendations on the how, we should first look at whom and proceed from there.

The group that we have been asked to speak to is really hyphenated. Although it is not written that way, it is in fact more like a hyphenated group than a description of a sub group of a larger category; it is Jewish and Post-Modern. As such, both sides of the hyphen need to be looked at and understood before postulating a communication plan.

Defining Jewish is very difficult. However, no matter how varied it seems to be, the Jewish community has at least three ideas that most, if not all, Jewish people have been socialized into.

The first is the Holocaust. To deny the Holocaust is to absent oneself from the Jewish people. (For the Post-modern Jew, this seems to be lessening.) Second is the State of Israel. All agree on its right to exist and some allegiance to it; there are some Hasidic groups that would take issue with the political state but still see Israel as their eventual homeland. Third is the rejection of Jesus. That rejection is in no small part because of the claims of the Deity of Jesus. According to Prothero's "American Jesus," over 50% of Jewish people in the USA accept that not only did Jesus exist, but that he was a good man and a teacher. It is His claims of Deity that are at issue with most Jewish people.

Of course we will always find exceptions to the rule. However, for the most part, a Jewish person in the United States, Australia, the UK and Turkey all have the same internalized understanding of themselves. The above three ideas are central to that. I have left out the Russian Jewish identity markers because, in places where there was a vacuum in socializing a subgroup like the Jewish people in the former Soviet Union, special case issues are pleaded.

I am not talking about religious convictions; I am speaking about the process of enculturalization that happens in spoken and unspoken communication patterns to members of a group. All groups have a process by which they determine who the "other" is in relationship to the group. The entire weight of language, lifecycle events, food and myth all go into forming group identity. In the latter part of the 20th and early part of the 21st century the three common factors in developing a Jewish identity have been the three items mentioned above.

Given the history of the Jewish people and our interactions with Christendom, the gospel message is perceived as a threat to the Jewish people. Groups have a tendency to attribute to their ancestors characteristics and motives that they may or may not have had. In the case of the Jewish people, it is part of the Jewish narrative that Jews in Europe all died as a result of resisting conversion. It would be seen as an act of tribal disloyalty to even entertain the truths of the message that the enemies of our people are presenting

All this is to say that the higher the Jewish identity the more resistant to the very message we are bringing. So if one has a high sense of one's Jewish identity, they will feel a stronger sense of loyalty to not engage with the Gospel message. They will also be more affected by the sanctions their community will wield against them to keep them conforming to the group thought.

The group in question is not static; it is dynamic, and its members are on many axes of a continuum. Therefore, this degree of Jewish identity changes as a person goes through crises. One may start out with very little Jewish identity only to find later in life a nostalgic connection to Jewish forms that draw them back into a higher sense of Jewish identity.

Conversely, one may start out with a very high sense of Jewish identity and go through some paradigmatic change and find that they have adopted another value than the one they were raised with, i.e., one that allows for a taboo that otherwise would never have been considered. Certainly many in the movement came into the hippie subculture that allowed Jesus a certain degree of acceptability. Their connection with that subculture, and willingness to accept the sanctions the greater society laid on them along with Jewish community's rejection, allowed many to find the truth that was kept from them by the larger Jewish community.

Other hyphens in an identity contribute or diminish to the level of resistance to a message. How Israeli-Jews understand their identity, as Jews will be different from how South African-Jews view theirs. Another important distinction germane to our discussion is what some of the characteristics of the other side of the hyphen are.

America values pluralism, and in the case of American Jews, those more connected to the American side of the hyphen will be less affected by the particularism of the Jewish side.

All these contribute to where on the continuum the person we are communicating with finds himself or herself. It will be far more difficult to speak to someone whose core understanding of himself is connected to the rejection of one of our central truths.

Much has been written on how to communicate our understanding of Messiah to our Jewish people. I will not take up more time in repeating what so many of us already know.

The point is, in any communication plan to present the deity of Messiah within the metanarrative, we must take the measure of where on the continuum of the Jewish side of the hyphen our post- modern Jewish person is. Doing so adjusts our communication accordingly; it will be equally true to locate our friend on where he or she may be on the postmodern continuum.

There are many different definitions of post modernity and this paper is not going to try to explore each of them. What is commonly held about post-modernity is one of its presuppositions that having absolute knowledge of truth is impossible; a reaction to the hubris of the modern world that believed that Reason was the metanarrative by which all other narratives can be measured. The post-modern recognized the pre-suppositional nature of any observer, and that the one asking the question is already located in his culture. To believe one could come only armed with Reason, to discover truth is to be naïve.

Dr. D.A. Carson has proposed that within the post-modern world there are at least two different kinds of post-modern thinkers: hard and soft. "Hard post-moderns" infer that because we cannot have absolute knowledge, we can know nothing. For them, there is truth but we can only know it subjectively, leaving us only meaning.

The other group, "soft post-moderns," is evidenced by recognition that although we cannot have absolute knowledge (only God is omniscient) that does not exclude the possibility of knowing.

The soft post-moderns are more likely to be the products of the culture they are raised in, while hard post moderns are those who write the philosophies and criticisms of modernity.

We will find those who reject our narrative do so because it makes truth claims that contradict the person's worldview about truth claims. Daniel Breslauer, (see Cohen's response) as Akiva has demonstrated, would be a classic example of a hard post-modern - someone so far on the post-modern side of the hyphen that the traditional Jewish objections he would have are almost nil. To the Daniel Breslauers of the world our approach will be different than to the majority of post-modern Jews we will encounter, who are somewhat towards the middle of the hyphen.

Depending on where on the continuum the person we are dealing with is, we may find great opportunity. One of the generally accepted values of the post-modern world is that everyone's story is valid and should have a right to be heard. Our story as Jewish believers has been marginalized and dismissed by the larger Jewish community, which allows us the status of outsider and disenfranchised. These are the very groups that the post-modern world finds worth championing. This is certainly one of the starting points we must find for our message.

A caution must be sounded here. When approaching a post-modern person with our story, we must be careful not to compromise our worldview in order to gain a hearing. We must not give up **the** truth to share **a** truth. Akiva has rightly pointed out the difficulty of interacting with someone like Kepnes, who would be glad to accept our text-centered approach, but reduces it to one of many meanings.

The typical Jewish- post-modern we will encounter will be someone who is in the middle of the hyphen. They will know that they are Jewish, but see themselves as part of other groups that will inform them of who they are. They will be committed to local and global issues, not only Jewish issues. They will see themselves as spiritual as opposed to religious. They are searching for the divine spark within, and the Awe of the transcendent. (What they are looking for is exactly what we are offering them in the Incarnation.)

Whatever Jewish religious forms they use, they will have redefined for their own purposes. All religious convictions will be seen as valid, as long as they are personal and do not enter the public arena. Intolerance will be the only taboo; all truths are personal truths.

Now to the how: We must see ourselves as cross cultural in our methods, although some in attendance may be more post-modern than not. I would recommend that we who are not post modern become students of post-modernity; In that we listen and engage rather than reject; that we find places where our story can make a difference in the lives of the people we are talking to. As for our place on the Jewish side of the hyphen we should continue being part of the community. The community's journey is our journey. The deity of Messiah is a very large, important part of our story, but it is not the entire story. The entire story needs to be encountered. **So that this is clear, the answer to presenting the mystery of God and the deity of Messiah is in the whole metanarrative of the scriptures, not the single propositional statements there in.**

In order to make our story more than just one of many we need to deal directly with the soft post modern's confidence with truth. We start by recognizing that we are indeed all located in our culture, but demonstrate that we can move from our fixed culture ever closer to the horizon of truth. And as we move closer and closer we gain more understanding of the horizon we are looking at, much like Asymptote graphs can be used in calculus to work with non fixed numbers so closely that we can make them work like they were certain and located.

Perhaps an illustration may help here. We help the soft postmodern see that there are things which can be known well enough to treat them as though they were absolutely true. The probability of one falling to ones death if one walks out of a window on the 10th floor is high enough, that even if you don't know for sure that it will happen you operate as though it will. The more we see things fall from the 10th floor of a building and what happens to them, the more sure we are that we should not do it.

With humility in our story telling, we talk about our unique story and journey to faith. We make sure that we integrate into our personal story the larger metanarrative of Scripture.

We do it with wit and perception into the heart as well as the head of the one we are talking to. Part of telling our story is listening to others' stories and finding where our stories intersect.

Let me tell you a story:

I remember flying back from San Francisco with the first assistant to the mayor of San Francisco, on a five-hour flight. I listened to her story and what she was passionate about. She was working on a major speech for the mayor on the place of cities in our nation's recovery. Eventually she asked where I was going and what I do. Knowing full well that the person I was speaking to was a typical Jewish postmodern, I chose to cause some dissonance. Earlier in our conversation it was clear that she saw all Christians as right wing Republicans. So when asked, I responded by saying "I am a born again, Bible believing, you fill in the derogatory remarks Christian." After the chuckle, came her next statement: "But you are obviously Jewish." Rather than jump right into my testimony, I went back to her issues with the cities and talked about how the Scriptures spoke to the place of cities. I explained that the problem of injustice is the problem of the Fall. I brought up the place of the cities of refuge in the Scriptures and how they represented a place for justice and grace. I pointed out how God was indeed interested in redeeming justice and the place of Israel in that plan.

At this point she asked if she could take out her computer and take some notes. This gave me a chance to deal with the direct felt need she had expressed, and to introduce the metanarrative that directs my life. I explained that my faith in Jesus was because I found that only the story of the God-Man giving his life to make right what is so wrong in this world fit my understanding of the world. I had been a member of SDS and thought that the solutions to man's problems were in revolution. I discovered the real problems are with in the heart of man, and only our creator could solve that problem. The incarnation, death, burial, and resurrection of the Son were the only way both God's justice and grace could be fully revealed. The deity of Messiah is imbedded in the narrative.

I know that there are many here who would take issue with calling themselves Christians. I find that the issue is not really about our labels, but about whom we really are. If you are Jewish, what ever you call yourself will be filled with the meaning you bring to the label. Labels will be redefined.

In another event I might have used another label to get behind the filters. On another trip I met a young Jewish woman who studied at Yeshiva University. She, unlike the woman in my last story, was very committed to her Jewish identity, and yet was also a post-modern. Our conversation started around our flight being delayed, and continued on to stories about our travels; she had just come back from Israel. I told her of my first time in Israel at her age and how I had volunteered on kibbutz, and we then talked about the book she was reading. I told her I had just finished reading "The Halachic Man" by Soloveitchik, and how unhappy I was it with it.

This opened up our conversation about the place of the Law in the Scriptures, and that led to how to interpret the text. She became very animated when we talked about hermeneutics, and was fascinated by the intent of the author as a key to understanding.

Her interest in better understanding the text, gave me an opening to show that the interpretation of any part must be consistent with the meaning of the whole. From there it was easy to walk her through the larger story of Creation, Fall, Redemption, and Consummation. I pointed out how there was a messianic hope that ran from the Law, Prophets and Writings. I went on to show her that the overall message of our Scriptures was the restoration of the *Malchut*- and that the King we are seeking to rule over us is none other that Ha Shem Himself. We had gone too far into our stories to stop listening. What a joy to be able to have someone so far on the Jewish side of the hyphen truly listen to the gospel.

Do you see how I used the metanarrative to help communicate the deity of Messiah? It was different in both stories but part of the greater story. In the first story, it was not hard to communicate the Fall; she knew there was evil in the world. She may not have taken personal responsibility for it, but she knew something was wrong. Connecting her understanding of the Fall, to the larger story is where I started.

With the second person I shared with her a common story, the Scriptures. It was helping my young Yeshiva student see how the text itself pointed to a transcendent God who was immanent. As we communicate the metanarrative the deity question will naturally fall into place and we deal with any objections at that point.

It is commonly understood that in order to effectively communicate to people who think they know what you have to say, you should not fulfill their expectations. I do not mean that you should lie or misrepresent who and what you believe. Rather, you should not answer with what is expected, and find a way to surprise the one you are talking to with your answer. That is why in my first story I used the very label that the listener would have least expected to hear.

Beyond the labels is the issue of meaning, and we have a story that answers the questions of meaning. It is not so much that we need to prove the Jewishness of our message about Jesus, as much as we need to make sure that our entire message communicates meaning to the listener. Depending on where on the axis we find them, our approach to the telling of the story varies to some degree.

I am also suggesting that to effectively communicate the mystery of God and the deity of Messiah to a Post-modern Jewish person, we should create communities where relationships are formed, stories shared and lived out.

The post-modern Jew is looking for the same thing that the post-modern gentile is looking for: meaning. For the most part they are looking for it not in propositional statements but in relationships. One of the governing principles in post-modern life is the community. It is here that the propositional truths of our faith must be lived out. We are to create *chavurahs* of meaning in which the metanarrative is told, repeated and fleshed out, where the Holy Spirit can work on the mind and heart of the person and the inevitable truth of the nature and person of the Messiah is understood within the larger story of redemption and consummation.

I applaud my friend Akiva's suggestion about creating communities with distinct Jewish behaviors and not just to evangelize. Certainly one of the bywords of the post-modern world is authenticity. If it is not authentic it will not be effective. I would take issue with my friend with his use of the word "pushing" when referring to other methods of proclamation. One can be authentic and effective when using other forms of communication.

Moving now on to what these communities should look like, there are a few specific things that these communities should have. These suggestions are birth out of a Shabbat fellowship that has been meeting in my home for the last three years, made up of both Jewish and gentile post moderns.

This fellowship has had a significant testimony to number of young Jewish post-moderns. And although most of the above observations made in this paper are most relevant to American Jews, many Israelis traveling in the US have been touched by the Shabbat fellowship.

1. The communities should have times of liturgical worship. The post-modern is drawn to the ancient. In line with authenticity, the worship should reflect the Jewish forms that the community is used to. The forms should not be artificial, but reflect the community's understanding of its Jewishness. This means that in certain communities the forms will follow more closely to the traditional forms of the synagogue whereas in other communities the forms might be more creative and will explore new ways to express old forms. These times of worship need not be in a traditional auditorium setting, but might work better around a table of food. A word about forms: There has been a debate among our messianic community regarding the use of rabbinic forms. I think that when it comes to life cycle events and calendar events, we must start with what have been historic behaviors. It is foolish to think that one can call something Jewish if it does not have some antecedent within historic Jewish behaviors. Given that creativity is one of the hallmarks of the post-modern generation, we should be creative in developing these historic forms for new communities. In our home we light the traditional Sabbath candles and recite the blessings for the challah and wine. We also sing Shabbat songs.

2.   The worship should be Christocentric; it must include worship that is reflective of the early faith community of the Messiah. By making our worship Christocentric and by focusing on the Father and the Son, we cover both Creator and Redeemer; this helps communicate the metanarrative. In our home Y'shua is part of all our prayers.

3.   These communities should be intentional in making hangout time for nothing more than hanging out and sharing stories. In our home people stay for hours just talking, playing music and board games. Many find their way to our front porch to continue discussing the text, and arguing about other meanings that may be found in the text.

4.   The Scriptures should be held within the community as authoritative in understanding faith and practice. There should be certain humility to approaching the text and the place of faith as well as reason to how one submits to God. There should be a time when the community encounters the hearing and expounding of the Word in a context of community, where discussion is encouraged. We need to avoid didactic pronouncements. We look at one section of the parsha for that week and look to how it points to the large story of scripture. Discussion is encouraged.

5.   Building into the community the telling of stories that relate to the roots of one's faith, connecting the community to a larger historic community and pre-Yavneh Judaism.

6.   These communities need to be connected to projects of social justice, like soup kitchens or making sandwiches to distribute to local homeless people, or direct help in Jewish causes, i.e., service in places where Jewish people are in need. Many in our group serve in soup kitchens, and have traveled for short-term ministry projects.

Through the efforts of Life in Messiah, Chosen People Ministries and Jews for Jesus a young Israeli that started attending out Shabbat fellowships did come to faith, my wife had the privilege of reaping the work of the whole community's witness. The young Israeli wanted the Shabbat Fellowship to be at his baptism, as he saw the Fellowship as his community of faith. It was glorious and all three ministries participated. He is now making application to attend Israel School of the Bible. It was through our walking together and living out the whole story that our friend came to see who the real Y'shua is.

The points listed above are only a few of the ways our communities will look as we speak to our post-modern Jewish sisters and brothers. I hope this short paper will stir up the wiser and more experienced of our numbers to add more to the list.

In the last analysis, communicating the Deity of Messiah to post-modern Jewish people is going to be imbedded in the communicating of the whole of our story and redeemed lives. The truth of the Gospel and the person of Jesus has passed through many periods of time and impacted our people in each age. His Spirit will not fail to make inroads into this current age.

COMMUNICATING THE DEITY OF YESHUA TO POSTMODERN JEWS

Akiva Cohen, Ph.D.

Former Dean of the Israel College of the Bible

אני מאמין באמונה שלמה שהבורא יתברך שמו אינו גוף ולא ישיגוהו משיגי
הגוף ואין לו שום דמיון כלל

I believe with complete faith that the Creator, blessed be His Name, is not corporeal, and that He is beyond all corporeal concepts, and there is nothing at all comparable to Him.

> —Maimonides, article no. 3 from his "Thirteen Articles of Faith" 12th Century CE[1]

"The Christian doctrines of the Incarnation and the Trinity present two main challenges to traditional Jewish study. One challenge is that the narrative of God's incarnation in one Jew belongs to a history that Jews do not share and cannot accept as part of their story. In this case, the Christian doctrine of the Incarnation appears comprehensible but simply wrong: the event did not occur. A second challenge is that the doctrine of God's having three identities appears incomprehensible: the Jewish biblical record does not speak of God in a way that allows us to characterize His nature as a relation among Father, Son, and Holy Spirit. . . . The traditional Jewish response is therefore to walk away from any discussion of such things . . . we must, instead, find a way to reason Jewishly about them."[2]

> —P. Ochs, in *Christianity in Jewish Terms*

"This final word of the credo of Jesus [the *Shem'a*] and all his brothers and sisters in the flesh, *echad,* which demythologizes and disdains every polytheism, appears to this very day in every Jewish prayer book in large-size bold print, for the final letter, daleth, can purely optically only all too easily be misread as resh—which would change 'One God' to 'another God' (*acher*), which according to rabbinic opinion could call forth the end of the world."[3]

—P. Lapide, in *Jewish Monotheism and Christian Trinitarian Doctrine*

"It is pleasing to know, that in our Land, this sign will never appear as a cross, rather it will always be slightly tilted to the side (see illustration). The reason for this is that we are living in a Jewish State."

—Israeli Driver's Manual 2010 (translated from the Hebrew)

My task in this session is to offer some suggestions as to how we may communicate the mystery of Yeshua's Deity with our 'postmodern Jewish community.'[4] My modest goal in this paper is to simply point to some of the signs on the postmodern Jewish road and offer some 'driving tips.'

The literature and prevalence of Postmodernism's (PM) influence on contemporary culture is vast. In a nutshell, PM is the rejection of several claims: the claim that truth is universal, absolute, and knowable, and that language is capable of conveying truth. PM deconstructs language as merely 'semiotics' (i.e., here: random signs resulting in language-games[5]). Truth claims are deconstructed as only 'socially constructed' and thus relative.[6] PM also rejects the heritage of the Western Canon of Literature (classic literature) and the Judeo-Christian meta-narratives[7] (the over-arching biblical stories for both Jews and Christians) as political texts that seek to maintain the oppression of 'minority voices.'[8] PM argues for dialogue with other community stories as all equally valid and '*true*' for each community.

I will begin with a cursory sample of two PM Jewish thinkers and then turn to the social characteristics of the current generation of youth growing up in the PM context. This will serve as an indication of the cultural soil with which we are seeking to be engaged. Then I will offer some suggestions as to how to communicate the Deity of Yeshua to the PMJ community.

Postmodernisms' Strange Jewish Garments: Doing Teshuvah and Wearing Sh atnez? [9]

According to Daniel Breslauer:

Jews in this new type of [postmodern] world require a new mode of constructing a Jewish identity, an

identity that is both recognizably Jewish but fluid
enough to evolve with time . . . Perhaps the most
important marker of such Judaism will be their lack
of 'religion,' their rejection of bonds preventing a
freely creative betrayal of the past. . . . Reading
Jewish stories as a means to criticize modernity, for
example, retains traditional sources but uses them in
postmodern ways. The stories that religion has
traditionally utilized to unite lives and provide a
fastening point for adherents no longer seem to
command attention or belief.[10]

Breslauer represents an extreme postmodern proposal,
namely, the creation of Judaism "without religion." Breslauer
argues that skepticism is already present in the Tanakh as
evidenced by the two versions of the Creation story in Genesis. In
Genesis 1:1–2:4 we have an evolution of undifferentiated darkness
to successive stages of differentiation culminating in the creation
of humanity. However, "Gen 2:4–3:24, tells of a devolution from a
complete and perfect beginning."[11] Breslauer notes, "both are
equally authoritative," and goes on to argue for continuing
examples (e.g., the schools of Hillel and Shammai; Ashkenazic
and Sephardic Jewish practice).[12]

Breslauer rejects all attempts at confining Jewish identity to
not only the traditional Jewish mindset, but also to the modern
worldview that argues for objective truth. "The choice of one act
to refer to Jewishness rather than another arises from the
subjective experience for the actor but is drawn from a community
of symbols and possibilities."[13] Breslauer's range of choices
includes not only the traditionally forbidden, but also an
unabashed exaltation in cultural *sh atnez*, "mixing types with
abandon."[14]

Breslauer enlists Buber's 'I-Thou'[15] theology applying it to
the postmodern value of 'awareness of the other' that calls for
tolerance of the other. According to Breslauer, such tolerance
demands a Judaism "that moves beyond religion," by which he
means freeing Jews from their tie to community with only other
Jews. Breslauer believes that only such a movement away can
facilitate a return.[16] Although I understand Breslauer's dilemma as
representing the PM Jewish search for meaning, one wonders if

such 'movement-away' really has the Jewish and spiritual vitality to bring about the envisaged 'return' of which he speaks.[17]

If Breslauer represents the radical edge of Jewish response to modernity's demise, Stephen Kepnes represents something of its creative forefront. Kepnes and his PMJ colleagues gladly dispense with 'the hegemony of the historical' by which Kepnes means that the dominant Jewish approach to texts (their dating, location, the meaning of the words, etc.) has now given way to *semiotics* (here: words as [random] 'signifiers' of the 'signified'), *discourse theory* (how writing, texts and discourse shape identity), and *deconstruction*[18] (every text contains contradictory meanings and thus is open to endless interpretation).[19] The exegetical application of these new theoretical approaches is often brought into contact with the biblical and rabbinic schools of interpretation.[20]

Kepnes sees postmodern Jewish thought as

> a kind of *teshuvah*, a return. . . . Jewish modernism at
> its root involves . . . a repression of the Jewish for the
> sake of the modern. . . . Modern Jews tried to replace
> Judaism with ethics and rationality . . . [P]ostmodern
> Judaism is its [Modern Judaism's] repair, return, and
> rehabilitation . . . a return to Torah, to revelation, to
> theology; it means a reappreciation, in a myriad ways,
> of rabbinic Judaism. . . . Postmodern Jews, Christians,
> and Hindus are no longer concerned with elevating
> their language-game to the status of the one true
> religion.[21]

It immediately obtains that on the one hand Yeshua-centered-Judaism shares some similarities with PMJ and on the other hand some extreme dissimilarities as illustrated in the following table. I have bolded concepts that have common discourse between both communities (even if *understood differently by each community*).

	Postmodern Jewish Community	MJ Community
Text-based 'readings'	*Open Canon of texts:* **Tanakh, Rabbinic Corpus,** **Hasidic** stories, Modern Jewish Literature Kabbalah, Secular Texts	*Closed Authoritative Canon:* **Tanakh** and the New Testament *Open Canon of (i)inspired Texts:* **Rabbinic Corpus, Hasidic Stories**
Hermeneutic Employed	Semiotics, Discourse Theory, Deconstruction, Feminist and Queer Theory, etc., **Rabbinic Hermeneutics,** Rejection of all meta-narratives **Community story** as one legitimating local worldview among many other diverse communities	Grammatico-Historical and Narrative Theology, **Rabbinic Hermeneutics** *Yeshua as the center* of the traditional Jewish meta-narrative God's Truth (Scriptures) as our **Community story** establishing a local and global incarnational expression of Messiah's body
Spirituality	Privatization of the sacred Sacred/Secular dichotomy, return to the (*reinterpreted*) tradition, **liturgy and Jewish lifestyle,** God of Israel as Jewish myth **Community-based**	Holistic view of the sacred Return to elements of (*reinterpreted*) tradition, **liturgy and Jewish lifestyle** God of Israel as Reality/Truth **Community-based**

MJ, for the most part, embraces a 'modernist' grammatico-historical hermeneutic re the historical Jesus, a modernist belief in objective truth and a pre-modernist belief in God and his 'supernatural' intervention into the natural order ('miracles'). Our faith rests upon the historical reality of the physical resurrection of Yeshua from the dead[22] and the actual indwelling of the Ruach HaKodesh as the seal of our faith.[23] Our hermeneutic stands at polar opposites to that of PMJ's private ritual piety, which is based upon a naturalist understanding of life.[24] MJ 'readings' of authoritative community texts (the Tanakh and the NT) and PMJ 'readings' (of eclectic and all equally [un]authoritative texts) cannot, for us, "both be the words of the living

God." Although the dominant hermeneutic in our modern movement has been more closely aligned with the Grammatico-Historical and Narrative Theology approaches, a promising approach towards finding common discourse with the PMJ community is through the use of Midrash. Midrash holds much promise as a fruitful rabbinic genre with which our community needs to become more familiar. A better acquaintance with Midrash can also teach us how to express our own theological perspectives in more Jewish ways.[25]

From a cultural standpoint, what 'language' may we employ to communicate our message to PMJs, and specifically the topic of this Symposium, the Deity of Yeshua? In order to answer that question we need to situate PMJs sociologically. Here I am especially thinking about the current up-and-coming generation who will be society's next cultural influencers.

The Social Location of (Young) Postmodern Jews

I believe that our communication of Yeshua's Deity needs to take place in Yeshua-Centered Jewish Community, engaged in Yeshua-Centered Jewish lifestyle and Yeshua-Centered Jewish belief.

Let me begin by briefly situating today's postmodern Jewish community in the larger categories of community (קהילה), lifestyle (הלכה) and faith (אמונה/belief) within the context of Jewish history and culture.[26] According to the late Mordecai Kaplan, z.l. founder of Reconstructionist Judaism, there are three possible ways of identifying with a religious community: *by belonging, behaving and believing.* Kaplan argued for 'belonging' as the primary Jewish category of Jewish identification, so that what we Jews believe and how we behave serve supportive roles to a shared destiny and sense of kinship.[27]

For the traditional Jewish community one's maintenance of a Jewish lifestyle is what defines one's *belonging* to the Jewish people. The theological outworking of Kaplan's perspective explains the emphasis of the Reconstructionist movement upon *community* as determinative for defining behavior.

Clearly, PM Jews are closer to the Reconstructionist/Reform *community-view* of Jewish identity than the more traditional *behavior-based* view of Jewish identity.[28] As we explore Jewish *belonging* the attraction of the younger generation to *community* (their Synagogue/Beit Midrash community connection is often 'Starbucks, Facebook,' etc.)[29] should not be missed by our attempts at 'connection.' Here I am thinking as a member of the last wave of baby boomers that overlap the Gen X'ers.[30]

Our audience is essentially generation X'ers, (who invented Google, MySpace, Facebook, Starbucks, etc.) and generation Y'ers,[31] who live in those physical and cyber-spaces and have now taken their generation to the next level of instant-and-continual-connection through *Twitter*.[32] So we have a technologically savvy, connection-obsessed generation whose postmodern education has conditioned them to doubt not only the authority of the Bible, but to view any meta-narrative[33] or claim to transcendent morality as simply a social construct.[34] Furthermore, for the most part their spirituality happens in/with less formally Jewish spaces/texts than Synagogue/Siddur.[35] How do we communicate with this mindset?[36] While any appeal to the Authority of the Tanakh (let alone an attempt to speak authoritatively to a PMJ from the NT!) has lost its binding address with this generation; we can engage PMJs with our story and our community.

Since our faith is based on *stories* about Yeshua, I believe that the Gospels are as relevant as ever as literary vehicles to communicate the truth of our faith. In addition to the Gospels, our personal 'life-story' provides us with the opportunity of sharing how we have found (Jewish) meaning in life. Our MJ communities are the social expression of community that provide opportunity for us to offer 'connection' with PMJs.[37] This may be likened to the current *Havurah* movement and its obvious appeal to young Jewish singles and couples. The motto of the National Havurah Committee is illustrative of my argument for communicating Yeshua's Deity from the place of authentic Jewish community: אין התורה נקנית אלה בחבורה "The Torah Cannot be Acquired Except through Fellowship."[38]

Another important development that continues to impact the Jewish community is a current interest in Yeshua's *Jewishness* as a result of the "Third Quest for the historical Jesus."[39] There are no doubt many Jewish University students who, as the result of taking some "Intro to Christianity" religion class, have come to find out about the interest of NT scholars in the Jewishness of Yeshua. Our 'assignment' as has been defined for this session, is "to suggest ways to communicate that Yeshua is more than just a Jewish teacher/Rabbi," i.e., his status as Deity.

I am suggesting in this paper that we cannot compartmentalize the communication of a *belief* apart from connection with a *community*. As PMJs come into contact with our story and with our community and its small Havurah-type groups, they are brought to the place where encounter *of* Yeshua (in all his fullness including his Deity) can begin to take place.[40]

However, even with our best efforts at building our MJ communities as part of our nexus of *belonging, behaving* and *believing*, I am cognizant of the fact that such an approach is viewed as repulsive and deceitful to the guardians of our wider Jewish community. I can easily articulate their typical objection: "Sure, reel them in to your wide-eyed 'loving' community and expose our assimilated and vulnerable Jewish youth to the Gospels and your *pseudo-Judaism*, and then spring the trap on them as you baptize them out of the Jewish community and into your thinly-disguised Christian community!"[41]

Here I gladly acknowledge that I strongly identify with those in our movement who are laboring to create authentic Jewish community. It is only from such a community setting that we can communicate the Deity of Yeshua in a properly Jewish manner.[42] This may be illustrated by referring to both the manner and the content of traditional Jewish prayer. Here "the medium is the message," namely, prayer as a community expression. This community ethos may be seen clearly in the *Shemoneh Esreh,* the Jewish community prayer *par excellence.*[43]

In this ancient prayer 'Israel' speaks to God both individually and corporately. The six corporate benedictions (#10-#15) focus exclusively upon community needs demonstrating that Jewish theology is essentially part of a community-based-liturgical construct. By the time we come to benediction #15 and pray for the צמח דוד עבדך (the branch of David your servant) to speedily flourish, it is abundantly clear that we are praying for Israel's Messianic King to bring about Israel's deliverance, for which *we* have waited all day.[44]

Now as to our challenge: Are there viable ways to bridge the gap between where most PMJ youth live and the Jewish heritage with which most of them are at best only vaguely acquainted? Of course the non-Messianic Jewish community faces the same challenges, namely, how does one hold forth a Judaism that is winsome to young PM Jews? Our answer is: come and meet Yeshua and his community and you will discover *why* your being Jewish actually matters! In other words Yeshua is (for us) the existential factor that (or better 'who') is able to connect PMJs to the God of Israel, to their heritage and to their calling to bear witness to him as Jews.

Many secular Diasporic[45] and Israeli youth are returning in various creative ways to Jewish heritage. They are hungry for connection with Jewish heritage and Jewish spirituality expressed in Jewish community. So if we have been reading the road-signs on the postmodern Jewish highway, we need to consider how to use *story* to communicate the Deity of Yeshua and to strive towards authentic Jewish *community* as the place from which we 'do' our theology and live it out. The Gospels provide an incremental revelation of Yeshua's Deity by their presentation of his words and actions, both of which receive a retroactive and definitive vindication by his resurrection. Exposure to Yeshua's teaching of Torah[46], his actions[47], his resurrection,[48] and our MJ communities are the invitation to young PMJs to 'encounter' Yeshua as Deity.[49]

What is the Concept/Doctrine We are Seeking to Communicate?

My brief paper will not allow me to address the question of how to communicate the Deity of Yeshua in terms of its *theological* articulation. I only offer here some brief comments. This central doctrine of our faith is agreed upon by virtually all Messianic Jews. Yet, *how* to explain that belief does not enjoy as much of a consensus. On the one hand, it is perhaps easier to say what we do *not* believe. We are certainly not advocating an adoptionist-type Christology that argues that Yeshua *became* divine.[50] It was the 'low' Christology of some first-century Jewish followers of Yeshua that provoked Patristic scorn of the 'Church of the Circumcision,' who they accused of being "paupers in their views about Messiah."[51]

Some in our movement may claim that the easiest way out of this difficulty is simply to state, "What the NT teaches is what we affirm." Such an approach tends to focus more upon Yeshua's functional subordination to the Father rather than upon his ontological status. By 'ontology' I mean who Yeshua is in the nature of his *being*, not just the way he *functions*, e.g., as the *representative* (Shaliah) of the Father. However, it is naïve to think that we can escape the task of theological articulation when trying to *explain* to someone *what* we believe about Yeshua's status vis-à-vis God without engaging in theological expression. When a Jew asks you "Is Yeshua God?" the minute you open your mouth and attempt to articulate your answer, you are 'doing' theology. So the only question becomes what is the *quality* of our theological expression, not, whether or not we think we need to engage in theological reflection and articulation.

Among the main voices of the MJ community, there are different approaches as to how we can best stay true to our calling as Jews and also remain true to what the NT teaches about Yeshua.[52] Some MJs would argue for a Maimonidian-type of negative theology and the kabbalistic idea of the אין סוף Ein Sof, ('The One who has no end') when talking about God, (or more accurately not talking about Him!). Yet, it is incorrect to claim that such an approach reflects a type of pure Jewish conceptual space. It is widely acknowledged that Maimonides was heavily influenced by Greek philosophical thought via the Muslim Arabic translations of the classical Greek philosophers.[53] Second, to claim that we cannot talk about God's positive attributes is an affront to God's "last [definitive] word" and revelation concerning His Son who is the exact representation of God's being (see Heb. 1:2-3; John 1:14, 18).[54]

The "high Christology" of the NT requires us to deepen our own understanding of who Yeshua is, and how to best explain that understanding to the wider Jewish community. E.g., it is now widely discussed by many scholars that Paul apparently had no problem inserting Yeshua into the *Shem a* (1 Cor. 8:6). And all are familiar with the way John begins his Gospel with the pre-incarnate *Logos* who was *with* God and *was* God and *through whom* all things were created (1:1–3). This same *Logos* became flesh (1:14).[55] How do we explain *that* to our Jewish contemporaries outside our MJ community?

Aside from the polemical use of rabbinic literature from medieval to modern times, there have been few creative proposals employing Jewish/rabbinic categories to articulate our understanding of the person of Yeshua. However, recent developments indicate promise for more mature MJ theological reflection on the subject of Christology.[56]

In our attempt to recover Jewish community and Jewish space, we need not be intimidated by the wider Jewish community's de-legitimation of our affirmation of Yeshua's Deity. It is not Greek (read: Gentile) idolatrous conceptual space to claim that Yeshua is Deity; rather, this is Hebraic revelation that Yeshua said is "from my Father in Heaven" (Matt. 16:17).[57] Furthermore, "in the fullness of time" the mystery latent in the Tanakh became explicit through the (Jewish) Apostolic witness.[58] In spite of our being misunderstood by the wider Jewish community our faith is still a monotheistic one. It is what Larry Hurtado calls a "mutation" of monotheism. Hurtado calls its earliest form "binitarian," that is Yeshua is worshiped alongside God, as opposed to "di-theism," which is the worship of two gods.[59]

Connecting with Postmodern Jews

Returning to my subject for this session, how do we communicate the truth of Yeshua's Deity with Jewish post-moderns? As I have already stated, there is no substitute for the hard work of community reflection and dialogue. In terms of how to best understand the way that PMs (including Jews) think, I believe we can learn some lessons from the Emerging Church[60] (EC) and its attempt to 'connect' with the PM mindset. However, we also need to be warned by the jettisoning of the historic faith by some of its more extreme proponents. Some positive aspects of the EC are: preference for dialogical witness, a focus on 'missional living' (as a result of their core conviction of the incarnation of Yeshua) and a focus upon temporal and social issues as opposed to a fixation on 'eternal salvation' at the expense of community connection and impact. Here the call is for a balance between 'proposition' and 'incarnation,' what Darrell Bock has called the need to retain both sides of the double helix (incarnational living and propositional truth).[61] I think we also can learn something from the EC's community ethos. For the type of thinking here, see Paul Hiebert's application of set theory to missiology, i.e., the distinction between a "bounded-set" (emphasis upon 'in' and 'out' definitions of whose 'in' the group and who is 'out') vs. a 'centered set' (although still holding to a clear sense of who is in the group and who is not; the emphasis is upon a relational movement towards the center).[62]

However, we need to stay clear of the difference between 'contextualization' and 'relativization.' Paul was willing to tell the Greek philosophers at Mars Hill that the God of Israel *is* the "Unknown God" that they had been ignorantly worshiping. He then filled that symbol/sign with *biblical content*, even as he employed some extra-biblical citations from their culture. What I am arguing for here is that in our attempts at communicating Yeshua's Deity in a Jewish manner (e.g., *Logos, Memra, Shekinah, Metatron, Sar HaPanim, Tzimzum*, etc.,)[63] we must remain faithful to the biblical witness in our use of contextualization.

Although Postmodernism has offered this generation new paradigms and ways of thinking humbly about life's big questions and what it means to live out one's faith; only the challenge of Yeshua to "take up one's cross and follow him," has the existential vitality to impart a vision worth living and dying for. God does not reveal his Son to the merely curious. But to those who are sincere seekers after the Truth, God is faithful to reveal the identity of his Son. And if there is anything that PMJs are lacking, it is a coherent vision of why their lives are ultimately significant. If we believe anything, it is that Yeshua is the existential answer to that need. Yeshua and the wonder and mystery of his person as Israel's promised Messiah: his pre-existent glory with the Father, his incarnation, life, call to self-denial and to "follow," his death and resurrection. That is our "story" about Yeshua, including his Deity. And this story needs to be told in the framework of Israel's history and destiny.

I must, of necessity, close even as I have barely begun to explore the issues under discussion. I believe that we need to be clear about what we believe; namely, that Yeshua is *the pre-existent and eternal Son of God.* Furthermore, our worship of the God of Israel *and* Yeshua remains in the category of monotheism.[64] It behooves us to 'speak' to fellow PMJs by demonstrating authentic Jewish community (in its many authentic—more traditional and less traditional—Jewish expressions), sharing our story (the Gospels and our personal-life stories), and allowing those 'encounters' with our community and story to lead to encounter with Him.

James Dunn, in his book, *A New Perspective on Jesus,* in which he discusses the much-publicized "Quest for the historical Jesus," states:

> As is well known, the quest began by way of reaction against the Christ of Christian dogma. The Christ of the Chalcedonian creed, "perfect in Godhead and perfect in manhood, truly God and truly man," was just too unreal a human being. The Pantocrator, the world ruler, of Eastern iconography was too far removed from the man who walked the shores of the Sea of Galilee. How can we believe in such a Christ when, according to the Letter to the Hebrews, he was able "to sympathize with our weaknesses [and] . . . in every respect has been tempted as we are" (Heb. 4:15)? It is the human Jesus, the one who truly knew and experienced the reality of everyday existence in first-century Palestine, the Jesus who lived among the poor, who counted people like Martha and Mary as his close companions, who was known as "a friend of tax collectors and sinners" (Matt. 11:19), that we prefer to

hear about. Is he not a more meaningful Savior than the almost mechanistic God-man or the remote Pantocrator? No wonder the cult of Mary, the mother of Christ, became so popular when her Son was so divine and so remote. The heart yearning for comfort and an inspiring role model needed a mother figure to intercede with this awe-inspiring Christ, needed to rediscover the human Jesus behind the divine Christ.[65]

Dunn's insight here is instructive to our community and to this Symposium. Namely, that it makes more sense to speak of Yeshua in terms of his *Jewish humanity* and then build upon that. We might call such an approach a 'bottom-up-Jewish' Christology, rather than a 'top-down-Creedal' Christology. If postmodernity and the Emerging church are supposed to teach us anything, perhaps it is that God is not under any obligation to follow our formulas. Nor is He obligated to our sense of how we 'think' someone (especially a *Jewish* someone) is supposed to come to comprehend the truth of Yeshua's Deity.[66]

To illustrate this on a personal note, I remember as vividly as if it were last month, that in 1979 as a 19 year old High School grad, I stood gazing in awe at the "Day of Judgment" fresco of Michelangelo magnificently painted on the huge side wall of the Sistine Chapel. As a Jewish adolescent trying to decipher the scene before my eyes, the thought began to dawn on me, that the guy sitting on the throne was, well, err . . . yes, Jewish!

Only moments earlier I had entered St. Peter's Cathedral spellbound at the perplexing scene before my eyes: Yeshua and his nail-pierced hands and feet sprawled in serene resignation upon Miriam's lap. Time seemed to stop as I starred at the uncannily real-to-life depiction carved by Michelangelo out of a slab of white-marble. Those 'encounters' with Yeshua constituted a formative experience that set my feet on a focused two-year journey that culminated upon my knees before the revelation of the Son of God.

My point is that I was as equally intrigued by the depiction of Yeshua as "truly God and truly man," the "Pantocrator," (although those theological terms would have been completely foreign to me) as I was with the far-more-accessible Yeshua lying so peacefully upon his mother's lap.

Thus, I really don't think there are any *formulae* that we can employ in communicating the Deity of Yeshua with our PM Jewish community. God can and does use, as he sees fit, any and every means at his disposal (e.g., our prayers and His good pleasure) to reveal Yeshua to the sincere and seeking heart.[67]

ENDNOTE

1. It has been noted that unlike the centrality of 'doctrine' to Christian theology and catechism, Maimonides' 13 principles of faith appear at the end of the Siddur's *Shahrit* service and the poetic version (*Yigdal*) sung at the beginning of Shahrit and by some at the end of *Ma'ariv* and the *Musaf* on Shabbat. This reflects the fact that the 13 principles are considered an optional part of the prayer service (Hasidic and many Sephardic Jews do not even sing *Yigdal* since in their eyes it diminishes the sanctity of the 613 commandments) indicating the peripheral and optional role of 'creed' in Jewish liturgy/theology. For the priority of 'commandment' over 'creed' in Judaism, see the typical ethos reflected in the following midrash, "Would that they abandoned Me, but kept My Torah—since by occupying themselves therewith, the light which it contains would have led them back to the right path" (Intro to Lam Rab, commenting on Jer 16:11).

2. P. Ochs, in T. Frymer-Kensky, et al., eds., *Christianity in Jewish Terms*, (Theology in a Postcritical Key; Boulder: Westview, 2000), 59. Och's mention of his difficulty in comprehending the Christian claim for the Trinity in the Tanakh should challenge us to careful reflection and articulation of our understanding of the subject. See B. Marshall, "Israel: Do Christians Worship the God of Israel?" in *Knowing the Triune God: The Work of the Spirit in the Practices of the Church* (Grand Rapids: Eerdmans, 2001), 231–64.

3. P. Lapide, "Jewish Monotheism," in Jewish Monotheism and Christian Trinitarian Doctrine: A Dialogue by Pinchas Lapide and Jürgen Moltmann (trans. L. Swidler; Eugene: Wipf and Stock, 2002 [1979]), 29.

4. Mark Twain's purported response to the announcement of his premature obituary in a newspaper that "the report was greatly exaggerated!" may be applied to Postmodernity: its burial of Modernity is premature. Note the brilliant tongue-in-cheek comment by one of my former teachers at Tel Aviv University, (in response to a postmodern ethno-musicologist guest lecturer from the USA), "Is what you are asking us to do, to simply go down to the Library and move all the books from the History section into the Fiction section?" The literature on Postmodernism is vast and impinges on all disciplines. Postmodernism in the West tends to focus more upon epistemology (the nature and limits of knowledge) whereas the European version has a stronger focus upon literary theory. The personification of the evil imperialist perpetrator of modernism: the 'dead white male' is now hackneyed to say the least. There are clearly positive aspects of postmodernism: openness to the 'other,' i.e., the 'minority voice,' awareness and analysis of 'interested' readings (read: 'white-male,' 'political,' 'chauvinist,' 'colonialist,' 'imperialist,' etc.) and literary works; pedagogical strategies of empowerment (e.g., in a technological environment that provides educational access through distance-learning, electronic access to eLibraries, Wikipedia, Google, Twitter, etc.). However, postmodernism also has weaknesses, e.g., jettisoning the Western Canon of Classics in favor of the all-too-often kitsch

'minority voice' literature and art, and an obsession with deconstructing art and literature to expose the lurking colonial, sexual and racial oppression *intended* (!) by the author/artist. As I just hinted at, Postmodernism's main weakness, which needs to be patiently explained to any avid enthusiast, is that it is a self-contradictory worldview. If the claim is made that "all truth/meta-narratives/'readings' are subjective/relativistic/etc.," than why should I believe *that*? For some basic orientation to the subject and some Evangelical and Jewish responses, see S. J. Grenz, *A Primer on Postmodernism* (Grand Rapids: Eerdmans, 1996); M. Erickson, *Postmodernizing the Faith: Evangelical Responses to the Challenge of Postmodernism* (Grand Rapids: Baker, 1998); idem, *Truth or Consequences: the Promise and Peril of Postmodernism* (Downers Grove: InterVarsity, 2001); For the negative impact of Postmodernism upon Education and Art, see R. Kimball, *Tenured Radicals: How Politics has Corrupted Our Higher Education* (rev. ed.; Chicago: Ivan R. Dee, 1998); idem, *The Rape of the Masters: How Political Correctness Sabotages Art* (San Francisco: Encounter, 2004). For Jewish engagement with postmodernism, see nn. 10, 19–21.

5. The term 'language-games' (*Sprachspiel*) was coined by the philosopher, Ludwig Wittgenstein (of Jewish ancestry and considered by some as one of the most influential philosophers of the 20th century). Wittgenstein used this concept to speak of simple forms of language as illustrated by songs children sing but do not understand the meaning of the words. Words are used in their simplest sense in grammatical rules that are likened to a sort 'move' on a game board. Jean-François Lyotard applied Wittgenstein's language-games to his postmodern discussion of the multiplicity of communities of meaning. E.g., applying language-games to the concept of justice, "A modernist might ask: 'is this good?' But a postmodernist might ask 'who/what is it good *for*?" (i.e., all ideals and values are equally valid). See G. Ward, *Teach Yourself Postmodernism* (London: Hodder & Stoughton, 2003).

6. A. Mohler, Jr. offered this succinct definition in an informal discussion on the subject viewable at http://www.youtube.com/watch?v=gv6uxCch7oc Mohler elsewhere states, "As Michel Foucault—one of the most significant postmodern theorists—argued, all claims to truth are constructed to serve those in power. Thus, the role of the intellectual is to deconstruct truth claims in order to liberate the society." Cited from Mohler's article, "Ministry is Stranger Than it Used to Be: The Challenge of Postmodernism," accessible on his web site www.albertmohler.com Although Mohler's comments on postmodernism are helpful, his warnings concerning the Emerging Church need to be nuanced by writers like Scot McKnight whom I will reference later in this paper.

7. See n. 33 for a definition of meta-narrative.

8. These texts, however, can be deconstructed and thus reinterpreted and liberated from their traditional oppressive and political exploitation of the minority voices.

9. *Sh □atnez* refers to the prohibition in Scripture (Lev 19:19; Deut 21:11) of wearing a garment in which wool and linen have been spun, woven, or sown

together. See A. Steinsaltz, *The Talmud: A Reference Guide* (New York: Random House, 1989), s.v. "שעטנז".

10. S. Daniel Breslauer, *Creating a Judaism without Religion: A Postmodern Jewish Possibility* (Lanham: University Press of America, 2001), 8.

11. Ibid., 10.

12. This type of statement is typical of postmodernism's celebration of antinomies ("contradictions between two apparently equally valid principles").

13. Ibid., 13. For Breslauer, the "community of symbols" of which he speaks is clearly the universal community and not a distinctive Jewish one. Breslauer's range of Jewish 'possibilities' include his affirmation of the famous Israeli transvestite Dana International's employment of Jewish symbols in her lyrics so that in her betrayal of Jewish tradition she has created "a new Jewish reality, a new possibility for Jewish living." It appears that the only thing 'Jewish' about Breslauer's vision for a "Judaism without religion" is its trendy deconstruction of anything that remotely resembles identifiable Jewish identity.

14. Ibid., 16.

15. Buber's "I-Thou" theology refers to his classic work by that name in which he articulates his concept of dialogue. God the "Eternal Thou" is always addressing us through the experiences of life which in turn demand a response from us. This process of dialogue is one in which each partner affirms the 'presence' of the other.

16. Ibid., 23. Breslauer's 'deconstruction' of Buber hardly represents the latter's theology,—although Buber did embrace freedom from Jewish 'law' but not freedom from the divine summons to the 'I-Thou' relationship—which certainly did not seek to free Jews from Jews! The author's call for the integration of women is applauded by this author and I believe by our movement which places a premium upon the model of Yeshua and Paul's high view of women (despite Paul's feminist accusers of his alleged misogyny). Breslauer's call to be open to sexually displaced Jews regardless of their sexual orientation should also, for our community, follow Yeshua's compassionate engagement for the displaced other without affirming a lifestyle choice that is dishonoring to God (cf. John 8:1–11 Yeshua and the adulterous woman).

17. For a 'snapshot' of a Jewish application of the postmodern turn, see Breslauer's postmodern reclamation of the quaint Hasidic story by the 'modernist' writer S. Y. Agnon. The story focuses upon a Rabbi Ezekiel who, while travelling in an open wagon, sought to light his pipe. After repeated failed attempts due to a strong wind, the Rabbi then recites a tale about a former *rebbe*. The said *rebbe* Menachem sought to kindle the Sabbath lights but the wind from the window immediately blew out the candles. R. Menachem then went to the window and declared, 'Master of the World, isn't it true that I must light these candles for the Holy Sabbath?' Immediately the wind, continuing to blow outside, did not blow through the house. Rabbi Ezekiel then orders his pipe to be lit and the wind does not blow it out, upon which he exclaims, "Do not think that a great miracle has occurred. It is rather that the power of stories is so great that telling of a righteous man's acts has an efficacious affect." [How much more when we tell the stories of

Yeshua?!] Breslauer then deconstructs the story as illustrative of his 'Judaism without religion.' Rabbi Ezekiel's lighting of his pipe replaces a traditional Jewish ritual act (lighting of the Sabbath candles) and becomes *a private Jewish ritual act*. The value of the act is created by its association with a Jewish text (story). Finally, the myth of the supernatural has been replaced by the natural (R. Ezekiel disavows any miraculous element in his act of lighting his pipe) (ibid., 9).

18. Jacqes Derrida (b. 1930, d. 2004) the French-Algerian scholar (of Jewish descent), is best known for his writing on Deconstruction. Derrida focused upon the instability and indeterminacy of meaning resulting in a loss of authoritative interpretation of texts and their consequent similarity to an arbitrary game. Derrida called into question what he called "Logocentrism" which is the idea that a word is 'present' to us in our minds prior to its communication to others; that words communicate fixed meanings. Derrida calls this belief "the metaphysics of presence," something he considered was one of the great illusions of Western thought. For a concise summary of Derrida's thinking (which I have drawn from here), see S. Sim, *Derrida and the End of History* (New York: Icon, 1999).

19. S. Kepnes, ed., *Interpreting Judaism in a Postmodern Age* (New York: New York University Press, 1996), 3. Missing from Kepnes work is the current darling of literary theory: Queer theory. 'Queer theory' functions as a hermeneutic to facilitate 'queer' readings of texts. I.e., gay, lesbian and feminist perspectives. The late M. Foucault, one of several cult figures for PMs, is hailed as one of the leading theorists/exponents of this approach. Current publications indicative of this approach are, D. Boyarin, ed., *Queer Theory and the Jewish Question* (New York: Columbia University Press, 2003); G. Drinkwater, J. Lesser and D. Sheener, *Torah Queeries: Weekly Commentaries on the Hebrew Bible* (New York: New York University Press, 2009). The latter book notes the penetration of Queer Theory into Jewish mainstream by reporting, "*Torah Queeries* includes the voices of some of the most central figures in contemporary American Judaism today, from the rector of one of Conservative Judaisms seminaries to the president of a national rabbinic association, highlighting, in some ways, just how central the topic of lesbian, gay, bisexual, and transgender (LGBT) inclusion has become, at least in the American Jewish world" (p. 5). For anyone in our movement who may be so out of touch with where the current generation 'lives,' that your only reaction to this is that you find yourself disgusted by this subject (rather than moved with compassion for our lost Jewish community) what will you do with Jesus' embrace of tax-collectors, prostitutes, lepers and the Samaritan woman [i.e., LGBT, or HIV infected Jews]? After I wrote these words I came across R. Newman's, helpful perspective from his *Questioning Evangelism*, "Why Are Christians So Homophobic?" (chap. 8; see n. 49 for the full reference).

20. For the integration of modern literary theory with traditional Rabbinic texts, see S. A. Handelman, *The Slayers of Moses: The Emergence of Rabbinic Interpretation in Modern Literary Theory* (New York: University of New York Press, 1982).

21. S. Kepnes, P. Ochs and R. Gibbs, *Reasoning after Revelation: Dialogues in Postmodern Jewish Philosophy* (Theology in a Postcritical Key; Boulder: Westview, 1998), 25–26.

22. 1 Cor 15:14, "And if Christ has not been raised, then our preaching is futile and your faith is empty" (NET).

23. Ezek 36:27, "I will put my Spirit within you; I will take the initiative and you will obey my statutes and carefully observe my regulations"; John 14:17, "The Spirit of truth, whom the world cannot accept, because it does not see him or know him. But you know him, because he resides with you and will be in you"; Rom 8:9, "You, however, are not in the flesh but in the Spirit, if indeed the Spirit of God lives in you. Now if anyone does not have the Spirit of Christ, this person does not belong to him"; Eph 1:13, "And when you heard the word of truth (the gospel of your salvation)–when you believed in Christ–you were marked with the seal of the promised Holy Spirit." (NET)

24. Rabbi Ezekiel's invocation of the power of story and PMJs denial of the miraculous (see n. 17).

25. See the contribution of Carl Kinbar who succeeds in engaging in a fruitful interaction with Midrash and the theological vistas it can open up for the development of Messianic theological perspectives. C. Kinbar, "Israel, Interpretation, and the Knowledge of God: Engaging the Jewish Conversation," Hashivenu Forum, 2010. I would argue further, that in spite of our very different epistemological frameworks, both PMJs and MJs share—in the words of Kepnes cited above—"a reappreciation, in a myriad ways, of rabbinic Judaism."

26. For the following I am indebted to N. Gillman, *Sacred Fragments: Recovering Theology for the Modern Jew* (Jerusalem: JPS, 1990), xvii–xviii.

27. Among Kaplan's works his magnum opus is, *Judaism as a Civilization: Towards a Reconstruction of American-Jewish Life* (repr.; Philadelphia: JPS, 1994 [1934]).

28. For a provocative analysis of Judaism's lack of appeal to many postmodern American Jews, see T. Zahavy, "The Predicament of the Postmodern American Jew," in C. Selengut, ed., *Jewish Identity in the Postmodern Age: Scholarly and Personal Reflections* (St. Paul: Paragon, 1999), 235–48. Zahavy places the blame for the problem of viable Jewish identity upon the leadership of the Jewish community. Using a market metaphor Zahavy blames the "corporate executives" of Judaism for a defective "product." While recognizing Lubavitch talent at "product development" and marketing, as evidenced by their increasing "market share," Zahavy comments that the Messianic dying-rising version of a marginal sector of Lubavitch failed to realize they "were supposed to be developing Judaisms, not Christianities!" Zahavy maintains that "such products need to be pulled from the market for product redesign." Zahavy further sees what he calls Holocaust-and-Redemption-Judaism, where, for example the Nazis replace the Egyptians, as starting out well but that the product remains in the *development* phase due to its overwhelming horror which keeps its reality distant from most Jews who prefer to remember it in superficial ways. Zahavy, notes J. Neusner's claim that this type of Judaism does not have the power to "transform the inner life of the Jew" (as does the Judaism of the dual Torah according to Neunser).

How much more should our Yeshua-centered Judaism have 'market-appeal' to transform the inner man! Zahavy also comments on 'Cyber Jewry' as cyber communities where "Jews online study Torah together, argue about politics, inter-marriage and the like, exchange recipes, find their roots, make dates and even find spiritual solace" (p. 245).

29. The Israeli equivalents are also Facebook (Hebrew interface) type connection sites and the ubiquitous Israeli coffee houses.

30. No, I never saw the Beatles in concert; yes I bought the Abbey Road LP, and turned my parents' stereo speakers way up to hear McCartney's awesome base lines and did the same for Jimi Hendrix's guitar licks. For those younger participants at the BPS, an LP ("Long Playing") is: a record that spins at 33⅓ rpm. For those who have never seen an LP, they look like this: (but is about 12 in [30 cm] in diameter).

31. Also called 'Millennials' since they have spent formative years around the turn of the millennium.

32. The potential for engaging GenY'ers through cyber-space—Facebook, You Tube, Chat-rooms, blogs, Google, Wikipedia, iPhone, iTunes, Kindle, eBooks, SMS, Twitter—type environments and Coffee shops is clear; note CPM's recent Coffee shop initiative in Tel Aviv and numerous Diasporic (mostly, but not exclusively North American) and Israeli MJ web sites. The traditional Jewish community (esp. Chabad!) seems to be out in front here, but see MJTI's network site and the UMJC site which is closing the gap e.g., see their 'Webinars.' I did a search at www.twitter.com and several hits came up for Messianic Judaism of which Beth HaDerech (which appears to be a Toronto-based Latino-Hasidic-style Messianic Jewish Congregation) was dominant and linked to their web site, which attempts to use Hasidic categories to communicate Yeshua. The site also makes disclaimers for their employment of Hasidic voices who are, nonetheless, not believers in "Maran Yeshua."

For the application of Twitter to Education, see e.g., the University of Texas at Dallas, where Twitter has been incorporated into the actual classroom setting with large groups of students. This innovative approach gives more students the opportunity to express their views in class discussions; furthermore, the limit of 140 characters forces them to get to the central point. For 'posting' in class, see the following video:
http://twitterforteachers.wetpaint.com/page/Twitter+in+the+Classroom.
Twitter's political power was demonstrated in the recent Iranian June 09 elections by protesters after the Government blocked other media outlets. I am not trying to suggest 'Twitter-tracts' should be sent to Jewish College students, (whose leaders are trying to 'block the message,' etc.), but some in our movement may not resist such evangelistic temptation! Clearly the GenY'ers cyber spaces present ethical issues for our community attempts at 'connection.'

33. Meta-narratives as defined by J. F. Loytard are large-scale theories and philosophies of the world, e.g., the progress of history, the claim by science of the knowability of everything, and the possibility of absolute freedom. See Jean-François Lyotard, *La condition postmoderne: rapport sur le savoir*. Paris: Minuit,

1979); Eng. trans., *The Postmodern Condition: A Report on Knowledge* (Theory and History of Literature, vol. 10; trans. B. Massumi; Minnesota.: University of Minnesota Press, 1984).

34. For all of postmodernism's claims to reject meta-narratives, I believe the case can be argued that it has one, namely, the predictable outworking of a Neo-Darwinist worldview: "That in the beginning there was always the multi-verse, and through time and chance, in a remote and lonely corner of one of an infinitesimal number of universes, on one teeny and otherwise wholly insignificant speck of a planet, in one small and unimpressive galaxy, the first living organic matter came into being. And then through random mutation and natural selection the first simple cells began to evolve until the appearance of *Homo sapiens. Homo sapiens* recently fell into the hubris of Modernity's veiled power-claims for rationality and progress, but has now evolved to recognize that there are no absolutes or meta-narratives with a binding address but only community stories that reflect the social location of each cultural group."

35. The following is simply illustrative of some of the (admittedly over-simplified) distinctions (from the Emerging Church's Perspective of the traditional Evangelical Church). My purpose in including this table is to suggest that we need to think and re-think how we are 'doing congregational meetings' in our Jewish cultural settings. I will briefly discuss the Emerging Church later in this paper. The content is based on a talk given by D. Carson, "Is the Emergent Church Biblical?" at the C. F. Henry Center for Theological Understanding on 9/21/2005, accessible at http://www.henrycenter.org

Emphasis on Propositional Truth	Experience Focused
Belief Focused	Belonging Focused
Traditional/Fundamentalist and non-ritualistic	Eclectic embrace of ritual/mystical Spirituality
Too polished/Performance Orientated (Mega-Church included here)	Participation-based
Showman/audience hierarchy	Relational Emphasis
Over-Cerebral/Rational	Embraces Feelings/Emotions
Intolerant of Others	Tolerant of Others

36. Cultural influence takes place on three levels: Level 1) theory/philosophy/epistemology, 2) the Arts and Humanities 3) popular 'coffee table' setting conversations. I realize that most people (PMJs included) live in between the 2nd and 3rd levels and this is where most of our congregational leaders live and rub shoulders with their communities. However, it is imperative that we address the 'level-one' thought-shapers/intellectual trendsetters of the Jewish

community, because it is only by interacting with PMJs' leading theorists that we can make an inroad that has the potential to filter down to the second and third level settings (the Arts and Humanities and coffee-table conversations).

37. I am fond of the model I have discussed with Jhan Moskowitz (my dialogical partner for this session) which both of us are applying (he in NYC and myself in Israel) of gathering in small groups around *meals* in homes to discuss texts. Jhan and I both found it ironic and challenging that our assignment has been how we communicate a doctrine in a generational *Zeitgeist* that shuns doctrinal orthodoxy [Emergents] or simply denies it exists [Postmoderns]).

38. The National Havurah Committee (NHC) uses this Talmudic saying (*b. Ber* 63b) as their motto. The NHC define themselves as: "a network of diverse individuals and communities dedicated to Jewish living and learning, community building, and tikkun olam (repairing the world). For nearly 30 years, the NHC has helped Jews across North America envision a joyful, grassroots Judaism, and has provided the tools to help people create empowered Jewish lives and communities." The Havurah movement began in the late 60s and 70s as a type of Jewish grass-roots revival movement protesting an overly institutionalized Judaism. These small egalitarian groups function without the employment of rabbis and are popular in the Reconstructionist, Reform and Conservative movements. The name derives from Havurah (חבורה) small groups of religious fellowships that originated in Second Temple times among the Pharisees. See the NHC website: http://www.havurah.org.

39. Both Christian and Jewish scholars are engaged in the "third quest." The three 'Quest's' for the historical Jesus are: First Quest) Mid-18th-mid-19th century. This quest used rational historical research to discover the historical Jesus as opposed to the "Christ of Faith." This Quest was effectively brought to an end by A. Schweitzer who demonstrated that the picture of Jesus that emerged from this quest was simply a reflection of the liberal scholars who projected their own humanistic image onto Jesus. Schweitzer introduced Jesus' Apocalyptic teaching and Jesus' expectation for the end of history into the discussion; Second Quest) In the 50s the quest was revived with the claim that there was historical data that could lead us to the historical Jesus. This quest sought to re-connect the Jesus of history to the Christ of Faith using existentialist categories; Third Quest) Since the late 70s this quest seeks to focus upon Jesus' Jewishness and Jewish context.

40. This relates to Paul Hiebert's model of a "centered-set," instead of a "bounded-set" model of community inclusion, *Anthropological Reflections on Missiological Issues* (Grand Rapids: Baker Books, 1994). Certainly the hope for any disciple of Yeshua is that they will come to understand and embrace his Deity as part of their understanding of his person, however, we need to allow people the space and pace to move towards that center as they participate in community life.

41. For a typical critique of "Jewish Christianity" and a warning to the Jewish community to beware of 'us' (!) from the distinguished Jewish spokesman of the Holocaust, see E. Wiesel, "The Missionary Menace," in *Smashing the Idols: A Jewish Inquiry into the Cult Phenomenon* (G. D. Eisenberg, ed.; New Jersey: Jason Aronson, 1988), 161−63.

42. Towards the conclusion of writing this paper, I received a copy of the (yet unpublished) paper by M. Kinzer, "Finding our Way Through Nicaea: The Deity of Yeshua, Bilateral Ecclesiology, and Redemptive Encounter with the Living God," 2010 Hashivenu Forum (Los Angeles): 1–32. Kinzer discusses the Nicene Creed and the *Ecclesia* of the Nations vis-à-vis its relationship to MJ. Kinzer sees our position as one of "dialectical ecclesial continuity," by which he means the unique vantage point of MJs situated in covenantal bond with *both* the Jewish and Christian communities. Re Kinzer's insight of the inextricable link between behavior and belief, the following is illustrative of his thoughts, "For the Jewish people, the chief community-defining positive commandment was 'You shall observe the Torah' and the chief negative commandment was 'You shall not believe that Jesus is the Son of God.' For the Christian Church, the chief community-defining positive commandment was 'You shall believe that Jesus is the Son of God' and the chief negative commandment was 'You shall not observe the Torah' " (p. 3). Kinzer's view of Nicaea is one of critical but affirming embrace, e.g., "Paul offers a Yeshua-faith interpretation of existing Jewish tradition [the *Shem á*], and the Nicene Creed offers an expanded interpretation of Paul's teaching" (16). Cf., the important article by C. Blaising, "Creedal Formation as Hermeneutical Development: A Reexamination of the Nicene Creed," presented at the Biblical Interpretation in Early Christianity session of the SBL Congress, 2008, and the Patristics and Medieval History Group at the ETS, 2008. Blaising draws upon letters written before and after the Nicene council which he believes demonstrate that the language of the creed (esp. the *"ousia"* language) is the result of a preoccupation by its framers with biblical hermeneutics rather than a particular system of ancient philosophy. The basic controversy is succinctly illustrated by the following claim/counter claims from one of Arius's letters: "The Son is from God Himself (ἐξ αὐτοῦ τοῦ θεοῦ)" is the view of Alexander (as cited by Arius's letter). "He [Yeshua] is from nothing (ἐξ οὐκ ὄντων ἐστίν)" represents Arius's view, *Letter to Eusebius of Nicomedia*, ca. 319 CE. See Blaising's article (9–13) for the way both parties sought to base their claims on reference to Scripture. The whole subject of the relationship of the Messianic Jewish movement to the historic Creeds of the Church and MJ Hermeneutics is a desideratum for a future Symposium.

43. Our individualistic Western predisposition leads us to place an over-emphasis upon Yeshua's instruction to pray "in secret," as if Yeshua, himself, did not pray in community! It is certainly reasonable to assume that Yeshua's custom growing up would have been to gather together with 'Israel' (in a *minyan*) to pray the *Amidah* in whatever form current in his day. As noted by modern commentators, Yeshua's emphasis re praying "in secret" is certainly not on prayer's *locus* but rather upon its *manner*. The early disciples of Yeshua (see esp. the book of Acts) hardly understood this as a literal command.

44. I am suggesting that Yeshua-Centered Jewish prayer/liturgy needs to 'spin around Yeshua' in the Jewish Yearly cycle. I am not advocating a wholesale renewal of the Siddur but I am advocating the adoption of a centering of Yeshua's death and

resurrection and the outpouring of the Ruach HaKodesh as an integral part of our liturgical cycle.

45. The "Taglit-Birthright" program (www.birthrightisrael.com) that brings young 18–26 year old Jewish youth to Israel for a free 10-day trip has achieved measurable success in connecting Jewish youth with their heritage. As of January 2010 (in which Birthright celebrated its 10 year anniversary), the program saw 250,000 young Jews and children of Jews from around the world come to visit Israel. Without any statistical data to reference I believe it is safe to say that for MJs the experience of coming to know Yeshua has been the major factor in their re-connection with Jewish heritage. The implication for covenantal theology related to Messiah (Messianic Jews) and the Land of Israel (for mostly non-Messianic Diasporic Jews) as the two main factors that have reconnected young Jews with their heritage is in itself a sociological/theological phenomenon that merits reflection and exploration.

46. For the new openness among Jewish scholars to 'reclaim' Jesus as 'ours,' see D. Hagner, *The Jewish Reclamation of Jesus: An Analysis and Critique of Modern Jewish Study of Jesus* (Grand Rapids: Zondervan, 1984; repr. Eugene: Wipf and Stock, 1997). See also the seminal study of S. Heschel, *Abraham Geiger and the Jewish Jesus* (Chicago: University of Chicago Press, 1998); Among many examples that continue to be published: G. Vermes, *Jesus in His Jewish Context* (Minneapolis: Fortress, 2003); D. Flusser, *Jesus*, (with S. Notley; Jerusalem: Magnes, 1997 [Ger. Orig. 1968; now in Hebrew trans. Jerusalem: Magnes, 2001]); A.-J. Levine, *The Misunderstood Jew: The Church and the Scandal of the Jewish Jesus* (San Francisco: HarperSanFransico, 2006). For the interest of the early Zionists in Yeshua, see the now the invaluable contribution of T. Sadan, *Flesh of our Flesh: Jesus of Nazareth in Jewish Thought* (Jerusalem: Carmel, 2008 [Hebrew]); see also *Jesus through Jewish Eyes* (A. Shinan, ed.; Tel Aviv: Yediot Ahronot, 1999 [Hebrew]).

47. What I like to call Yeshua's 'c.v.' sent back to John the Baptist from Isa 61 and Isa 35 (see Matt 11:2-5): Yeshua's 'acts' consist of proclaiming God's good news to Israel, healing the sick, giving sight to the blind, causing the deaf to hear and the lame to walk, healing lepers, and raising the dead.

48. For a succinct and cogent articulation of the arguments for the truth of Jesus' resurrection, see W. L. Craig, *Reasonable Faith: Christian Truth and Apologetics* (3d ed.; Wheaton: Crossway, 2008), Chap. 8 deals with the Resurrection of Jesus. Craig's approach is important for our postmodern Jewish audience (for whom the authority of the Tanakh let alone the NT Scriptures does not have intellectual purchase) since his appeal is *not* based on the *divine inspiration* of the Scriptures, but rather an examination of the NT as an *historical document*. Craig argues persuasively from the inference to the best explanation re the following three points: 1) The Fact of the Empty Tomb 2) The Postmortem Appearances 3) The Origin of the Christian [faith in Yeshua as Messiah and Lord] faith. As I note in n. 4, postmodernists need to be shown the self-contradictory nature of their own worldview. Once this is done they can be challenged to examine the evidence for the Resurrection and come to their own conclusions after a careful perusal of the

NT corpus. For a philosophical defense of Yeshua as God incarnate, and the atonement and resurrection, see R. Swinburne, *Was Jesus God?* (Oxford: Oxford University Press, 2008).

49. I believe that as we tell the story of Yeshua it remains useful to refer to Messianic prophecy to convince PMJs even though they don't believe in Yeshua (since they are Jewish) or the concept of a Messiah whose coming was prophesied in the Tanakh (since they are PMJs)! See M. Rydelnick, "The Ongoing Importance of Messianic Prophecy for Jewish Evangelism in the New Millennium," in D. Bock and M. Glaser, eds., *To the Jew First: A Case for Jewish Evangelism in Scripture and History* (Grand Rapids: Kregel, 2008), 261–91; However, Rydelnick's case needs to be complimented by an informed sensitivity to the current worldview shift of postmodernism, see W. E. Brown, "Theology in a Postmodern Culture: Implications of a Video-Dependent Society," [first published in 1995! So read "DVD/Streaming Video-Dependent" for "Video-Dependent"!] in D. S. Dockery, *The Challenge of Postmodernism* (2d ed.; Grand Rapids: Baker Academic, 2001), 169–83, e.g., "No longer is the question, 'Is there a God?' but rather, 'Which God?' The question is not 'Was Jesus the Son of God?' but 'How can I believe there's just one way to heaven?' 'Is the Bible true?' has become 'Is there truth?'" (179). The Jewish versions of these can be easily adapted, e.g., not 'How can I believe that Jesus is *our* Messiah,' but 'How can *you* believe that there *is* an actual Messiah!' Brown also notes, "Rather than telling people what to believe — a didactic approach — people must now be led to discover the truth for themselves through a more Socratic method" (ibid.). See also the articulation by one of our most gifted and seasoned communicators, R. Newman, *Questioning Evangelism: Engaging People's Hearts the way Jesus Did* (Grand Rapids: Kregel, 2004).

50. This early heresy that Yeshua was a man who became God by adoption is found in the *Shepherd of Hermas* (ca., 150 C.E.), and then by Theodotus around 190 C.E. who came to Rome from Byzantium and believed that Yeshua was virgin born, but that only after he was tested did he become the Christ at his baptism when the Spirit descended on him, and then only after his resurrection became fully God.

There is no space in the current paper to explore what J. D. Dunn and others have referred to as a 'two-stage' Christology. See Dunn's exposition of Romans, (Word Biblical Commentary: vol. 38a; Dallas: Word, 1988), esp. ad loc, 1:3-4, περὶ τοῦ υἱοῦ αὐτοῦ τοῦ γενομένου ἐκ σπέρματος Δαυὶδ κατὰ σάρκα, τοῦ ὁρισθέντος υἱοῦ θεοῦ ἐν δυνάμει κατὰ πνεῦμα ἁγιωσύνης ἐξ ἀναστάσεως νεκρῶν, Ἰησοῦ Χριστοῦ τοῦ κυρίου ἡμῶν, (concerning his Son who was a descendant of David with reference to the flesh, who was appointed the Son-of-god-in-power according to the Holy Spirit by the resurrection from the dead, Jesus Christ our Lord, NET) where Dunn's discussion of ὁρισθέντος "designated," (RSV) "declared to be," (BGD [BDAG], NEB, NIV) is instructive, e.g., the Old Latin tradition prefixed προ- ("a point of time prior to another point of time") to the verb so that the "appointment" of Yeshua as υἱοῦ θεοῦ (Son of God) is moved 'back' to eternity. Paul's understanding of Christology is also developed in the following phrase ἐν δυνάμει (in power), see Dunn's discussion and his explanation that such a Christology is *not* to be equated with adoptionism.

L. Hurtado has written extensively on the early worship of Jesus within the context of Second Temple monotheism. Hurtado is also recognized for having overturned W. Bousset's theory that Jewish worship of Yeshua developed in a Gentile-Hellenistic environment. E.g., Bousset's theory has no explanation for the use by early Jewish followers of Yeshua of the Aramaic liturgical expression: μαράνα θά (*maranatha*) "O Lord, Come!" [1 Cor 16:22] and the very early worship of Yeshua alongside God among his *Jewish* followers.

51. Eusebius, History of the Church, Book III, 27, pp. 91–92. Cited by G. Nerel in the following important article, "Eusebius' *Ecclesiastical History* and the Modern Yeshua-Movement," *Mishkan* 39 (2003): 65–86, (here, 83).

52. It is instructive to look the UMJC and the IAMCS statements of faith with regard to Christology. The UMJC lists their "statement of shared convictions" as affirmed by their delegates in 2003 (which they are careful to note does not replace their doctrinal statement) about Yeshua as:

Cited from: http://www.umjc.org/resources-mainmenu-101/documents-mainmenu-110/cat_view/119-theology

"The Union of Messianic Jewish Congregations holds that the One GOD, the GOD of creation, the GOD of Israel, the GOD of our ancestors, of Whom our tradition speaks, reveals Himself uniquely, definitively, and decisively in the life, death, resurrection, and return of Yeshua the Messiah.

Yeshua is the incarnation of the Divine WORD through Whom the world was made, and of the Divine GLORY through Whom GOD revealed Himself to Israel and acted in their midst. He is the living Torah, expressing perfectly in His example and teaching the Divine purpose for human life. Yeshua is completely human and completely divine.

As the risen Messiah and the heavenly Kohen Gadol (High Priest), Yeshua continues to mediate GOD's relationship to His people Israel, to those of the nations who have joined the greater commonwealth of Israel in Him, and to all creation. GOD's plan of salvation and blessing for Israel, the nations, and the entire cosmos is fulfilled only in and through Yeshua, by virtue of His atoning death and bodily resurrection, and GOD's gift of life to both Jews and Gentiles, in this world and in the world to come, is bestowed and appropriated only in and through Him."

The relevant section of the official UMJC doctrinal statement reads:

"We believe in the deity of the L-RD Yeshua, the Messiah, and His virgin birth, in His sinless life, in His miracles, in His vicarious and atoning death through His shed blood, in His bodily resurrection, in His ascension to the right hand of the Father, and in His personal return in power and glory."

The MJAA lists their congregational network (IAMCS) doctrinal statement about Yeshua as follows:

Cited from http://www.iamcs.org/WhatWeBelieve.php

GOD THE SON (HaBen)

The Son is God (Deity), and is worshipped as God, having existed eternally [Ps. 110:1 (cf. Heb. 1:13); Isa. 9:6–7; Matt. 28:18–20; Phil. 2:5–11; Col. 1:15–19; Rev. 3:21 (Heb. 1 - worshipped by angels); Rev. 4:8, 5:5-14].

The main difference between the UMJC and the IAMCS doctrinal statements re Yeshua is that the IAMCS statement speaks of Yeshua as "God" whereas the UMJC statements retain a more nuanced distinction. Although the UMJC statement does speak of Yeshua as "deity," and in their more recent addition as "completely divine," it does not refer to him as "God," although one use of the word typed "L-RD" (instead of "L-rd") does seem to go as far as one can go (in English) without actually saying that Yeshua is "God." I think that this illustrates the difficulty for many MJs to adopt a Nicene articulation of "very God of very God" and thus makes it imperative that we engage in the hard work of theological reflection, discussion and articulation of this central belief of our faith.

53. Maimonides' 'negative theology,' or 'apophatic theology' (an attempt to describe God through negation), follows the Islamic Neo-Platonic tradition, that one cannot predicate anything of God as that would suggest a limitation in God. All that may be predicated of God is that "He exists." Maimonides denied that God has attributes. For a fascinating angle on this whole question, see now Kinzer's article, "Finding our Way," in which he notes the similar theological move between the Kabbalists' view of the unity of the Ein Sof and the *Sefirot* against the Jewish Philosophical writers (i.e., Saadia Gaon/Yehuda HaLevi/Maimonides) avoidance of recognizing an uncreated hypostasis. Kinzer likens the Kabbalists' theological move to that of Nicaea's defense against an Arian view of a separate hypostasis. *In this sense* the Kabbalists are closer to our concept of God than the Jewish philosophers, however, their use of Ein Sof is noted here as a further example of negative theology.

54. That negative theology (the Ein Sof, etc.) can be a helpful cross-cultural conceptual voice to speak to Hasidic Jews is not what I am addressing here.
At the 12th Annual Hashivenu Forum (the same day I had to submit this paper!) entitled "Encountering the God of Israel in the Messiah of Israel," there was a fruitful discussion of how we, as Jews, can best engage in the theological articulation of Yeshua's status vis-à-vis God. Perhaps the most fruitful suggestion was the integration of Liturgy and our confession about Yeshua in Scriptural terms (e.g., Phil 2 passage) woven into our liturgical worship. This parallels the singing of the creeds by many "High church" traditions and the Eastern Church. I mention this here also because of the Postmodern Jewish and Christian penchant for sacred and mystical space including the liturgical creation and expression of such 'spaces.'

55. That Yeshua's speech was understood by the Jewish leadership as a claim to Deity is explicitly stated in John's Gospel, "For this reason the Jewish leaders were trying even harder to kill him, because not only was he breaking the Sabbath, but he was also calling God his own Father, thus making himself equal with God." (John 5:18); 'Jesus said to them, "I have shown you many good deeds from the Father. For which one of them are you going to stone me?" The Jewish leaders replied, "We are not going to stone you for a good deed but for

blasphemy, because you, a man, are claiming to be God [or 'a god']" ' (John 10:32–33). M. Kinzer speaking of the *taxis* (cf. τάξις, Eng., 'taxon,' order of relationship) between the Father and the Son, emphasizes Yeshua's Deity as articulated by the Nicene Creed, "Though the Son is ordered after and in relationship to the Father, he is not a demigod, a secondary divinity at a lower level of being from the Father." ("Finding our Way," p. 18). This limited 'sounding' on the topic is clearly not the place I can develop this. Suffice it to say here that some central Pauline texts, such as the *hymn to Yeshua*, embedded by Paul in Phil 2:6–11, is a rich early text that bears witness to the faith of the earliest community in Yeshua and hearkens back to Isa 45:23 where the reference is clearly God Himself. See the works of L. Hurtado, e.g., his only work currently translated into Hebrew: *How on Earth Did Jesus Become God? Historical Questions about Earliest Devotion to Jesus* (Grand Rapids: Eerdmans, 2005); the Hebrew translation כיצד הפך ישוע לאל published by Ben Gurion University of the Negev Press, 2006. This opens the whole discussion of Jewish texts that reflect mediator figures and the extent of God's mediated or unmediated manifestations. For one such reflection on the subject see the parallels between Metatron and Jesus as discussed by A. Segal, "Ruler of This World: Attitudes about Mediator Figures and the Importance of Sociology for Self-Definition," in E.P. Sanders, ed., *Jewish and Christian Self-Definition: Aspects of Judaism in the Graeco-Roman Period* (Vol. 2; London: SCM, 1981), 245–68; For Segal's discussion on the Two Powers heresy in Rabbinic Judaism, see his, *Two Powers in Heaven: Early Rabbinic Reports About Christianity and Gnosticism* (Leiden: Brill, 1977).

56. See R. Harvey, *Mapping Messianic Jewish Theology: A Constructive Approach* (Milton Keynes: Paternoster, 2009), chapter 5 (96–139) entitled "Yeshua the Messiah: The Shaping of Messianic Jewish Christology." As I have noted in this paper, Kinzer's "Finding our Way," paper has certainly advanced this discussion in many helpful ways.

57. See O. Skaursaune, *In the Shadow of the Temple: Jewish Influences on Early Christianity* (Downers Grove: InterVarsity, 2002), esp. ch. 3; and chs. 15-16; idem, "From the Jewish Messiah to the Creeds of the Church," *Evangelical Review of Theology* 32 (2008): 224–37, "To those who perceive the Christology of the Nicene creed as very Hellenistic or Greek, I have one basic challenge: how do you then explain that all Greek writers we know of, reacted with an instinctive disgust to the most obvious implication of the Nicene Creed, namely that it portrayed a God who suffered in his Son, of one essence with him? If there was one theological dogma shared by all educated Greek men and women, it was the impassibility ["incapable of suffering or of experiencing pain"] of God or the divine nature." Having acknowledged Skaursaune's point concerning Christology, the same cannot be said of conceptuality: see Hiebert, *Anthropological Reflections*, 125, "While the Greeks saw God in intrinsic terms, as supernatural, omnipotent, and omnipresent; the Israelites knew him in relational terms, as Creator, Judge, and Lord. They also referred to him as "the God of Abraham, Isaac, and Jacob, our forefathers."

58. Some of the ways that the Gospels imply Yeshua's Deity are: his act of forgiving sins, his miracles (e.g., commanding the storm to be still, walking on water, raising the dead), the Transfiguration, his unique filial relationship with the (his "own") Father (esp. in the Gospel of John), his claim that the final destinies of people rest on their response to him, and his parabolic teaching. For the latter, see P. B. Payne, "Jesus' implicit claim to deity in his Parables," *TJ* 2 (1981): 3–23. Other Jewish 'storylines' that I believe ultimately are 'fulfilled in Yeshua' are Buber's "I-Thou" (as a reflection of the Eternal Relationship between *the Father and the Son*), Heschel's "God in Search of Man," (Yeshua *is* the ultimate expression of that search and esp. God in search of lost *Jewish man* [Israel], see Matt 10:5); Borowitz's Covenant Theology reflects the way that the covenant has become an existential reality for us in our encounter with Yeshua . . .).

59. L. Hurtado, *How on Earth*, 48.

60. It is important to distinguish between the 'Emergent' Church and the 'Emerging' Church. The former refers to "Emergent Village" (www.emergentvillage.com, where they define themselves as: "a growing, generative friendship among missional Christians seeking to love our world in the Spirit of Jesus Christ"). 'Emerging Church' is "the wider, informal, global, ecclesial (church-centered) focus of the movement, while Emergent is an official organization in the U.S. and the U.K." described by S. McKnight in the linked Christianity Today article cited in n. 59. McKnight notes that there is much confusion amongst Evangelicals re the difference between 'Emergent' and 'Emerging.' The latter, McKnight notes, is really more about ecclesiology than epistemology.
McKnight's lecture on the Emerging Church at Westminster Seminary in 2006 may be accessed at http://www.foolishsage.com/wordpress/wp-content/uploads/McKnight%20-%20What%20is%20the%20Emerging%20Church.pdf

61. D. Bock, posting "Christology and the Emergent Movement," posted May 2, 2008, http://blog.bible.org/primetimejesus/content/christology-and-emergent-movement-may-2
For an informative summary and assessment of the positive aspects of the emerging church, see S. McKnight, "Five Streams of the Emerging Church," http://www.christianitytoday.com/ct/2007/february/11.35.html McKnight lists these as 1) Prophetic: Emerging Christians believe the church needs to change, and they are beginning to live as if that change had already occurred. 2) Postmodern, citing L. Shults, "The truly infinite God of Christian faith is beyond all our linguistic grasping, as all the great theologians from Irenaeus to Calvin [include here Rambam?] have insisted, and so the struggle to capture God in our finite propositional structures is nothing short of linguistic idolatry." 3) Praxis-oriented: how faith is lived out. 4) Worship: esteem for sacred space and ritual that is not afraid to ask questions like: "Is the sermon the most important thing on Sunday morning? If we sat in a circle would we foster a different theology and praxis?" 5) Orthopraxy: how a person *lives* is more important than what he or she *believes*. 6) Missional: participating, with God, in the redemptive work of God in this world and in the community where God's redemptive work occurs. Holistic:

ministering to the whole being. This emphasis finds perfect expression in the ministry of Jesus, who went about doing to bodies, spirits, families, and societies. 7) Post-evangelical by being Post-systematic theology, God didn't reveal a systematic theology but a storied narrative, and no language is capable of capturing the Absolute Truth who alone is God. 8) Skeptical of an "In versus Out" mentality. [I believe the following self-critique by McKnight, a respected Evangelical scholar who is also aligned with the Emerging Church applies equally to our movement.] "This emerging ambivalence about who is in and who is out creates a serious problem for evangelism. The emerging movement is not known for it, but I wish it were. Unless you proclaim the Good News of Jesus Christ, there is no good news at all—and if there is no Good News, then there is no Christianity, emerging or evangelical." 9) Political in the sense (as I understand McKnight here) of focusing on ministering to the poor and working *for* social justice rather than just being *against* abortion or homosexuality.

Of interest is the following self-description that employs the 'emergent' language for Messianic Jewish Congregations from one of Kesher's recent articles (http://www.kesherjournal.com/Issue-23/Complexity-in-Early-Jewish-Messianism): "Joshua Brumbach recently relocated to Washington, DC where he and his wife are the founders of Yinon, an organization committed to revitalizing congregations and planting *emergent Messianic Jewish communities* that inspire young Jews toward a vision of Jewish life that is progressive and engaging, rooted in the enduring legacy of Mashiach (emphasis mine)."

62. P. Hiebert, *Anthropological Reflections*. As far as I know Hiebert (d. 2007) was not aligned with the Emergent or Emerging Church, however, his missiological insights are highly relevant to some of their thinking about paradigms. Hiebert argues for Yeshua, Paul, and the Hebraic mindset as a "centered set," i.e., "people in covenant relationship with God, and therefore as people-in-community."

63. See J. Fischer, "Yehsua: The Deity Debate," *Mishkan* 39 (2003): 20–28. (The whole issue is dedicated to the Divinity of the Messiah).

64. See Paul's 'filling out' of the *Shem'a* in 1 Cor 8:6 where he includes Yeshua into Israel's central creedal declaration.

65. J. D. Dunn, A New Perspective on Jesus: What the Quest for the Historical Jesus Missed (Grand Rapids: Baker, 2005), 16–17.

66. Usually spoken of by postmoderns as the need for modernists/traditionalists to humbly acknowledge a sense of "chastened epistemology."

67. My story is the story of a 'modern' Jew who climbed (traditional) Mt. Sinai at the age of 19 that set me on my two-year all-consuming search for God that took me through geographical journeys: Israel, Europe, Canada, South Africa, and spiritual ones: Reform Judaism, Orthodox Judaism, Eastern Religion, to faith in Yeshua as my Messiah and Lord. I would further argue that faith in Yeshua (including belief in his Deity), ironically, is the answer to Emil Fackenheim's call (as a response to the Holocaust) to fulfill the 614th commandment: Jewish survival. Now, more than a quarter of a century after first trusting in Yeshua for forgiveness of my sins, I am as passionate as ever about embracing my Jewish identity and celebrating the riches of Jewish heritage in my life journey. My zeal

and conviction for the preservation and celebration of Jewish peoplehood and heritage is not *in spite* of Yeshua but *because* of him! (To use Rosenzweigian terms, if Judaism is the sacred fire and the Gentile church is the flame of God's salvific light, then Yeshua is *the blue center of the flame*).

The challenge I have presented in this paper is to develop authentic Jewish community and lifestyle from which our contextualized theology re Yeshua's Deity can take shape. Our communities will share continuities with our Jewish past, and by virtue of our Yeshua-centered Judaism, stark discontinuities. Nonetheless, whatever our Yeshua-centered Jewish communities end up looking like, we need to take seriously the (tendentious but inescapable) conclusion of L. H. Schiffman, *Who was a Jew? Rabbinic and Halakhic Perspectives on the Jewish-Christian Schism* (New Jersey: Ktav, 1985), 77, "In retrospect, the *halakhot* we have studied were what maintained the identity of the Jewish people. Had the rabbis relaxed these standards, accepting the semi-proselytes or the earliest Gentile Christians into the Jewish people, Christians would quickly have become the majority within the expanded community of 'Israel.' Judaism as we know it would have ceased to exist even before reaching its codification in the Mishnah ... observance of the commandments of the Torah would have disappeared within just a few centuries ... In short, it was the *halakah* and its definition of Jewish identity which saved the Jewish people and its heritage from extinction as a result of the newly emerging Christian ideology."

The other side of Schiffman's claim is complemented by noting that the Apostolic council in Jerusalem (Acts 15) came to the same conclusion that he advocates for the Jewish people as also relevant (as understood by Yeshua) for Messianic Jews. (As is well known the question of *Jewish* observance of Torah's commandments was not even a discussion item at the Jerusalem Council). This is no less than a properly contextualized understanding of what Yeshua was asking of Israel, "[T]he primary kind of conversion to Jesus is intensification, that is, the revitalization of a previously existing Jewish faith. In light of this general orientation to the mission of Jesus it needs to be said that Jesus' strategy was not so much evangelization (as defined by most today) as *the attempt to awaken Israel,* especially marginalized Galileans, to his prophetic vision for Israel. This vision was not just for the Galilee; he had a mission for the entire nation." S. McKnight, *Turning to Jesus: The Sociology of Conversion in the Gospels* (Louisville: Westminster John Knox, 2002), 148 (emphasis original).